Behaviour Problems
in School

a source book of readings

Edited by Phillip Williams

HODDER AND STOUGHTON
LONDON   SYDNEY   AUCKLAND   TORONTO

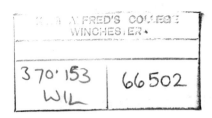
Acknowledgments

The editor and publishers are grateful to the following for permission to reproduce copyright material: 1 Reprinted by kind permission of E. K. Wickman; 2 Reprinted by kind permission of E. K. Wickman; 3 Copyright © 1970 The Society for Research in Child Development, Inc. Reprinted by permission of the publisher and A. Ziv; 4 Reprinted by permission of the *Journal of Child Psychology and Psychiatry* and T. Moore; 5 Reprinted by permission of the *British Journal of Educational Psychology* and L. B. Birch; 6 Reprinted by permission of the *Journal of Child Psychology and Psychiatry* and M. Rutter; 7 Reprinted by permission of the *British Journal of Educational Psychology* and Sheila Mitchell; 8 Reprinted by permission of the *British Journal of Educational Psychology* and J. Tizard; 9 Reprinted by permission of the *British Journal of Psychology*; 10 Reprinted by permission of the *Journal of Child Psychology and Psychiatry* and M. L. Kellmer Pringle; 11 Reprinted by permission of The Council for Exceptional Children and H. Goldenberg; 12 Reprinted by permission of *Behaviour Research and Therapy* and E. E. Levitt; 13 Reprinted by permission of the *Journal of Child Psychology and Psychiatry* and M. Shepherd; 14 Reprinted by permission of The Council for Exceptional Children and K. A. Allen; 15 Reprinted by permission of the *Journal of Special Education* and W. C. Becker.

ISBN 0 340 16770 X Boards

ISBN 0 340 16771 8 Unibook

Copyright © 1974 Hodder and Stoughton Ltd

First published 1974: second impression 1976

Printed in Great Britain for
Hodder and Stoughton Educational,
a division of Hodder and Stoughton Ltd, London,
by J. W. Arrowsmith Ltd., Bristol

Contents

General Introduction

The purpose of this book is to bring together a collection of readings which have something useful to say about children's behaviour in school. The readings are drawn primarily from the field of educational psychology, where there is a large corpus of published work concerned with children's behaviour. But much of this material is not directly relevant to the behaviour of children in the school setting. Yet it is behaviour in the school and in the classroom which is of specific interest to teachers and to their colleagues in social work, counselling, medicine and child guidance who collaborate with teachers in dealing with children's school problems. This reader selects from published research and enquiry in educational psychology some excerpts which reflect this interest.

For ease of reference the book has been divided into four sections. Section A deals with the nature of children's behaviour problems—not only the sorts of behaviour which concern teachers, but also those aspects of school which children themselves find troublesome. Section B deals briefly with the ways that teachers can use to identify and assess the seriousness of the behaviour which children show, whereas section C looks in more detail at the range of causes which lie behind some of the difficulties. The last section, D, is concerned with the different ways in which behaviour problems can be treated. The first two articles in this section review aspects of the established techniques for coping with problems in schools, whereas the second two illustrate the newer behaviour modification approach for dealing with behaviour problems in the classroom. An introduction to each section contains a commentary on points to be borne in mind in reading the articles.

In bringing together this collection of readings, an important factor has been the level of specialization which is sometimes shown by research articles. These papers have been chosen so that they can be read by persons who are not as yet fully conversant with educational research design and statistics. Some technical terms and concepts are necessarily retained but in general the reader is advised to concentrate on the principles illustrated by the articles, not the more technical details.

This book does not aim to proffer direct advice on handling behaviour problems: it is not a practical manual. Other texts try to meet this aim. The book stems from the conviction that it is not sensible to deal with behaviour problems without first being aware of and alert to some of the main issues revealed by published work. The articles have been chosen in no small measure for their ability to generate questions for discussion in courses concerned with children's behaviour in the classroom. In order to facilitate the use of the material for seminar work, some examples of questions and activities have been listed at the end of the book.

Finally, a word about the terminology used by the writers. Behaviour problems, problem behaviour, maladjustment, maladaptive behaviour and deviant behaviour are all examples of terms used by different authors. The existence of such a variety of overlapping terms illustrates some of the difficulties in delineating the general area of behaviour problems with which the book deals. This is reflected in the section titles—it seems more sensible for each section title to retain the terminology mainly used in the articles of the section, rather than repeat the title of the text. But the reader is alerted to the fact that different authors have different criteria for deciding the kinds of behaviour with which they deal. This issue of definition—which several of the authors discuss—needs to be kept in mind.

The contents are pointed very much at behaviour in school. Although the school is not the sole setting for all the articles, nevertheless they are all of relevance to the behaviour problems that teachers meet in schools and the decisions that they have to take for dealing with them.

The Nature of Behaviour Problems

Introduction

The first two extracts in this section are taken from one of the classical studies of children's behaviour in schools, carried out by E. K. Wickman in 1928. This is an old study but it is one which has been very widely quoted and has stimulated a lot of interesting work in the field of teacher perception of children's behaviour.

Although Wickman's methodology has been criticized, there is no doubt that most of the workers who have attempted to repeat his enquiry have largely corroborated the order of seriousness of children's behaviour which he found. However, there have been some changes. The article by Ziv, which follows the Wickman extracts, first summarizes another aspect of Wickman's work—the correspondence between ratings made by teachers and by mental hygienists, or child guidance staff. Ziv then examines the extent to which the difference reported by Wickman can be substantiated in Israel today, and finds that the orders of seriousness as given by teachers and psychologists have now moved much more closely together than in the Wickman study. Ziv also examines the seriousness of children's behaviour from a different standpoint by asking the children themselves what they feel about the importance of different sorts of behaviour in the classroom. His comparison between the views of the teachers and the views of children is an interesting one.

This 'consumer reaction' approach is followed in the next paper, by T. Moore, in which the difficulties experienced by children in the school situation are studied in some depth. Not only do teachers find aspects of children's behaviour troublesome: children themselves find aspects of school quite disturbing. This article indicates which of the different aspects of the primary school are worrying to children and also indicates the way in which their dislikes and anxieties change over the years of primary school.

This section ends with a short article which focuses in some detail on one single element of behaviour: nail-biting. The article shows how an aspect of behaviour which is sometimes regarded as rather unusual and indicative of unnecessary anxiety, is in fact widely distributed in the school population. This is not a comment on the seriousness or otherwise of the habit, but an indication that some knowledge of the incidence and extent of children's behaviour is often enlightening. It provides us with an informative backcloth against which we can set those elements of behaviour with which we ourselves in the classroom may be particularly concerned.

WICKMAN, E. K.

1. Teachers' List of Undesirable Forms of Behaviour

To enquire into the social dicta on what constitutes undesirable conduct is a necessary starting point for any objective study of the behavior disorders of children. Most textbooks on discipline and child training are written from the point of view of the author's individual judgments about desirable and undesirable, healthy and unhealthy behavior. Relatively few studies are available in which the opinions of a social group have been collected on this subject.

In the studies of behavior problems of children conducted in the two elementary schools in Minneapolis and Cleveland, the investigation was first directed to securing the individual and combined opinions of the teachers on what constitutes undesirable behavior. This was accomplished by means of a schedule on which the teachers were requested to list all the kinds of behavior problems which they had encountered in their teaching careers.

In analyzing the data obtained from these reports with reference to what they may reveal in the way of teachers' attitudes toward children's behavior, we shall first present the tabulated list of behavior problems reported by the teachers in the Cleveland school. This list will then be compared with the reports from the teachers in the Minneapolis school and with the list of behavior problems for which children were referred by parents, teachers, and social agencies to a child guidance clinic.

The twenty-seven teachers in the Cleveland school who reported on this questionnaire submitted a long list of behavior problems which they had encountered in their professional experience. There was a total of 428 items in the reports from these twenty-seven teachers. When

Wickman, E. K. (1928) 'Teachers' list of undesirable forms of behavior,' in *Children's Behavior and Teachers' Attitudes*. New York: The Commonwealth Fund, Chapter III.

duplications were eliminated, there were 185 separate items of undesirable behavior. Not all the returns will be reproduced here; but an abridged list, wherein many of the individual descriptions are omitted, was arranged by classifying the responses according to similar types of problems. The classification is composed of seven major groups, each containing sub-classifications. These groups are quite arbitrarily determined and were established for convenience in analyzing the results and for obtaining a comprehensive classification of behavior problems in which synonymous and closely related descriptions were combined. It should be noted that this classification was not indicated on the questionnaires to the teachers. By permitting the teachers to make spontaneous replies, it was hoped that they would record freely the kinds of behavior which they considered and treated as undesirable and that thereby they would reveal the nature of their distinctions between wholesome and unwholesome, desirable and undesirable conduct in children.

In the following classified list of problems reported by the group of teachers, the behavior descriptions in italics indicate the author's terminology in establishing groupings. In some instances a single descriptive term appearing in the teachers' reports was adopted for the caption of a sub-group; and in that case the term is not italicized. The numbers that follow the behavior descriptions signify the number of times the problems were reported. It will be noted that numbers appear both after the group captions and after the individual descriptions of undesirable behavior within these groups. The former indicate the total frequency with which problems classified within these groups were reported; the latter specify the frequency with which the particular descriptive terms were recorded. In many instances a teacher reported the same general type of behavior problem more than once by describing different ways in which the problem might be manifested; as for example, one teacher described three forms of dishonesty by listing 'lying', 'evasion of the truth', and 'attempt to deceive'; another teacher reported twenty-five kinds of disorderliness in the classroom.

GROUP I

Violations of General Standards of Morality and Integrity (76)

Stealing 11: Stealing 9, Theft 2.

Dishonesties 44: Lying 7, Untruthfulness 7, Dishonesty 3, Deceitfulness 6, Evasion of truth 2, Cheating 7, Falsehood 1, Bluffing 2, Untrustworthiness 2, Pretense 1,

Fabrication 1, Exaggeration 1, Copying from other's papers 1, Hypocrisy 1, Lack of honor 1, Forgery 1.

'Immorality' 12: Bad Physical habits 3, Immorality 4, Obscenity 2, Unclean Thoughts, Glances, Notes 1, Vulgarity 1, Sex problems 1.

Profanity 4: Swearing 2, Profanity 2.

Smoking 2.

Miscellany 3: Unlawfulness, Lack of Ideals, Unjustness.

GROUP II

Transgressions Against Authority (27)

Disobedience 13, Disrespect to authority 4, Defiance 4, Impertinence 1, Slowness in obeying instructions 1, Refusal to do things when asked 1, Wilful misconstruction 1, Refusal to do anything that is right unless forced 1, Insubordination 1.

GROUP III

Violations of General School Regulations (30)

Truancy 16.

Tardiness 11.

Irregularity in attendance 1, Taking articles home 1, Destroying materials 1.

GROUP IV

Violations of Classroom Rules (70)

Disorderliness 33 (Many individual descriptions of petty behavior annoyances or failure to comply with school routine, e.g. playing with pencil, disorderly lines, unnecessary noise, etc.)

Restlessness 4.

Interruptions 16.

Too social 9; Whispering 6.

Lack of supplies 2.

Miscellaneous 6.

GROUP V

Violations of School Work Requirements (41)

Inattention 13: Inattention—inattentiveness 11, Lack of concentration 2.

Lack of Interest 4: Indifference 3, Lack of interest 1.

Carelessness 11: Carelessness 6, Irresponsibility 2, Unreliability 1, Lack of pride in work 1, Inaccuracy 1.

Laziness 13: Laziness 4, Lack of effort 1, Idleness 1, Dawdling 1, Procrastination 1, Refusing to form habit of preparedness 1, Indolence 1, Lack of initiative 1, Shirking 1, Evades duties 1.

Difficulties with Other Children (38)

Annoying Other Children 24: Annoying 11, Cruelty 3, Roughness 3, Fighting 4, Bullying 2, Punching 1.

Tattling 6.

Miscellany 8: Disregard of rights of others 2, Getting others into trouble 1, Quarrelsomeness 1, Coloreds and Whites fighting 1, Laughing at others' mistakes 1, Imposing on others 1, Interfering with the work of others 1.

GROUP VII

Undesirable Personality Traits (136)

Negativisms 27: Stubbornness 16, Sulkiness 3, Sullenness 1, Contrariness 2, Obstinacy 2, Disposition to argue 1, Hectoring 1, Persistency 1.

Unacceptable Social Manners 19: Impudence 6, Impoliteness 5, Rudeness 3, Discourtesy 3, Uncivil 1, Sarcastic 1.

Self-Indulgences 15: Selfishness 9, Unsportsmanship 2, Jealousy 1, Greediness 1, Not altruistic 1, Lack of loyalty 1.

Arrogance 14: Overbearing 2, Forwardness 2, Overconfidence 2, Domineering 1, Feeling of superiority 1, Boastfulness 1, Dictatorialness 1, Always wants to lead 1, Pride 1, Conceited 1, Too independent 1.

Diffidence 14: Bashfulness 4, Shyness 3, Sensitiveness 2, Too dependent 2, Self-conscious 1, Too timid 1, Failure to join group 1.

Evasions 11: Evasiveness 1, Lack of forthrightness 1, Insincere 1, Sneakiness 1, Failure to confess fault 1, Over-critical of others to hide faults 2, Evades punishments 1, Thoughtlessness 2, Forgetting 1.

Interferences 12: Destructiveness 5, Curiosity 2, Meddlesomeness 2, Gossiping 2, Inquisitiveness 1.

Lack of Emotional Control 13: Temper 6, Lack of Self-Control 5, Crying 2.

Undesirable Mental States 3: Dissatisfied 1, Unhappy 1, Resentful 1.

Miscellany 8: Uncleanliness of habits and personal appearance 2, Lack of pride in self 2, Listlessness 1, Silliness 3.

Not all of the twenty-seven teachers recorded items in each of the seven groups of problems. The items under the classification of violations of classroom rules were reported by sixteen teachers; transgressions against authority, by seventeen; evasions of school work requirements, by eighteen; difficulties with other children, by twenty; infractions of general school regulations, by twenty-one; violations of general moral standards, by twenty-two; but all twenty-seven contributed one or more items under the classification of undesirable personality traits. Only four of the teachers enumerated items in all of the seven major groups of problems. No single teacher's report approached the range of problems described by the entire group.

On first reading, the above may appear to be a rather impressive list of kinds of undesirable behavior and may arouse sympathy for the child who must run the gauntlet of these teachers' inspections of his behavior as he passes through the grades. If we can take these declarations of behaviour problems at their face value, it would seem that the child who escapes the frowns and disapprovals of the teachers must be the exception. A child entirely free from all of these behavior disturbances might very well be regarded with some alarm. The extensiveness of this list of problems raises the question whether the teachers who declared it were an unusually 'strict' group of disciplinarians.

However, when we compare these reports obtained from the teachers in one representative school in Cleveland with the responses secured by similar methods from the teachers of another representative school in a city 600 miles distant, the two lists are found to be in essential agreement. With some differences in terminology the items of problem behavior reported by the teachers in the Minneapolis school covered all of the seven major groups and their sub-headings in the above classified list. There is only one minor exception. The list prepared by the teachers in Minneapolis contains no item describing the 'dissatisfied' or 'unhappy' child; but this exception is negligible inasmuch as both of these items were declared only once and by the same teacher in the Cleveland school. A few additional descriptions of behavior problems appear in the Minneapolis teachers' list which are here presented with the numbers indicating the frequency with which they were reported by the twenty-nine teachers in this school:

Nervousness 4; Inferiority complex 1; Fatigue 2; Stupidity 1; Unwillingness to work at hard tasks 1; Poor posture 1; Naughtiness, a form of impatience 1; Dreamer 1; Inability to conform to the group 4; Ill-breeding 1; Hereditary criminal tendencies 1; Self-abuse 3; Clashing of personalities 1; Forming of gangs 1; Desire to be center of attraction 1; Speech defects 1; Religion 1; Dislike for school 1.

For a further check on the adequacy of the above list of recognized behavior problems in children, we may utilize the records of behavior clinics to which parents, teachers, social agencies, and juvenile courts refer behavior-problem children. A search through these records (the records include 367 cases referred to the demonstration child guidance clinic in Minneapolis during 1924, and 756 cases refered to the demonstration child guidance clinic in Cleveland during 1925–6) reveals that all of the items of undesirable behavior designated by the teachers in the two schools in Minneapolis and Cleveland were variously reported in the cases of children referred to the clinics. There were, of course, minor differences in terminology and many of the individual descriptions of problems were reported for only a few of the thousand clinic cases; but all of the major groups and sub-groups of problems, as classified above, were richly represented. In addition some problems were designated in the clinic cases which do not appear in the teachers' lists. These additions for the most part appeared in cases referred to the clinic by parents and it is interesting in this connection to observe the differences between the general types of behavior disorders for which parents referred their children and the problems reported by our teachers.

In making this comparison it appears that both parents and teachers recognize problems involving violations of standards of morality and integrity, disobedience and disrespect for authority, overactivity and lack of concentrated interests, temper outbursts, quarrelsomeness and difficulties with other children, as well as certain undesirable personality traits, more especially contrariness and obstinacy. Parents, however, seem to be much more concerned than teachers with neurotic habits of children, such as enuresis, nail-biting, thumb-sucking, fears, nervousness, tics, problems of eating and sleeping.

Parents also add to the teachers' list the following: suspicious attitudes, not confidential, being easily influenced by companions, fearlessness, lack of appreciation of danger and harm, cowardliness in physical activities, muscular inability and incoordinations.

It is probable that parents are in a better position than teachers to observe most of these problems, and perhaps they are more concerned with such conditions in their children; but it is noteworthy that none of the teachers in either school listed neurotic habits or the particular difficulties in social adjustments. As might be expected, teachers seem to be more aware than parents of problems relating to the school situation such as truancy, tardiness, inattention, laziness, and especially disorderliness. They also stress the problems of impoliteness, selfishness, and boastfulness in children. There is a suggestion that parents may be more concerned than teachers with the oversensitive and unhappy child.

These suggestive differences between the teachers' and parents' recognition of behavior disorders in children require more extensive investigation before valid conclusions can be drawn. Such an investigation might be undertaken with considerable profit. No attempt has been made in our study to secure experimental evidence on the peculiar characteristics of teachers' reactions to child behavior as different from parental or social reactions generally. Beyond the above observations, the position is taken that attitudes as discerned by the methods employed in this investigation are not restricted necessarily to teachers, but that they reflect possibly the prevailing attitudes of the general social order.

Judging from the comparisons just made between the list of behavior problems of children prepared by the teachers of the two schools and the problems recognized by parents, we may conclude that the teachers in the Cleveland school are not exceptional in their declarations concerning undesirable behavior as tabulated above. Moreover, it appears that when the items of problem behavior enumerated by the entire teaching staff of a representative school are assembled, the list is a fairly inclusive inventory of the entire range of conduct disorders recognized by parents and teachers generally. But this completeness of the list is obtained only by combining the judgments of the entire group of teachers. When we study the reports submitted by the individual teachers, we find highly individualized and specialized responses. The fact that no single teacher's report in either the Cleveland or the Minneapolis school approached the general range of problems enumerated by the group, is indicative of differences in attitudes or at least of individual sensitivities toward problems in child behavior. Only five teachers in both schools submitted items for all of the seven major groups. Of the rest, the majority listed problems mostly classifiable under four or five sub-groups, while many of the teachers' reports were confined to items in only two or three sub-groups. Though nearly all teachers listed some item in the general group of undesirable personality traits, even here they individually stressed specific types of difficulties. The individual teacher seemed to be concerned mostly either with the stubborn, the disorderly, the irresponsible, the untruthful, or the disobedient child. A few reports from individual teachers are here reproduced to illustrate these individual differences.

A teacher in the Minneapolis school, who submitted the following list, seems to be chiefly concerned with problems of obedience and honesty. Note that the first seven items are all descriptive of a pupil's antagonism toward the teacher's authority:

Determination to have own way

Contrariness

Antagonistic attitude toward teacher and others in authority

Disobedience

Stubbornness

Conceitedness

Self-pity, feeling of not getting a square deal

Indifference

Laziness

Dishonesty

Tendency to lie

Sneakiness

Tendency to steal

Another teacher in the Minneapolis school concentrates attention on problems which offend her standards of morality. Her entire list was as follows:

Stealing of money and such things as pencils, pens, etc.

Telling lies

Cheating

Swearing

Telling obscene stories

Writing obscene notes

Drawing obscene pictures

Smoking cigarettes, chewing tobacco, drinking whisky and liquor

Destroying property wilfully

Carrying dangerous weapons

Boys who bully smaller boys and molest girls

Children always quarreling with other children

Truancy

Laziness

Sullenness

Insolence

Runaways from home

Ungovernable temper

Cruelty, such as tying cans to cat's tails, getting dogs to chase cats, getting dogs to fight each other, killing birds and stealing birds' eggs

It is possible to discern a dominant note in all of the items enumerated by this teacher in the Cleveland school, though she is one of the five teachers whose descriptions of undesirable behavior are sufficiently extensive to be classifiable under the seven major groups of problems:

Falsehood

Immorality

Bluffing

Unjustness

Profanity

Vulgarity

Truancy

Tardiness

Indolence

Carelessness

Lack of pride in work

Wilful misconstruction

Wilful disobedience

Refuses to do anything that is right unless forced to do so

Harrassing others

Always getting others into trouble

Quarrelsomeness

Tattling

Uncleanness of habits and personal appearance

Sneakiness, i.e. waiting until someone's back is turned to do petty things

Demanding constant attention by thrusting themselves forward, or pert actions

Stubbornness

Obstinacy

Hectoring

Discourteousness

Rudeness

Pretense

Forgery of parent's name

Forgery of other people's names

Deception

Cheating

Theft

Impudence

Persistency

Impoliteness

Selfishness

Boastfulness

Resentfulness

Gossiping

Lack of self-control

Failure to confess a fault even when they know they have been found out

Lack of pride in self

Overcritical of others to hide their own faults

Dictatorialness

Domineering

Talkativeness

Boisterousness

Interrupting

Restlessness

Untidiness of desks

Impromptu recitations

Shoving and pushing to get ahead of someone else

Those who will not sit still at least two minutes

There is little doubt as to the type of discipline maintained by the Cleveland teacher who submitted the following:

Telling an untruth

Copying from some other person's paper

Truancy

Laughing at other's mistakes

Excusing themselves from trouble by blaming someone else

Whispering when child should be working

Not putting pens down when told in writing lesson

Raising hands when standing

Standing on wrong side of seat when ready to answer

Not standing still when ready to answer

Casting side glances to another child

Snickering

Noise when getting books out of desk for next class

Turning around in seat

In a music lesson to hum or sing aloud when asked to study

Wasting time when coming into the room

Writing notes

Playing with pencil, ruler, etc.

Disorderly lines when passing

Asking to leave room when not necessary

Not getting to work upon coming into the room

Talking when not being called upon

Erasing board when asked to leave work there

Talking in the hall

Talking aloud in library

Unnecessary noise in coming up steps

Failure to bring required materials

Failure to have necessary materials ready for work

Watching other people instead of taking care of own work

Fine deductions concerning the nature of teachers' attitudes cannot be drawn, to be sure, from a rough inspection of their statements about the types of undesirable behavior which they have encountered in their teaching careers. However, a perusal of the list of behavior problems, so obtained, gives a definite impression of a general pervading characteristic in the problems enumerated. With very few exceptions they represent disturbances. Either the behavior violates the teacher's principles of morality, her authority, the school and classroom order, the required standards of study, or it disturbs through difficulties with other children. Even the personality traits enumerated are limited almost entirely to those which are disagreeable and annoying. The majority of the items represent what children do that is undesirable, not what they fail to do. Behavior problems, in the teachers' estimations, thus appear to be active disturbances that attack the standards of morality, obedience, orderliness, and agreeable social conduct.

In the teachers' list there is a conspicuous paucity of items describing child problems which are indicative of social and emotional maladjustment but which are not directly disturbing to school routine. Those individual problems of the child which do not cause active annoyance to the teacher appear only casually in the teachers' reports. Such personal problems are described in the few items of shyness, sensitiveness, unsocialness, and unhappiness which were recognized by eight of the twenty-seven teachers of the Cleveland school and by only three of the twenty-nine teachers of the Minneapolis school. It is possible, however, that the wording of the questionnaire did not elicit responses indicating the recognition of these kinds of problems.

The suggestive findings obtained from this initial approach to the study of teachers' attitudes toward child behavior raised important questions for further investigation for which more refined methods of enquiry were necessary. For example: Are behavior problems in school children diagnosed by the immediate effect of the behavior on the teachers? Is the problem child in school identified chiefly by annoying, aggressive, disobedient behavior? Are problems of shyness, dependency, and retirement in children regarded by teachers as important problems in behavior?

WICKMAN, E. K.

2. Teachers' Reactions to Behaviour Problems of Children

The data thus far presented on the subject of teachers' reactions to the behavior of their pupils have related to an analysis of the kinds of behavior which identify the problem child to the teacher. The evidence indicated that the teachers who cooperated in the experiments reacted differently to various types of troublesome behavior, and suggested that such differences in reaction were determined by the immediate effect of the behavior disorders upon the teachers themselves. The individual behavior problems of the child which had the least effect upon the teachers' moral sensitivities and immediate teaching purposes were submerged apparently under the weight of the more overt forms of undesirable conduct. Such problems were considered relatively unimportant and therefore more desirable modes of behavior.

It now remains to verify these observations by more direct measurements of the teachers' reactions to the various types of behavior problems. Such measurements were sought by sounding the teachers' attitudes toward the relative seriousness, unwholesomeness, or undesirableness of troublesome forms of child behavior. In this connection it was necessary also to consider how typical were the attitudes of the small group of teachers in the one Cleveland school in which this study originated. Here the questions arose whether the reactions of these teachers could be considered representative of the reactions of teachers generally, and whether we would be justified in drawing any general conclusions from our investigation. To answer such questions an effort was made to elicit the reactions of many and heterogeneous groups of teachers.

Two methods were employed in the Cleveland school for measuring

Wickman, E. K. (1928) 'Teachers' reactions to behavior problems of children', in *Children's Behavior and Teachers' Attitudes*. New York: The Commonwealth Fund, Chapter IV.

the teachers' attitudes toward the relative seriousness or unwholesomeness of the different kinds of problem behavior. The first method
consisted of a rating scale on which the teachers recorded their beliefs
and opinions about the relative seriousness of fifty types of problems
considered abstractly when occurring in any child. This scale was later
employed in educing the judgments of teachers from different schools
in various communities. The second method was incorporated in the
schedule on which the teachers in the Cleveland school evaluated the
seriousness of any form of troublesome behavior whenever they reported
its occurrence in an individual child under their care. The difference
between the first and second methods is that in the former the teachers
estimated the seriousness of any form of behavior in the abstract as it
might occur in any child, while in the latter method the individual
teacher indicated her reactions to the seriousness of a specified problem
observed in a particular pupil in her room. The results from the
application of the first method will be presented here. Data from the
second method are confined to reports from the Cleveland experiment
while the results from the first method include data from the control
groups.

Teachers' Ratings on the Relative Seriousness of Behavior Problems

As previously described, the investigation undertaken in the Cleveland
school began with a questionnaire to teachers on which they were
requested to report all the kinds of behavior problems in children
which they had encountered in their teaching experience. Two weeks
later, a rating scale was administered for the purpose of measuring
the teachers' reactions to the different kinds of behavior problems. This
schedule contained a list of fifty items of troublesome behavior which
had been established by classifying the teachers' responses on the
previous questionnaire, compared with and supplemented by responses
obtained by similar means from the teachers in the Minneapolis school
and by the list of problems for which the first 300 children had been
referred to the child guidance clinic in Cleveland. On this rating scale
the teachers were asked to make two judgments with respect to each
of the fifty problems. First they were directed to record their opinions
on the incidence of these problems among school children. Second,
they were asked to make a judgment on the relative seriousness of the
problems whenever they occurred in any child. Both ratings were made

with reference to their occurrence in boys and girls separately. One
week later the rating scales with slight changes in directions were
administered a second time in order to correct an obvious error in the
interpretation of the directions by three teachers on the previous ratings
and to secure a check on the reliability of the ratings.[1]

The data with which we are here concerned relate to the teachers'
ratings on the relative seriousness of the fifty items of troublesome
behavior. The term 'seriousness' was set up for the teachers as equivalent to the undesirableness of the various behavior problems, the
difficulty encountered in coping with them, and the evidence of child
maladjustment represented by them. The printed directions defined the
term by directing the teachers to respond to the question, 'How serious
is it for the individual child who shows this behavior? In other words,
how much does it make him a problem child, disturbing or a misfit?
This amounts to the same thing as asking, "How undesirable is this
behavior in the school child?" ' The teachers recorded their judgments
on a graphic rating scale with four calibrations that corresponded to
captions describing the following degrees of seriousness:

> Of no consequence*
> Of only slight consequence
> Makes for considerable difficulty
> An extremely grave offense[2]

To indicate their judgments about the seriousness of a problem, the
teachers were directed to make their ratings at any point on the scale
used in Chart 2.1, p. 20, either at one of the four designated points
corresponding to the descriptive captions or anywhere in between. This
permitted them to make finer distinctions in their judgments about the
seriousness of the different problems than would have been possible
by limiting their ratings to the four fixed degrees.

The teachers were not informed that the rating scale was primarily
designed to measure their attitudes toward the behavior problems. Such
a statement would have aroused an intellectual control over their
ratings and would have stimulated their personal and professional pride
to make judgments according to ideas of 'right' or 'book-perfect'
responses. Efforts were made to avoid establishing a 'mental set' for
making ratings that would please the investigator or show up well in
a report. The real purpose of the scale was to measure the teachers'

---

* This particular calibration is not shown on the charts in the text—ed.

customary habits of thinking about and reacting to the occurrence of troublesome forms of behavior in their pupils. For this reason the rating scale was introduced to them with the statement that it represented an effort to secure necessary information in evaluating the seriousness of behavior problems in children, and the terminology employed in setting up the scale included such words as serious, undesirable, misfit, disturbing, problem child, maladjusted. Stress was laid on the degree of undesirableness of a particular behavior problem in a child and the amount of difficulty produced in coping with the problem, with the hope that, by so directing them, the teachers' emotional reactions to the problems might be elicited. The assumption was that the degree to which teachers considered a particular form of behavior undesirable represented the energy they exerted toward the modification of such behavior. As will be seen later, this method also afforded an insight into the teachers' requirements of classroom behavior and into their habits of treating the behavior symptoms of maladjustment.

One additional point of technique was employed to reduce the tendency to intellectualize or rationalize in making ratings of this kind. A time limit of thirty minutes was imposed for reading the directions and making the two hundred ratings required on the two scales (frequency of occurrence and seriousness) of the fifty problems as they occurred in boys and girls separately. Moreover, the teachers were urged to make their ratings as rapidly as possible.[3] By securing their first immediate reactions to the problems without permitting much time for rationalization, it was hoped that their everyday responses would be elicited rather than their studied intellectual responses indicating what their attitudes 'ought' to be.

An element of rational control undoubtedly entered into the teachers' ratings despite our precautions. In view of the results obtained, however, the allowance for this factor in the interpretation of the data would only lend further support to the conclusions that will be drawn. For conservative interpretation we shall consider the ratings as representative of the teachers' everyday reactions to the problems listed in the scale.

The results obtained from the twenty-eight teachers in the Cleveland school are graphically displayed in Charts 2.1 and 2.2. The ratings on the seriousness of each of the fifty items of troublesome behavior were scored by means of a calibrated rule. The length of the bars in the charts represents the average of the ratings of the twenty-eight teachers

CHART 2.1

TEACHERS' RATINGS ON THE RELATIVE SERIOUSNESS OF BEHAVIOR PROBLEMS WHEN
OCCURRING IN A BOY
(RATINGS OF 28 TEACHERS, CLEVELAND SCHOOL)

Rated Seriousness of Problem

Rating Scale

Type of Problem	Average Score	Of Only Slight Consequence 4·5	Makes for Considerable Difficulty 12·5	An Extremely Grave Problem 20·5
STEALING	16·9			
HETEROSEXUAL ACTIVITY	16·9			
OBSCENE NOTES, TALK	15·6			
UNTRUTHFULNESS	15·6			
MASTURBATION	15·5			
DISOBEDIENCE	15·1			
PROFANITY	14·9			
IMPERTINENCE, DEFIANCE	14·5			
CRUELTY, BULLYING	14·3			
CHEATING	14·0			
TRUANCY	13·9			
DESTROYING SCHOOL MATERIALS	13·9			
SMOKING	13·9			
DISORDERLINESS IN CLASS	13·8			
UNRELIABLENESS	13·5			
TEMPER TANTRUMS	13·0			
QUARRELSOMENESS	12·8			
IMPUDENCE, RUDENESS	12·3			
LAZINESS	12·0			
CARELESSNESS IN WORK	11·9			
SUGGESTIBLE	11·9			
LACK OF INTEREST IN WORK	11·5			
INATTENTION	11·3			
RESENTFULNESS	11·2			
SULLENNESS	11·0			
UNHAPPY, DEPRESSED	11·0			
DOMINEERING	11·0			
STUBBORNNESS	10·8			
WHISPERING	10·6			
EASILY DISCOURAGED	10·5			
PHYSICAL COWARD	10·4			
SELFISHNESS	10·3			
INTERRUPTING	10·3			
SLOVENLY IN APPEARANCE	10·3			
ENURESIS	10·2			
TARDINESS	10·2			
DREAMINESS	9·8			
NERVOUSNESS	9·7			
ATTRACTING ATTENTION	9·4			
TATTLING	9·3			
RESTLESSNESS	9·2			
OVERCRITICAL OF OTHERS	8·7			
THOUGHTLESSNESS	8·4			
SUSPICIOUSNESS	8·4			
IMAGINATIVE LYING	8·3			
FEARFULNESS	8·2			
UNSOCIALNESS	7·8			
SENSITIVENESS	7·7			
INQUISITIVENESS	7·5			
SHYNESS	6·7			

CHART 2.2

TEACHERS RATINGS ON THE RELATIVE SERIOUSNESS OF BEHAVIOR PROBLEMS WHEN
OCCURRING IN A GIRL

(RATINGS OF 28 TEACHERS, CLEVELAND SCHOOL)

Rated Seriousness of Problem

Rating Scale

Type of Problem	Average Score	Of Only Slight Consequence 4·5	Makes for Considerable Difficulty 12·5	An Extremely Grave Problem 20·5
HETEROSEXUAL ACTIVITY	16·6			
OBSCENE NOTES, TALK	16·2			
STEALING	16·1			
SMOKING	15·7			
PROFANITY	15·0			
DISOBEDIENCE	14·9			
MASTURBATION	14·9			
CHEATING	14·3			
UNTRUTHFULNESS	13·9			
UNRELIABLENESS	13·5			
TEMPER TANTRUMS	13·3			
TRUANCY	12·9			
CRUELTY, BULLYING	12·8			
IMPERTINENCE, DEFIANCE	12·7			
IMPUDENCE, RUDENESS	12·5			
DESTROYING SCHOOL MATERIALS	12·2			
STUBBORNNESS	12·2			
QUARRELSOMENESS	12·0			
DISORDERLINESS IN CLASS	11·9			
SUGGESTIBLE	11·7			
LAZINESS	11·5			
SULLENNESS	11·4			
LACK OF INTEREST IN WORK	11·1			
CARELESSNESS IN WORK	10·9			
SLOVENLY IN APPEARANCE	10·9			
INATTENTION	10·8			
UNHAPPY, DEPRESSED	10·7			
WHISPERING	10·7			
SELFISHNESS	10·7			
DOMINEERING	10·5			
RESENTFULNESS	10·4			
TATTLING	10·4			
INTERRUPTING	10·4			
THOUGHTLESSNESS	10·2			
EASILY DISCOURAGED	10·0			
ENURESIS	9·9			
INQUISITIVENESS	9·7			
ATTRACTING ATTENTION	9·6			
RESTLESSNESS	9·6			
TARDINESS	9·6			
NERVOUSNESS	9·4			
OVERCRITICAL OF OTHERS	9·0			
SUSPICIOUS	9·0			
UNSOCIALNESS	9·0			
PHYSICAL COWARD	9·0			
IMAGINATIVE LYING	8·6			
DREAMINESS	8·6			
SENSITIVENESS	8·2			
FEARFULNESS	8·0			
SHYNESS	7·5			

on each of the items. Chart 2.1 shows the average ratings on the seriousness of these problems when occurring in a boy, Chart 2.2 when occurring in a girl.

It should be realized that the data portrayed in the graphs, being confined to the averages of ratings from twenty-eight teachers, are apt to be misleading in that they show *apparent* differences between the rated seriousness of most of the fifty items of behavior which are not always *significant* or very *reliable* differences. Two factors enter into these ratings which affect the significance of the observed differences. They are: (1) the small number of teachers rating and (2) the lack of entire uniformity in the ratings made by the different teachers. The first factor was checked by obtaining ratings from many more teachers, and data from these extended investigations will be presented later in this chapter. But, even without this supporting evidence, it is still possible to draw some deductions from the results obtained in the one Cleveland school in which this study of attitudes originated, if we observe the necessary precautions of interpretation imposed by the limitations of the data. A statistical check made on the significance of the apparent differences in the average ratings as shown in the charts, which took into account both of the aforementioned limiting factors, indicated that any difference amounting to approximately 3 of the raw units of the scale between the average ratings of any two items could be interpreted as a significant difference. Such a criterion warranted the prediction that there would be better than 99 chances in 100 of obtaining a difference (either smaller or larger) in the same direction, if the experiment were repeated under the same standard conditions. To be more explicit, though we may observe an apparent difference in Chart 2.1 between the teachers' ratings on the seriousness of 'stealing' (average rating, 16·9) and 'untruthfulness' (average rating, 15·6) the difference between the averages of these ratings amounts to only 1·3 units of measurement which is not sufficiently significant to justify the conclusion that the teachers as a group considered 'stealing' more serious than 'untruthfulness'. On the other hand, 'stealing' may be said to have been considered more serious than 'truancy' (average rating, 13·9) and all the succeeding items in the list because the difference between the average ratings is 3 units or over. The point which we wish to emphasize here is that apparent differences in average ratings observed by simply reading the charts are not always significant or reliable differences when the data are treated statistically.

With this limitation imposed upon the data, our interpretations will be confined to an observation of the tendencies in the teachers' ratings of the seriousness of the various behavior disorders. Some extremely significant facts may be deduced from just such observations.

The most striking fact to be noted in the ratings is the agreement between the results obtained by this method and our previous methods of measuring teachers' reactions. The active, aggressive, overt forms of troublesome behavior were regarded in each instance as more serious than the inhibitive, repressive, inactive, personal problems of children. Indeed, the former were rated at the top of the scale as the most serious of all problems while the latter were considered least serious and of little consequence. In the following analysis of the teachers' ratings we have listed in the first column the items of behavior which were rated as the most serious of all problems for both boys and girls. In the second column are listed all the items which were considered of least consequence and which, according to the statistical criterion, were rated reliably less serious than any and all of the problems enumerated in the first column.

ANALYSIS OF PROBLEMS RATED MOST AND LEAST SERIOUS
BY TEACHERS IN THE CLEVELAND SCHOOL

Problems Rated as Most Serious	*Problems Rated as Reliably Less Serious, and Least Consequential of all Problems*
Stealing	
Heterosexual activity	Shyness
Obscene notes, talk	Fearfulness
Masturbation	Sensitiveness
Profanity	Imaginative lying
Smoking	Unsocialness
Disobedience	Suspiciousness
Untruthfulness	Overcritical of others
Cheating	
Unreliableness	
Temper tantrums	
Truancy	
Cruelty, bullying	
Impertinence, defiance	
Impudence, rudeness	
Destroying school materials	
Quarrelsomeness	
Disorderliness in class	

Considering the manner in which this scale was set up for the teachers, we should conclude from their ratings that they found the aggressive, antisocial, attacking activities of children the most difficult and undesirable of all behavior problems and that they devoted their major attention to the correction of just such forms of troublesome behavior. On the other hand, they regarded the unsocial, inhibitive forms of behavior as the least serious among the fifty problems listed and as relatively more desirable forms of behavior.

Nearly all the items describing undesirable personality characteristics of children, whether descriptive of attacking or withdrawing traits, are confined in the lower half of the lists of items in the two charts which designate the problems considered to be the less serious. The upper half of the lists, on the other hand, contain with few exceptions only overt forms of undesirable behavior.

For purposes of analyzing the teachers' attitudes toward certain related types of problems, we have arbitrarily drawn from the entire list of items a number of problems that are closely associated as regards the general character of the troublesome behavior which they represent, and we have then compared the group of problems so established with the remaining items in the list that are reliably distinguished in having been rated either more serious or less serious. A number of such groups of related problems have been established in this fashion. The first column in each of the following groups contains the arbitrarily selected problems of a related kind. The second column then contains all problems which were rated significantly less serious (for both boys and girls) than any and all of the items so selected; and the third column includes all problems rated significantly more serious.

PROBLEMS RELATING TO IMMORALITY DISHONESTY, ETC.	Problems Rated Reliably Less Serious	Problems Rated Reliably More Serious
Heterosexual activity	Shyness	(None)
Obscene notes, talk	Sensitiveness	
Masturbation	Fearfulness	
Stealing	Unsocialness	
Untruthfulness	Imaginative lying	
Cheating	Suspiciousness	
Profanity	Thoughtlessness	
Smoking	Overcritical of others	
	Restlessness	

Tattling
Nervousness
Attracting attention
Inquisitiveness
Dreaminess
Tardiness
Enuresis
Slovenly in appearance
Interrupting
Selfishness
Physical cowardliness
Easily discouraged
Whispering

PROBLEMS RELATING TO DIFFICULTIES WITH AUTHORITY	Problems Rated Reliably Less Serious	Problems Rated Reliably More Serious
Disobedience	Shyness	(None)
Impertinence, defiance	Sensitiveness	
Temper tantrums	Fearfulness	
Impudence, rudeness	Unsocialness	
	Imaginative lying	
	Suspiciousness	
	Overcritical of others	
	Dreaminess	

PROBLEMS RELATING TO DIFFICULTIES IN APPLICATION TO SCHOOL WORK	Problems Rated Reliably Less Serious	Problems Rated Reliably More Serious
Inattention	Shyness	Stealing
Lack of interest	Sensitiveness	Heterosexual activity
Carelessness	Fearfulness	Obscene notes, talk
Laziness		
Unreliableness		

PROBLEMS DESCRIBING AGGRESSIVE AND ANTAGONISTIC PERSONALITY TRAITS	Problems Rated Reliably Less Serious	Problems Rated Reliably More Serious
Resentfulness	Shyness	Stealing
Sullenness		Heterosexual activity
Domineering		Obscene notes, talk
Stubbornness		Masturbation
		Disobedience

PROBLEMS DESCRIBING WITHDRAWING AND RECESSIVE PERSONALITY TRAITS	Problems Rated Reliably Less Serious	Problems Rated Reliably More Serious
Shyness	(None)	Stealing
Sensitiveness		Heterosexual activity
Fearfulness		Obscene notes, talk
Unsocialness		Masturbation
Dreaminess		Disobedience
Imaginative lying		Profanity
Physical cowardliness		Smoking
Suspiciousness		Untruthfulness
Easily discouraged		Cheating
Unhappy, depressed		

In addition to the groups above, we may note that the single item describing disorderliness in class was rated fairly high in the scale of seriousness for both boys and girls. Only the problems of 'stealing' and 'heterosexual activity' were rated reliably more serious than 'disorderliness'. 'Whispering', which might be considered a specific form of disorderliness, was rated reliably less serious than 'disorderliness' when occurring in a boy but not when occurring in a girl. Moreover, 'whispering' was rated significantly more serious than 'shyness' for both boys and girls.

In comparing the teachers' ratings on the seriousness of the problems as they occur in a boy and as they occur in a girl, (Chart 2.1 compared with Chart 2.2), it appears by inspection that some problems were rated differently in the two sexes. But when the differences are submitted to the statistical check for the reliability of the difference, only one item, 'inquisitiveness', is found to have been rated with a fairly significant difference in seriousness. This one problem was rated more serious when occurring in a girl than when occurring in a boy. Considering that all the raters were women, this single fairly reliable difference in rating the behavior in the two sexes represents possibly a sex-determined response, but the difference is not sufficiently great to venture an interpretation of its significance, and the difference did not appear again in the ratings obtained from the control groups. On the whole, the rank-order arrangements of the seriousness of the fifty problems when occurring in a boy and when occurring in a girl are quite consistent.[4]

To summarize the above analyses of the ratings made by the teachers in the Cleveland school, we may note simply the direction of the teachers' reactions to the seriousness of the fifty behavior problems. From problems considered most difficult and undesirable to those regarded as least significant, the order is as follows:

Sex problems, stealing, dishonesty, truancy, disobedience
> *more serious than*

Problems of classroom order and application to school tasks
> *more serious than*

Antagonistic, aggressive personality traits
> *more serious than*

Withdrawing, recessive personality traits.

The reliability of the distinctions in teachers' ratings between the seriousness of adjacent groups in the above order is not definitely established by the ratings obtained from the small group of teachers in this school but it is confirmed between the seriousness of alternate groups; and when the number of raters is increased, as will shortly be evident in examining the ratings from the second control groups of teachers, the above order is reliably established.

Data from First Control Groups of Teachers

The same rating scale as employed in the Cleveland school, adapted with such minor changes as were necessary for introduction to control groups, was administered to three groups of teachers as follows:

Group I. Thirty experienced teachers enrolled in the author's class (1925–26) at Senior Teachers College, Cleveland, in a course entitled 'Behavior Problems of School Children'. The class was composed of three supervisors, three principals, and twenty-four teachers in public schools.

Group II. Forty-one experienced teachers enrolled in a class (1927) of Dr Ruth Andrus, at Teachers College, Columbia University.

Group III. Ten men teachers in a progressive private school for boys. (1927).

These three groups were selected because of availability for control ratings. They were composed of teachers with heterogeneous viewpoints, training, and interests. On the whole the teachers who composed Groups II and III would be considered rather advanced in points of view regarding methods of teaching and classroom management. We should suppose that any marked differences in reactions to behavior problems of children from those of an average group of teachers would be found in just such teachers as were represented in these two groups who had the advantage of highly specialized training and progressive viewpoints in education.

B

The rank-order arrangements of the seriousness of the fifty problems as rated by each of the three groups are presented in Charts 2.3 and 2.4. The items are arranged in rank-order from those rated most serious to those rated least serious. The same caution of interpretation mentioned in connection with the results from the Cleveland school apply as well to these control ratings. Small differences in the average rating of problems are not significant, and might be obliterated in securing ratings from larger numbers of raters. Only the general tendency of rating which can be observed in the types of problems rated from most serious to least serious may be legitimately interpreted.

In comparing these results with those obtained in the Cleveland school, it will be noted that a number of problems are ranked in somewhat different order of seriousness. However, taken as a whole, the agreement is fairly close[5] and the general direction of rating is basically preserved. The problems relating to sex, stealing, dishonesty, disobedience and truancy were again rated as the most serious and difficult problems while most of the recessive, withdrawing traits and the purely personal problems of children were rated reliably less serious than the attacking forms of behavior, and were ranked toward the bottom of the scale where they were considered to be of comparatively little significance. A few exceptions in these control ratings to the order of rating established by the teachers in the Cleveland school, however, deserve attention.

In the results from Control Group I, the problem of masturbation was ranked comparatively low in seriousness, quite differently than by any of the other groups of teachers. It so happened that the scale was administered to this particular group of teachers some time after the course work for which they were enrolled had begun. The course was conducted on a seminar-laboratory scheme of instruction in which the members of the class themselves submitted the types of behavior problems which they wished studied in class. The first topics requested were the problems of sex and disobedience.

Both of these problems had been discussed in relationship to actual cases of problem children and some reading assigned, before the rating scale was administered. The aim of the course was to reduce the teachers' emotional reactions to these forms of undesirable behavior by working through to the natural causes that operated in the production of the problems and the adult attitudes toward them. From the teachers' ratings it will be observed that in the case of masturbation this method

CHART 2.3

TEACHERS' REACTIONS TO BEHAVIOR PROBLEMS OCCURRING IN BOYS,
SHOWING RANK-ORDER ARRANGEMENTS OF RATINGS OF PROBLEMS FROM
MOST TO LEAST SERIOUS

Control Group I Teachers College, Cleveland	Control Group II Teachers College, Columbia	Control Group III Private School for Boys
Cruelty, bullying	Masturbation	Stealing
Untruthfulness	Heterosexual activity	Untruthfulness
Disobedience	Stealing	Masturbation
Impertinence, defiance	Destroying school materials	Heterosexual activities
Obscene notes, talk	Untruthfulness	Obscene notes, talk
Truancy	Cheating	Cruelty, bullying
Unreliableness	Obscene notes, talk	Destroying school materials
Heterosexual activity	Truancy	Quarrelsomeness
Stealing	Temper tantrums	Cheating
Cheating	Smoking	Easily discouraged
Destroying school materials	Unreliableness	Impertinence
Smoking	Unhappy, depressed	Disobedience
Profanity	Easily discouraged	Suggestible
Quarrelsomeness	Suggestible	Selfishness
Temper tantrums	Profanity	Temper tantrums
Suggestible	Physical coward	Domineering
Inattention	Nervousness	Resentfulness
Disorderliness in class	Resentfulness	Tardiness
Laziness	Selfishness	Unsocialness
Selfishness	Enuresis	Stubbornness
Impudence, rudeness	Impudence	Unreliableness
Lack of interest in work	Disobedience	Physical coward
Domineering	Carelessness	Truancy
Sullenness	Quarrelsomeness	Profanity
Carelessness in work	Domineering	Carelessness in work
Physical coward	Fearfulness	Sullenness
Stubbornness	Impertinence	Impudence
Easily discouraged	Cruelty, bullying	Unhappy, depressed
Resentfulness	Lack of interest in work	Smoking
Unhappy, depressed	Laziness	Slovenly in appearance
Interrupting	Sullenness	Disorderly in class
Overcritical of others	Unsocialness	Tattling
Masturbation	Suspiciousness	Enuresis
Nervousness	Tardiness	Inattention
Enuresis	Disorderly in class	Interrupting
Thoughtlessness	Stubbornness	Laziness
Restlessness	Inattention	Thoughtlessness
Tardiness	Sensitiveness	Suspiciousness
Suspiciousness	Shyness	Imaginative lying
Slovenly in appearance	Tattling	Lack of interest
Attracting attention	Slovenly in appearance	Overcritical of others
Fearlessness	Thoughtlessness	Nervousness
Unsocialness	Overcritical of others	Attracting attention
Dreaminess	Imaginative lying	Sensitiveness
Whispering	Dreaminess	Restlessness
Sensitiveness	Attracting attention	Inquisitiveness
Inquisitiveness	Inquisitiveness	Whispering
Tattling	Whispering	Dreaminess
Shyness	Restlessness	Fearfulness
Imaginative lying	Interrupting	Shyness

CHART 2.4

TEACHERS' REACTIONS TO BEHAVIOR PROBLEMS OCCURRING IN GIRLS,
SHOWING RANK-ORDER ARRANGEMENTS OF RATINGS OF PROBLEMS FROM
MOST TO LEAST SERIOUS

Control Group I
Teachers College, Cleveland

Stealing
Obscene notes, talk
Heterosexual activity
Impertinence
Cruelty, bullying
Cheating
Unreliableness
Disobedience
Truancy
Temper tantrums
Destroying school materials
Untruthfulness
Smoking
Lack of interest in work
Profanity
Domineering
Selfishness
Laziness
Quarrelsomeness
Easily discouraged
Carelessness
Inattention
Slovenliness
Impudence
Overcritical of others
Suggestible
Unhappy, depressed
Resentful
Nervousness
Tattling
Thoughtlessness
Enuresis
Sensitiveness
Interrupting
Slovenly in appearance
Physical coward
Unsocialness
Disorderliness in class
Stubbornness
Fearfulness
Whispering
Suspiciousness
Attracting attention
Dreaminess
Masturbation
Tardiness
Inquisitiveness
Restlessness
Shyness
Imaginative lying

Control Group II
Teachers College, Columbia

Heterosexual activity
Stealing
Masturbation
Cheating
Untruthfulness
Obscene notes, talk
Cruelty, bullying
Temper tantrums
Suggestible
Smoking
Nervousness
Unhappy, depressed
Truancy
Resentfulness
Unreliableness
Enuresis
Disobedience
Profanity
Easily discouraged
Destroying school materials
Impertinence
Fearfulness
Selfishness
Suspiciousness
Quarrelsomeness
Domineering
Laziness
Slovenly in appearance
Carelessness in work
Disorderliness
Impudence
Unsocialness
Physical coward
Lack of interest in work
Sensitiveness
Inattention
Sullenness
Thoughtlessness
Stubbornness
Overcritical of others
Tardiness
Tattling
Imaginative lying
Dreaminess
Shyness
Attracting attention
Restlessness
Inquisitiveness
Interrupting
Whispering

of study had apparently altered their reactions inasmuch as they weighted it a less serious problem than did any of our other groups of teachers. Their reactions to 'disobedience', on the other hand, were still very determined, for they rated this item as one of the most serious of all problems. Indeed, this problem remained the principal topic of discussion for the entire term, at the end of which most of the members of the class ranked it less serious than at the beginning, though a few contended to the end that disobedience in children could not be dealt with except through some form of punishment.

The data from Control Group II show the greatest deviations in ratings from those of the other groups of teachers. The members of this group were enrolled in a class at Teachers College, Columbia University, and their ratings reveal, more strikingly than those of any other group, certain influences of modern educational methods, e.g. the encouragement of greater freedom and social expression in the class-room, the adaptation of teaching methods to the individual differences of children. Thus, the items of interrupting, restlessness, whispering, inquisitiveness, attracting attention, were rated at the very bottom of the scale of seriousness as the least difficult of all problems, replacing the items of shyness, unsocialness, sensitiveness, and fearfulness which were awarded that position by other groups of teachers. Disobedience and disorderliness, too, were rated somewhat lower in the amount of difficulty which these problems produced for the teachers in this group than for those in other groups. Likewise, problems relating to difficulties in adjusting to school tasks, like carelessness, lack of interest, inattention, were slightly reduced in degree of seriousness. Though most problems representing withdrawing and recessive tendencies in children were rated comparatively low in the scale of seriousness, there was a noticeable inclination in the ratings of these teachers toward ranking them as slightly more important problems than in the ratings made by any other group of teachers, except Control Group III. In fact a few items like unhappiness and easily discouraged and physical cowardliness were considered to be fairly serious problems. But the behavior difficulties relating to sex, stealing, untruthfulness, truancy were ranked at the very top of the list as the most serious of all problems in entire agreement with the ratings made by all groups of teachers examined.

The significant differences in the ratings made by the teachers in the progressive private school for boys (Control Group III) from those of other groups affected the following problems: unsocialness was rated more serious, physical cowardliness was rated slightly more serious, and truancy was rated considerably less serious. As in Control Group II, disorderliness in class and the problems relating to lack of application to school tasks were ranked comparatively low in the scale of seriousness; while being easily discouraged was rated as a serious problem. But all problems affecting stealing, sex, untruthfulness, disobedience were rated characteristically as the most serious while shyness, fearfulness, dreaminess, sensitiveness were considered to be the least difficult of all problems.

As in the experimental group, in the ratings from Control Groups I and II the differences between the seriousness of problems when occurring in a boy and when occurring in a girl were not significant.[6]

On the whole the ratings from the three control groups corroborate the general conclusion reached from the findings in our experimental group, namely, that teachers consider the inhibitive, recessive, unsocial forms of behavior to be of comparatively little consequence while the antisocial, attacking types of conduct are regarded as extremely serious problems. There was a tendency among teachers in Control Groups II and III, however, to discount the seriousness of problems relating to difficulties in the application to school tasks and to disturbances in the routine of classroom management. This tendency is suggestive of less rigidity in methods of instruction, and of tolerance toward greater freedom in the classroom on the part of teachers in the two control groups than obtained in the other groups of teachers examined.

Data from Additional Control Groups of Teachers

The teachers who composed the first three control groups could not be considered very representative of teachers-at-large, and their ratings reflected some differences in reactions to behavior problems of children. It was desirable, therefore, to obtain control ratings from other groups of teachers in elementary schools who would be more nearly representative of the teaching profession. Accordingly, ratings on the seriousness of the fifty problems were secured from the entire teaching staffs of thirteen elementary public schools in various communities. The entire number of teachers who rated was 511. The schools in which the teachers were located are designated for convenience by letters as follows:

School	Location	Number of Teachers Rating
A	Newark, N. J.	53
B	Newark, N. J.	38
C	New York City	44
D	New York City	63
E	New York City	82
F	New York City	57
G	Cleveland, Ohio	21
H	Cleveland, Ohio	35
I	Cleveland, Ohio	19
J	Cleveland, Ohio	64
K	Three villages in ⎤	
L	Minnesota and ⎬	35
M	New York State ⎦	

The only essential change made from the scale used in the experimental and first control groups was the substitution of the term 'problem' for the word 'offense' in the last descriptive degree of seriousness in the graphic rating scale used. As previously mentioned, the change in terminology was made in order to avoid the influence of the ethical implication in the term 'offense'. As in the other rating scales the teachers were requested under time pressure to rate the seriousness of the fifty items of behavior problems; and the term 'seriousness' was defined by the phrases 'undesirable behavior', 'consequence', 'difficulty produced', 'grave problem'. Because no significant differences were obtained in the experimental and first control groups between the ratings of the seriousness of the problems when occurring in a boy and when occurring in a girl, the teachers in the second control groups were directed to rate simply the seriousness of the problems when occurring in any child.

The methods of scoring and treating results were the same as employed previously. The averages and standard deviations of the ratings made by the teachers in each school indicated that the groups of teachers representing the various schools agreed very closely with each other in the ratings of the seriousness of the different problems. Coefficients of correlation on the rank-order arrangements of the seriousness of the problems between the groups of teachers ranged from 0·79 to 0·90.

The averages of the ratings made by the entire group of 511 teachers are graphically displayed in the accompanying Chart 2.5.[7] Though the caution against interpreting apparent differences in the rated seriousness of the fifty problems applies in principle here as in the results obtained from the experimental group of teachers, the much larger number of raters in these control groups permits the drawing of somewhat finer distinctions between the recorded seriousness of the various problems. The statistical check on the reliability of the difference between two obtained averages indicates that a difference of approximately one unit (instead of three units as in the ratings from the experimental group) on the scale of measurement between the average of the ratings of any two problems may be regarded as a significant difference in *direction* of rating.

The very close agreement between the ratings made by the twenty-eight teachers in the experimental group and the 511 in the thirteen schools of these control groups is apparent by comparing Charts 2.1 and 2.2 with Chart 2.5, and is statistically verified.[8] Only a few exceptions to the rank-order arrangement of the seriousness of the fifty problems as rated by the experimental group need to be pointed out in these control ratings. The items profanity, smoking, sullenness, interrupting, tattling, restlessness were ranked somewhat, but not very markedly, lower in seriousness by the 511 teachers than by the teachers in the one Cleveland school. Whispering was the single item that was ranked at all significantly lower. Three items—enuresis, lack of interest, nervousness—were rated somewhat more serious by the 511 teachers than by the twenty-eight teachers in the original experiment. These are, on the whole, minor changes and do not alter the general conclusions drawn from the results in the experimental group; and the tendencies in the teachers' ratings are essentially the same. The overt forms of behavior, like sex problems, stealing, untruthfulness, truancy, cruelty, disobedience, temper outbursts, were regarded as the most undesirable and serious of all problems. The items relating to disorderliness and to difficulties in adapting to school work requirements were rated about midway on the scale of seriousness. With the exception of the items of unhappiness, easily discouraged, and selfishness which were considered to make for some difficulty, all the personality traits were rated toward the lower end of the scale. The recessive, withdrawing traits were rated on the whole as of somewhat less consequence than the extravagant, aggressive characteristics.

Summary

In drawing together the findings from the various applications of our

CHART 2.5

TEACHERS RATINGS ON THE RELATIVE SERIOUSNESS OF BEHAVIOR PROBLEMS IN SCHOOL CHILDREN
(RATINGS OF 511 TEACHERS)

Type of Problem	Average Score	Rated Seriousness of Problem — Rating Scale
		Of Only Slight Consequence 4·5 — Makes for Considerable Difficulty 12·5 — An Extremely Grave Problem 20·5
HETEROSEXUAL ACTIVITY	17·3	
STEALING	17·0	
MASTURBATION	16·7	
OBSCENE NOTES, TALK	16·6	
UNTRUTHFULNESS	15·8	
TRUANCY	15·6	
IMPERTINENCE, DEFIANCE	15·0	
CRUELTY, BULLYING	14·8	
CHEATING	14·7	
DESTROYING SCHOOL MATERIAL	14·3	
DISOBEDIENCE	14·1	
UNRELIABLENESS	13·9	
TEMPER TANTRUMS	13·0	
LACK OF INTEREST IN WORK	12·8	
PROFANITY	12·3	
IMPUDENCE, RUDENESS	12·2	
LAZINESS	12·2	
SMOKING	12·0	
ENURESIS	11·8	
NERVOUSNESS	11·7	
DISORDERLINESS IN CLASS	11·7	
UNHAPPY, DEPRESSED	11·5	
EASILY DISCOURAGED	11·5	
SELFISHNESS	11·3	
CARELESSNESS IN WORK	11·3	
INATTENTION	11·2	
QUARRELSOMENESS	11·1	
SUGGESTIBLE	11·0	
RESENTFULNESS	10·8	
TARDINESS	10·5	
PHYSICAL COWARD	10·4	
STUBBORNNESS	10·3	
DOMINEERING	10·3	
SLOVENLY IN APPEARANCE	10·1	
SULLENNESS	9·9	
FEARFULNESS	9·7	
SUSPICIOUSNESS	9·1	
THOUGHTLESSNESS	8·7	
ATTRACTING ATTENTION	8·5	
UNSOCIALNESS	8·3	
DREAMINESS	8·3	
IMAGINATIVE LYING	8·1	
INTERRUPTING	8·0	
INQUISITIVENESS	8·0	
OVERCRITICAL OF OTHERS	7·9	
TATTLING	7·5	
WHISPERING	7·5	
SENSITIVENESS	7·0	
RESTLESSNESS	6·9	
SHYNESS	5·4	

methods in measuring teachers' reactions to the behavior problems of school children, we call attention to the fact that the teachers in the one Cleveland school, who composed our original experimental group, consistently distinguished between the seriousness of various types of behavior problems. If we may be permitted to adopt the mathematical symbol (>) used in designating inequalities to express differences in the teachers' weighting of certain related types of problems, we can formulate the direction of their reactions to the seriousness of behavior disorders as follows:

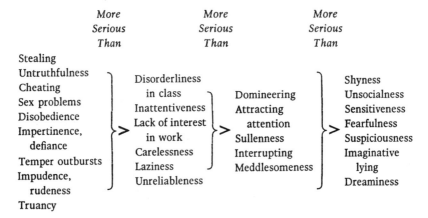

By interpretative classification of the groups of problems, the above formulation becomes:

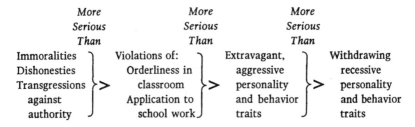

The tendency toward weighting the seriousness of problems in the order illustrated was observed both in the teachers' evaluations of the degree of difficulty they experienced in coping with the occurrence of these problems in individual pupils under their care, and in their judgments on the relative degree of seriousness of the particular behavior traits rated in the abstract when occurring in any child.

The same relative weighting of the problems was observed in the control ratings secured from 511 teachers who composed the entire teaching corps of thirteen elementary public schools in various communities. Control ratings obtained from selected groups of teachers who had been more or less exposed to advanced viewpoints in education showed slight differences in the weighting of the behavior items. But even these teachers clearly distinguished the greater seriousness of problems relating to sex, dishonesty, disobedience, and failures in application to school work over the withdrawing, recessive personality disorders.

The findings suggest that teachers' reactions to the behavior problems of children are determined in direct relation to the immediate effect of the behavior upon the teachers themselves. Those problems which transgress the teachers' moral sensitivities and authority or which frustrate their immediate teaching purposes are regarded as relatively more serious than problems which affect for the most part only the welfare of the individual child. All the experimental methods employed in this investigation lead to this conclusion.

If we might project the tendencies observed in the teachers' reactions to the seriousness of different kinds of troublesome behavior in children to their attitudes toward more acceptable behavior traits, we would be led in the direction of compliant, submissive, dependent behavior as more desirable to teachers than aggressive, experimental, independent behavior.

Notes

1 Even with the necessary changes in directions, the group of teachers rated fairly consistently in the first and second administration of the scales. The coefficient of correlation on the rank-order arrangements of the rated seriousness of the fifty behavior problems (rated as occurring in a boy) between the first and second ratings was 0.90 ± 0.028.

2 The term 'offense' has an implication that was unfortunate for purposes of measuring the teachers' judgments about the seriousness of the problems irrespective of ethical connotations. The term 'problem' was substituted in the rating scale administered to the 511 teachers in the second control groups. But this change in terminology did not result in any observable changes in the ratings secured from the control groups over those secured from the experimental group. It would seem that the terms 'offense' and 'problem', as used in this rating scale, tend to elicit very much the same kind of response from teachers.

3 Only two teachers did not finish their ratings in the time allotment and were permitted a few minutes additional time. One of them complained, 'This is too serious a matter for such rush.' Interestingly enough both teachers were found during the course of the experiment to be distinguished from all the teachers in the amount of difficulty they experienced in classroom discipline and in the numbers of children they reported for behavior problems.

4 The coefficient of correlation (Spearman's rank-order formula) was 0·94 ± 0·017.

5 The coefficients of correlation between the rank-order arrangements of the seriousness of the fifty problems as determined by the ratings of the four groups of teachers are:

	Problems Rated as Occurring in—	
Teachers in	*A Boy*	*A Girl*
Cleveland school and Control Group I	0·897	0·762
Cleveland school and Control Group II	0·727	0·670
Cleveland school and Control Group III	0·762	—
Control Group I and Control Group II	0·691	0·696
Control Group I and Control Group III	0·732	—
Control Group II and Control Group III	0·771	—

6 The coefficients of correlation between the rank-order arrangements of the seriousness of the fifty problems as occurring in a boy and in a girl were: Control Group I, 0·888; Control Group II, 0·92.

7 Ratings on problems relating to sex were not made by teachers from the New York public schools. The averages of the ratings on seriousness for these problems were computed on returns from teachers in the remaining ten schools.

8 The coefficients of correlation on the rank-order arrangements of the rated seriousness of the fifty problems between the results obtained from the experimental group and the group of 511 teachers is 0·895.

3. Children's Behaviour Problems as Viewed by Teachers, Psychologists and Children

In 1928 Wickman made his famous research comparing teachers' and 'mental hygienists'' attitudes toward children's behavior problems. Wickman called a group composed of eight psychiatrists, four psychologists, thirteen psychiatric social workers, and five teachers with social work background 'mental hygienists'. By means of a checklist of 50 behavior problems, Wickman examined teachers' versus mental hygienists' behavior appraisal. A negative but low correlation was found between their rankings. (In Wickman's first research the correlation was -0.22, and with the full sample, -0.11.) Teachers ranked misbehavior in the classroom as the most serious problem, while mental hygienists rated personality and emotional problems as most severe. Based upon the findings in his research, Wickman recommended that teachers attempt to modify their attitudes to be more like those of the mental hygienists. Since he believed the mental hygienists' outlook to be ideal, he suggested that teachers concern themselves more with children's developmental and adjustment processes and less with learning and behavior problems in the classroom.

Wickman's research, and particularly its methodology, was widely criticized. Yet, even today, his classic study and recommendations are quoted in many new child-psychology textbooks in order to stress the differences between teachers' and psychologists' points of view (Garrison, Kingston, and Bernard, 1967; Johnson and Medinnus, 1965; Thompson, 1962; Watson, 1965).

Watson (1933) criticized Wickman's research on the following points: (a) Mental hygienists and teachers were given different instructions; the former were asked to rank the problems with a view to future

Ziv, A. (1970) 'Children's behavior problems as viewed by teachers, psychologists and children'. *Child Development*, 41, 871–9.

adjustment, and the latter according to importance within a school framework. (b) Teachers were limited in time; mental hygienists had no time limit. (c) Problems were presented without definitions, thus eliciting varied interpretation. (d) Differences in ranking may not have indicated teacher insensitivity to emotional problems of children. Since no proof existed to show the mental hygienists' view to be better, there was no reason to demand any change in teacher outlook.

Following Watson's criticisms, many new researches on the same subject, with methodological modifications, were conducted. The heterogeneous group of mental hygienists was generally replaced by psychologists. Beilin, in 1959, reviewed and reported on 47 studies dealing with the subject. In spite of the differences, Wickman's findings were generally substantiated. Notable among those studies which took into account the problem of different instructions were Del Solar (1949), Ellis and Miller (1936), Hunter (1957), Mitchell (1942), Sparks (1952), and Stouffer (1952, 1956). Subsequently, analyses of the ranking differences between teachers and psychologists were made. Worthy of note among these are Peck (1935), who found 'undesirable personality traits' of prime concern to teachers, with 'aggressive behavior' ranking lowest; and Clark (1951), who explained that teachers show greater concern for peer-group relations than teacher-pupil relations.

Other studies took into account socio-economic status, age, and sex differences (Hildreth, 1928; McClure, 1929; Snyder, 1934). In spite of the many and varied analyses of results, the researches which followed Wickman's continued to strengthen and confirm his conclusions.

In more recent research, the gap between teachers' and psychologists' points of view seems to have narrowed. Nevertheless, teachers still rank as most serious overt aggressive behavior problems, while psychologists rank the problem of withdrawal as most severe.

In Israel, where teachers and psychologists cooperate closely, we were impressed by the great similarity between these two groups' attitudes toward children's behavior problems. This corresponding point of view should be most apparent with psychologists who as a rule work with teachers, and less so with psychologists who do not usually work with teachers. Taking this into consideration, it seemed that a study should be made in Israel concerning teachers' and psychologists' points of view.

A dimension not studied in the United States was the comparative points of view of professionals (teachers and psychologists) and children. As teachers are important factors in children's socialization processes, it seemed reasonable to expect children's opinions of behavior problems to resemble those of the teachers more closely than those of the psychologists. With this consideration in mind, the following hypotheses were articulated:

1. There will be a positive relation between teachers' and psychologists' rankings of children's behavior problems.

2. The correlation between children's and teachers' rankings will be higher than the correlation between children's and psychologists' rankings.

3. The correlation between teachers' and educational psychologists' rankings will be higher than the correlation between teachers' and clinical psychologists' rankings.

Method

Subjects

The subjects were: 82 teachers in elementary schools in the central Tel Aviv area; 165 eighth-grade children from the same schools (93 girls, 72 boys); and 45 psychologists (17 clinical psychologists working in hospitals and mental health clinics and 28 educational psychologists working in schools).

Materials

A list of 30 behavior problems was compiled, based upon Wickman's 50-problem checklist. We shortened the list for two reasons. First, after a pretest of a 50-problem checklist, we noted a tendency to rank with less care in the middle of the list. Second, Wickman's list contained problems too similar for differentiation; the same problem appeared under a different name, for example, 'disobedience—disorderliness in class'; 'nervousness—restlessness'; 'carelessness in work—laziness—lack of interest in work'.

The checklist was given to the subjects with the following instructions: 'The following is a list of 30 behavior problems of schoolchildren. The problems are arranged in alphabetical order. Please rank them according to their degree of severity. Number the problem which, in your opinion, is most serious number 1, the second most serious number 2, etc. The problem which in your opinion is the least severe will therefore be numbered 30.'

The problems were:

1. Aggressiveness	16. Lack of interest in work
2. Cruelty	17. Laziness
3. Dependency	18. Nervousness
4. Depression	19. Overcritical
5. Dishonesty	20. Overinterest in sexual activities
6. Disobedience	21. Resentfulness
7. Domination	22. Sensitiveness
8. Dreaminess	23. Shyness
9. Easily discouraged	24. Stealing
10. Egocentricity	25. Stubbornness
11. Enuresis	26. Suggestibility
12. Fearfulness	27. Tattling
13. Hyperactivity	28. Temper tantrums
14. Impertinence	29. Truancy
15. Irresponsibility	30. Unsociability

Procedure

Teachers, psychologists, and children were given the checklist with the above-mentioned identical instructions. All groups worked without time limit. Children worked in groups; teachers and psychologists were given the checklist individually. We tried to avoid the problem of interpretation by defining each of the behavior problems listed. For example, 'laziness—does not work, does not prepare his lessons'. In spite of this, we were aware that, because words denote different meanings to people, a fact brought out in many semantic studies, this interpretation problem was difficult to surmount.

Results

The average ranking for each group was computed and compared, using the Spearman rank correlation. The results appear in table 3.1.

TABLE 3.1

COEFFICIENTS OF CORRELATION BETWEEN RANKINGS OF DIFFERENT GROUPS

Group	Psychologists (General)	Educational Psychologists	Clinical Psychologists	Children†
Teachers	0·49**	0·40*	0·51**	0·84***
Psychologists (general)	...	0·71***	0·65***	0·18
Educational psychologists	...	...	0·77***	0·27
Clinical psychologists	...	...	...	0·15

† The correlation between boys and girls was 0·985

* $p < 0.05$ ** $p < 0.01$ *** $p < 0.001$

1. *Correlation between teachers and psychologists*

The results as seen in table 3.1 are completely different from those obtained by Wickman and others. As previously noted, in Wickman's research and the studies following his, the correlation between teachers' and psychologists' rankings was negative. In our study, the correlation between psychologists' and teachers' rankings was significant at $p < 0.05$, which indicated a similar point of view regarding problems of schoolchildren. This is in accordance with our first hypothesis, which is therefore accepted.

When we studied the 10 problems ranked as most serious by teachers and psychologists, we observed some differences, which can be seen in table 3.2.

TABLE 3.2

TEN MOST SERIOUS PROBLEMS AS RANKED BY TEACHERS
AND PSYCHOLOGISTS

Teachers	Psychologists
1. *Cruelty*	1. *Cruelty*
2. *Dishonesty*	2. Depression
3. *Aggressiveness*	3. *Nervousness*
4. *Stealing*	4. *Aggressiveness*
5. *Temper tantrums*	5. *Temper tantrums*
6. Egocentricity	6. Shyness
7. Disobedience	7. *Stealing*
8. Tattling	8. Hyperactivity
9. *Nervousness*	9. Easily discouraged
10. Impertinence	10. *Dishonesty*

Problems common to both groups are in italics

There were 12 problems in which there was a higher than eight-point discrepancy between the rankings of teachers and psychologists. Teachers ranked as more severe, disobedience, impertinence, tattling, and overcritical. Psychologists noted as more severe dishonesty, depression, hyperactivity, easily discouraged, enuresis, shyness, dependency, and dreaminess.

2. *Correlation between children and professionals*

In accordance with our second hypothesis, we found that the correlation between children's ranking and teachers' ranking was highly significant ($p < 0.001$), whereas that between children and psychologists was nonsignificant.

When considering discrepancies higher than eight points between teachers' and children's rankings, we found only four such problems. Teachers ranked as most severe 'temper tantrums', 'nervousness', and 'depression', while children ranked as most severe 'resentfulness'.

As for the discrepancies between psychologists' and children's rankings, since the correlation between the two groups was very low, we considered only those problems where the differences in the ranking were above 14. We found seven such problems. Psychologists noted as more severe 'depression', 'shyness', and 'dependency'; children noted 'impertinence', 'over-interest in sexual activities', 'domination', and 'laziness'.

3. *Correlations between teachers, clinical psychologists, and educational psychologists*
Our third hypothesis was rejected since there was no significant difference between the correlation of the rankings of teachers and clinical psychologists ($\cdot$51) and teachers and educational psychologists ($\cdot$40).*

Discussion

Several factors may explain the similarity we found between teachers' and psychologists' rankings of behavior problems. One explanation for this could be the fact that in the schools where the checklist was given the psychologists and teachers cooperate closely in their attempt to understand and solve the children's behavior problems. They discuss the problems and, as a result, make joint decisions as to their severity and the methods advised for handling them. When referring children to a psychological center for diagnosis or treatment, teachers must complete questionnaires compiled by psychologists. Perhaps, while filling in the forms, teachers are influenced by their terminology and tend to analyze the child in a psychologist's frame of reference. In addition, teachers in Israel demonstrate very active interest in psychology. This is evidenced by the predominance of psychological articles in their professional journals and by the fact that teachers participate in many extracurricular psychology and education courses.

It should also be remembered that the checklist and the request for ranking it were made by psychologists. It is possible that this factor might have influenced the teachers' ranking to meet what they thought

* Note the direction of the difference—ed.

were the psychologists' expectations.

When we studied qualitatively the differences among the 10 problems ranked as most severe by the two groups (see table 3.2), it appeared that what characterized the problems ranked by teachers as most severe is that they are school-oriented problems of teacher-pupil relations or peer relations. On the other hand, what characterized the psychologists' ratings were problems in the personality field and not necessarily overt problems ('depression', 'hyperactivity', 'shyness', 'easily discouraged'). It is possible that, in spite of the identical instructions given, psychologists could not free themselves of the psychopathological or prognostic meaning of each term. This may be due to the normally different points of view of the two groups. While the teachers consider what disturbs them within the classroom framework (pupil behavior), the psychologists consider the 'whole' and 'overinterest in sexual activities', which is taboo. On the other hand, psychologists are again characterized by their discernment of personality problems which are not always overtly expressed and therefore do not elicit a reaction from teachers or children. Since these are problems to which no attention is given in the school framework, it is obvious why they are not considered worthwhile ranking by the children.

A possible explanation for our third finding, that is, no difference between the correlation of teachers' and educational or clinical psychologists' rankings, is that in Israel educational psychologists have a clinical background and all psychologists work closely with teachers.

Our research has shown that, in Israel, teachers and psychologists have similar points of view concerning the severity of children's behavior problems, and children view the problems more like the teachers than like the psychologists.

MOORE, T.

4. Difficulties of the Ordinary Child in Adjusting to Primary School

Problem

At a time when primary education in Britain is under scrutiny, it is pertinent to examine the consumer's point of view. Few studies have been made of the problems faced by the ordinary child in coping with everyday school life. Educationists have been tireless in describing the situation as seen by adults, and latterly systematic observation and analysis have been applied to classroom interaction between teacher and child (Gallagher and Aschner, 1963) and between peer group and individual (Brinkmann and Brinkmann, 1963). Children have been asked their opinions on specific aspects, such as what constitutes good teaching (Taylor, 1962), and about their anxieties in tests and other situations (Sarason *et al.*, 1960); and there is an extensive literature on school phobia, well reviewed by Frick (1964). The present report is an analysis of difficulties which did not lead to outright refusal, encountered by ordinary children aged 6 to 11 in English schools and made known to their mothers.

That the emphasis is on difficulties is in no sense to discount the vast amount of good work being done in schools throughout the country. During our interviews many mothers made remarks such as 'He loves school'; 'can't get there quick enough'; 'wouldn't miss a day'; 'looks forward to returning after the holidays'; 'is devoted to his teacher'. Such testimony is heartening to receive. This report concentrates on the less satisfactory side of the picture, because it is here that attention must be drawn if improvements are to be made.

The validity of parents' testimony in this field may be called in question. Mothers do not witness what goes on in school, nor can they

Moore, T. (1966) 'Difficulties of the ordinary child in adjusting to primary school. *Journal of Child Psychology and Psychiatry, 7,* 17–38.

be strictly impartial; their attitudes reflect their own school experiences, their feelings about education generally, their contacts (often very limited) with the principal and staff of their child's school, and the degree of their identification with the child. Nevertheless, to dismiss their testimony as worthless would be to ignore one side of a question on which truly impartial evidence is scarcely to be had. For teachers also, being human, select what they perceive; and children do not reveal all their feelings to them, or to any investigator operating in the school environment.

Parents commonly remark how little the child says about school life, even when he is patently enjoying it. But when he is not, his mother is the likeliest person to detect signs of tension and unhappiness, and to elicit the reasons as the child sees them. How far his reasons are well founded is a separate question which would require careful investigation in each particular case; this we have not been able to undertake. It is the child's view of the situation, as expressed to his mother and reported by her, with which we are here concerned.

Method

The sample

At the Centre for the Study of Human Development a sample of London children, recruited before birth and studied longitudinally with contact not less than once a year, have now passed through their primary schools. For details of sampling and data collection procedures see Moore, Hindley and Falkner (1954), and Moore (1959). For present purposes all those children are included for whom information was available at any given age from 6 to 11. Although born in one area, the sample so dispersed that the 164 children were scattered in 115 schools of all sizes, types and philosophies (excluding the radically progressive). Only 13 (8 per cent) attended private schools. Inevitable losses over the years have not materially altered the social balance of the sample, which, as will be seen in table 4.1, continues to represent all classes of the urban population, though not in stratified proportions. Because of the demands of the programme, the mothers have to be cooperative and interested in their children. One might have expected their intelligence to be above average, but their mean score on the Mill Hill Vocabulary Test (Form B) was 30·45, which corresponds closely to the median reported by Raven (1958) for subjects aged 25–45. The children's intelligence, as measured by the abbreviated version (starred items) of the Revised Stanford–Binet scale, Form L, at 8 years, is widely dispersed about a mean above the 1937 norms: boys' mean I.Q. 121·2, S.D. 20·5; girls' mean I.Q. 111·5, S.D. 20·9. Comparative figures for the London school population are not available. The sex difference is significant ($p < 0.01$), and consistent with the boys' higher mean social class.

TABLE 4.1

SOCIAL COMPOSITION OF THE SAMPLE AT THE BEGINNING AND END OF THE PERIOD UNDER CONSIDERATION*

Father's occupational class at child's birth*	Age 6				Age 11			
	Boys N=85 (%)	Girls N=79 (%)	Total 164 (%)		Boys N=75 (%)	Girls N=64 (%)	Total 139 (%)	
Class I	2·4	3·8	3·0 ⎫		1·3	4·7	2·9 ⎫	
			⎬ 20·1				⎬ 21·6	
Class II	21·2	12·7	17·1 ⎭		22·7	14·1	18·7 ⎭	
Class III	61·2	59·5	60·4		62·7	57·8	60·4	
Class IV	11·8	17·7	14·6 ⎫		10·7	14·1	12·2 ⎫	
			⎬ 19·5				⎬ 18·0	
Class V	3·4	6·3	4·9 ⎭		2·6	9·3	5·8 ⎭	

* Registrar General (1950)

The data

Information was collected each year in the following way. Shortly before the child's birthday a form was sent to the parents enquiring about major events in the child's life. These included any change of school, class or teacher, and any absence of two weeks or longer. During a subsequent interview the mother was asked about the child's reaction to any such change, and on returning after absence. She was also asked whether he had shown any dislike of school, been reluctant to go or voiced any specific complaints, at any time during the past year. If he had school dinners she was asked whether these had given rise to any trouble. At four ages (6, 7, 9 and 11) a question was inserted as to any complaints by the child about the school toilets. Any difficulty once reported was followed up by enquiry the following year.

In the present analysis disturbances are classified in eight areas, as follows:

A. Reluctance to go to school, with or without explicit reason.
B. Difficulties in child's relationship to teachers, including Head Teacher.
C. Difficulties in relationships with other children in school.
D. Difficulties relating to school dinners or milk.
E. Dislike of school toilets.
F. Difficulties relating to work.
G. Difficulties relating to physical education.
H. Miscellaneous troubles.

Three grades of severity were used in coding:

marked   = severe disturbance extending over two months or more.
unqualified = intermediate, or duration unspecified.
milder   = lesser disturbance lasting under 1 month.

In the examples given below, lower-case letters indicate the area of disturbance, + means 'marked' and — means 'milder' as defined.

The relevant information was extracted from the protocols, classified and graded independently by two assistants; all differences of interpretation were arbitrated by the writer. Severity was estimated conservatively; any unqualified coding represents a definite disturbance, and 'milder' codings imply some degree of emotional upset, not mere passing whims. Since the difficulty had to be verbalized by the child to the mother, recalled by her and reported to the interviewer who then discussed it with her, the chances of spurious problems reaching the coding stage are almost certainly less than the chances of genuine difficulties failing to do so: the incidences given can thus be taken as fair minimal estimates of the number of complaints made, and disturbances shown, by the children.

Results

1. *Incidence of difficulties in general*
Table 4.2 shows, for boys and for girls at each age, the total number of disturbances of each grade of severity, and the average number of areas of difficulty per child. The falling trends, from 6–10 in girls and from 7–10 in boys, are doubtless due to adaptation and increasing confidence as the children get older. The average for girls is consistently a little lower than for boys.

Figure 4.1 presents in visual form the distribution of children by number of difficulties at each age. The proportion reporting difficulties in three or more areas decreases somewhat in both sexes, while the proportion having no difficulties increases in girls but not in boys. The sex difference in number of difficulties is significant only at age 10 ($p < 0.05$). Table 4.3, showing the number of interviews at which *any* difficulty was mentioned, makes clear how few children go through primary school without encountering some disturbance thought worthy

TABLE 4.2

INCIDENCE OF DIFFICULTIES

| | BOYS | | | | | |
	6 yr	7 yr	8 yr	9 yr	10 yr	11 yr
No. of children	85	81	81	70	75	75
No. of difficulties						
marked	11	10	14	3	3	5
unqualified	49	67	50	44	42	31
milder	81	70	56	56	52	71
Total	141	147	120	103	97	107
Average no. of areas of difficulty per child	1·66	1·81	1·48	1·47	1·29	1·43
	GIRLS					
No. of children	79	74	72	67	63	64
No. of difficulties						
marked	10	5	6	5	4	4
unqualified	47	41	43	38	37	29
milder	67	57	44	46	31	42
Total	124	103	93	89	72	75
Average no. of areas of difficulty per child	1·57	1·39	1·29	1·33	1·14	1·17

TABLE 4.3

NUMBER OF INTERVIEWS IN WHICH ANY DIFFICULTY WAS REPORTED
(COMPLETE RECORDS ONLY)

No. of interviews	Boys	Girls
6	36	22
5	9	11
4	14	8
3	3	10
2	4	6
1	0	2
0	1	2
Total 67		61

Sex difference not significant

TABLE 4.4

SCHOOL DISTURBANCE SCORES (NUMBER OF CASES IN BRACKETS)

	6–8 yr				9–11 yr				6–11 yr			
	Boys		Girls		Boys		Girls		Boys		Girls	
	Mean	S.D.	Mean	S.D.	Mean	S.D.	Mean	S.D.	Mean	S.D.	Mean	S.D.
A. By Sex and Occupational Class												
I—II	48·30	21·75	39·92	29·21	39·33	18·31	37·17	28·08	44·21	15·77	38·33	27·03
	(20)		(13)		(18)		(12)		(19)		(12)	
III	44·86	24·60	39·43	28·28	34·30	19·25	26·90	22·77	39·83	19·34	34·23	24·09
	(51)		(44)		(47)		(39)		(48)		(40)	
IV—V	30·85	24·57	27·24	18·93	35·11	29·45	33·87	24·88	33·20	26·05	30·94	14·52
	(13)		(17)		(9)		(15)		(10)		(16)	
Total	43·51	24·33	36·72	26·78	35·62	19·92	30·35	23·98	40·05	19·52	34·18	22·60
	(84)		(74)		(74)		(66)		(77)		(68)	
Sex x class interactions	n.s.				n.s.				n.s.			
Sex differences	n.s.				n.s.				n.s.			
Class differences	$p < 0·05$				n.s.				n.s.			
B. By Sibship Status at 6 yr												
Only	54·12	27·08	41·30	25·27	41·53	26·22	32·67	25·37	49·88	25·41	37·10	26·83
	(17)		(10)		(15)		(9)		(16)		(10)	
Eldest	41·30	21·05	33·23	32·88	35·00	17·98	29·90	21·14	39·00	16·99	33·40	25·53
	(20)		(13)		(19)		(10)		(19)		(10)	
Middle	32·27	24·48	24·00	17·68	29·57	18·40	24·35	20·36	28·80	15·69	24·17	13·51
	(15)		(19)		(14)		(17)		(15)		(18)	
Youngest	44·22	21·20	44·25	27·09	·35·92	19·12	33·20	27·26	41·22	16·56	39·47	23·50
	(32)		(32)		(26)		(30)		(27)		(30)	
Sibship differences	$p < 0·01$		$p < 0·10$		n.s.		n.s.		$p < 0·05$		n.s.	

of mention by their mothers. The preponderance of mentions for boys over girls does not reach significance.

For closer study, each child's difficulties were scored (*a*) from 6–8 years, (*b*) from 9–11 years, and (*c*) for the whole period. In scoring, each 'marked' difficulty was counted 4 points, unqualified codings 3 points, and 'milder' difficulties 2; this reflected a subjective estimate of their relative importance. One missed interview in either 3-year period, or two in the 6 years, was allowed for by averaging each child's scores over the interviews completed; but any case lacking more than this was excluded. The total score for each period was multiplied by

FIGURE 4.1
School disturbance: incidence by age

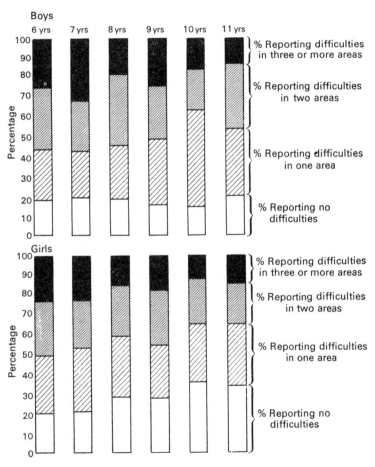

10 to remove decimals; thus a score of 30 represents an average of one unqualified difficulty (3 points) per interview. These scores were used in the following analyses:

By interviewer. Two interviewers (both male psychologists) took part in the programme. No significant difference in mean or variance of scores for any period was found between cases interviewed predominantly by one or the other.

By sex and social class. Two-way analyses of variance by sex and social class revealed no significant interaction nor sex difference at any age (table 4.4A). Variance attributable to occupational class was significant ($p < 0.05$) for the 6–8 year period, with little difference between Registrar General's classes I–II and III but a markedly lower incidence of disturbances reported in the manual working class IV–V; but insignificant for 9–11 years and for the total period. If the working-class scores were an underestimate owing to poor communication (between child and mother, or mother and interviewer) one would expect the difference to persist. Since, as we shall see, the professional-class children have more difficulties with other children and to some extent over questions of work, it seems likely that higher parental expectations and internalized standards cause them more anxiety in the early school years, which is gradually mitigated with increasing age, confidence and adaptation to the (often socially mixed) peer group.

By intelligence. The correlation between I.Q. and total school disturbance was insignificant in both sexes when the effect of social class was partialled out (boys: $r_p = 0.15$; girls: $r_p = 0.19$).

By mother's education. Analysis of variance revealed that this was not related to school disturbance for any period in either boys or girls.

By private vs. public education. The 13 children who attended private schools showed no significant or systematic difference in amount of disturbance from children of comparable social background attending state schools.

By sex and sibship. Boys and girls were grouped according to their status as only, eldest, middle or youngest children in the family at the age of 6 (table 4.4B). For the 6–8 year period, analysis of variance of the boys' scores showed a significant variation, with 'only' boys having the most disturbances and 'middle' boys least ($F = 4.362$, $df.$ 3, 80: $p < 0.01$). With the girls the variation was of borderline significance ($F = 2.604$, $df.$ 3, 70: $p < 0.10$), with the 'youngest' having slightly more disturbance than the 'only' girls (both being lower than 'only' boys) and the 'middle' again having least. For the period from 9–11 years the pattern remained unchanged, but the variation between groups decreased to insignificance. For the total period it reached the 5 per cent level in boys but was insignificant in girls. Hersov (1961a) found only and youngest children to be the most prone to school phobia.

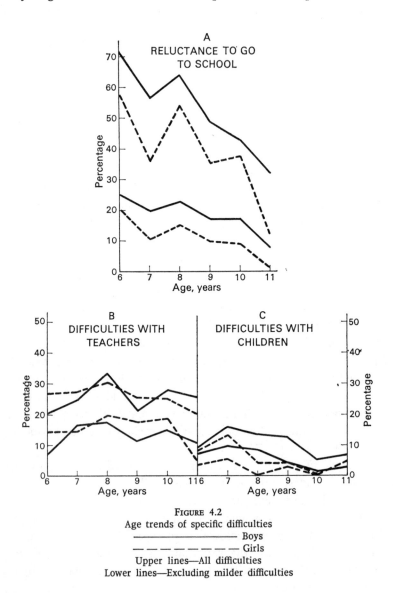

FIGURE 4.2
Age trends of specific difficulties
———————————————— Boys
— — — — — — — — Girls
Upper lines—All difficulties
Lower lines—Excluding milder difficulties

2. *Specific difficulties*

Age trends of each type of disturbance for boys and girls are shown in figures 4.2 and 4.3. These are given in terms of percentage incidence, (i) in total irrespective of grade of severity (upper lines) and (ii) excluding the 'milder' category for a more stringent criterion (lower lines).

The number of difficulties elicited by interview is well known to depend in part on the questions asked. Since the questions in this study varied in directness from one area to another, comparisons of incidence as between areas have little meaning. While overestimation is unlikely for reasons already given, it will become apparent that the probability of underestimation is greater in areas C, D, F and G than in areas A, B and E. But as the basic questions were the same for all mothers and throughout the age period, comparisons by age and sex within each area can be regarded as valid.

A. *Reluctance to go to school*. The basic question was 'Has your child shown any dislike of school at any time in the past year?' This commonly elicited a statement of the children's general attitude, whether positive, indifferent or negative, and sometimes specific problems as well. The latter were coded in the appropriate area; a coding of A was added only where the problem led to a dislike of going to school. In other cases the mother knew of nothing at school to account for the dislike; in some overdependent children the difficulty was clearly in leaving home and coping with the pressures of the wider world. These problems were also coded A. This area is therefore unlike the others in reflecting the child's general attitude rather than any particular aspect of school life.

Examples

Boy 522, 8yr   'Never wants to go to school; feels he wants to be sick, or go to toilet. . . . But insists on being on time, won't take notes to teacher, or ask her anything. . . . Finds children rough and noisy.' (Coded a+, b+, c.) (This feeling had existed in mild form at the child's first school, was aggravated on transfer to this larger, rougher school and persisted at a somewhat lower intensity to 10yr.)

Boy 694, 8yr   'Dislikes school in general. Very slow in getting up and dressing on school mornings. Doesn't feel very well at least once a week. Has bitten nails right down since transfer from previous school. Dislikes sums, is afraid of not doing them well.' (Coded a, f—.)

(Nervous, overdependent child. Difficulty had started at previous school and persisted throughout.)

Boy 852, 8yr   On transfer to a preparatory school 'cried every morning for a month. Said he hated it, had no friends, disliked being called by surname . . . Felt it was a long way from home, afraid bus would break down. Better when Mother learned to drive and collected him. Made friends in about one month, and became more cheerful.' (a, c.) But never really liked school; at 10yr: 'Any excuse not to go; says he loathes it, though goes now without fuss. Says he wouldn't prefer any other school, just dislikes schooling generally.' (a—.)

Girl 632, 7yr   This child normally enjoyed school, but on returning after nearly a term's absence owing to a series of infections, feeling nervous about the amount she had missed, her mother reported: 'She found her beloved teacher absent. The unimaginative Headmistress, exceptionally stern and cold, only made her worse. Thankfully another teacher had the right touch, and after a week of nerve-racking scenes which almost reduced me to a nervous wreck, she settled down as if by magic to enjoy school again.' (a, b—). No recurrence of trouble.

Figure 4.2A shows that this kind of trouble affects a majority of children in some degree at 6 years, decreases at 7, rises to a secondary peak at 8 and then dwindles steadily to 11, though even then one boy in three is still showing some reluctance. The increase at 8, if significant, is probably due to transfer from infant to junior school, where expectations tend to be higher and discipline stricter. Hersov (1961b) found a peak of school refusal following this transfer.

Whether we consider real aversion, as indicated by the lower curves, or mere reluctance, included in the upper ones, a negative attitude to school is shown consistently by more boys than girls at every age. The difference in total scores for this area is significant by the t-test ($p < 0.01$). Analysis of variance shows that it is not accounted for by social class differences in the sampling; in these scores class differences are insignificant. The sex difference is consistent with boys' more frequent recourse to truancy or outright school refusal (Hersov, 1961a). Several possible explanations suggest themselves. Is it that boys, being more active, find it harder to accept the immobility enforced, much of the time, in most schools? Or that they rebel against the curtailment of their freedom of choice, while girls conform more readily? And are there in addition, as Levy (1943) found, more boys than girls whose relationships with their mothers are so mutually dependent that they find it difficult to exchange the safety of home for the hurly-burly of school life?

B. *Difficulties with teachers.* These were elicited by the neutral question, 'Has he changed his teacher this year? How did he take the change?' supplemented as necessary by enquiries into past and present relationships. Some complaints came from children who had incurred punishment, but at least as many from the relatively innocent who shrank under discipline intended to impress the recalcitrant few. Shouting, smacking and grumbling; favouritism and reprimands perceived as unfair; failure to make work interesting and failure to explain clearly were among the commonest complaints. (But children's dislike of unsuccessful teaching is easily matched by their enthusiasm for the teacher who succeeds in capturing their interest and affection.)

Examples

Girl 744, 8yr 'Child feels she can do nothing right with this teacher; lost interest in work and became very nervous, sobbing in bed, twisting her hair, biting her nails and not wanting to go to school. Considerable improvement after Head spoke to the teacher, who was known to have serious personal difficulties, tended to have a "down" on certain children and talked quite inhumanly to them.' (Coded b+, a+.)

Girl 888, 8yr 'Reluctant to go to school while with previous teacher; used to complain of headaches and tummy-aches. The teacher was very severe, used to pull children's hair. Child wanted to change school.' (Coded b+, a.) This child thoroughly enjoyed school with certain teachers, but at 10yr: 'Says her new teacher is "miserable", never enjoys a joke, grumbles and smacks.' (b.)

Boy 586, 9yr 'Likes his new teacher less than the previous one; she is unresponsive, never praises, and criticizes him in class. The Headmaster is given to ranting and shouting at the children, who talk about him with no respect at all.' (b.)

Boy 758, 11yr 'Liked former teacher very much. Dislikes present one: says he leaves the class to itself, doesn't teach enough. Child is worried lest he be told off after occasional days' absence due to tummy upsets.' (b.)

Figure 4.2B shows that the peak for complaints about teachers comes at 8 years, when they are reported from one child in three, perhaps again because of the sterner attitude in the junior school; but the incidence never falls below 20 per cent, although serious disturbances are fewer. There is no significant difference between boys and girls, nor between social classes.

C. *Difficulties with other children.* Specific enquiry in this area was made only if the child had been transferred to a different group; but mothers could be expected to report any real problem in discussing adjustment to school generally. Trouble with contemporaries is commonly experienced by the overdependent child, especially the boy who lacks a satisfactory relationship with his father (Levy, 1943). Complaints are usually of roughness or bullying which tends to be attracted by the timid or over-fastidious child, or the 'teacher's pet'. Unpopularity for other reasons, such as bossiness, is occasionally reported. In a few schools, prefects or older monitors invested with authority are feared by the younger children; but this occurs less commonly than in the secondary school. Unhappiness due to loss of friends on regrouping is sometimes mentioned, but appears to be ephemeral as a rule.

Examples

Boy 852, 7yr 'Child complained of a boy who kept threatening to hit him. He went through a phase of wanting mother to meet him daily, which she did for 4 or 5 weeks. Trouble ceased when he made friends with the boy.' (Coded c.)

Boy 522, 7yr 'Both he and his brother (aged 8) are scared stiff and hate the school. They fear the monitors who are "everywhere" and the atmosphere generally.' (a+, c+.) Difficulty persisted to 10yr.

Boy 586, 7yr 'Found it difficult to face up to the rough children at his large new school; dislikes the long lunch-hour break. Sometimes comes in crying, saying he has been hit, or a bully has broken something of his.' Mother added: 'Perhaps he invites bullying; he has no sense of humour, just like his father.' (c.) The same complaint was made at 9yr, but on transfer to another school, he declared that the boys were rougher, and that there had been only one rough one at the previous school. At 11yr, he still complained of the boys, would not stand up for himself and had no particular friends. At home, where there was much parental friction, this boy was extremely aggressive to his mother.

Girl 832, 6yr 'Not keen on school, and reluctant to stay for dinners. Always wants it to rain, so she need not spend the hour in the playground with the rough boys.' (a, c.)

Girl 878, 7yr 'Put up to a higher group twice, leaving a friend behind—cried about this 1 or 2 days. Doesn't mix easily. Says boys are rough.' (c−.)

The incidence of this type of complaint (depending mainly on spontaneous information) is not very high (figure 4.2C); it may be underestimated owing to the lack of a specific question, but it may also be that most children prefer to make their own way with their contemporaries without adult intervention. Difficulties are reported for 16 per cent of the boys and 13 per cent of the girls at the peak age of 7 yr, drop sharply between 9 and 10, and finish around 6 per cent at 11, when the children are the oldest in the primary school and have generally had several years to find a *modus vivendi* with their group.

The boys' curves remain consistently higher than the girls', the sex difference in total scores being significant by the *t*-test: $p < 0.05$, and recurring in each occupational class. The demands of the male peer group may well be more exacting, involving as they do a degree of toughness impossible for a boy in the absence of an adequate model for male identification, or for one who has subordinated his aggression to the will of a domineering mother.

More difficulties in this area were experienced by children from socially superior homes (table 4.5). This probably reflects the earlier freedom of the streets accorded to the working-class child.

TABLE 4.5
DIFFICULTIES WITH OTHER CHILDREN, BY OCCUPATIONAL CLASS

Occupational class	N	Mean score
I–II	31	3·23
III	88	2·09
IV–V	26	1·00

$F = 3.178$; $df.2, 142$; $p\ 0 < 0.05$

D. Difficulties relating to school dinners and milk. The question was asked: 'Has he stayed to school dinners? Has this given rise to any trouble?' Difficulties were coded conservatively, ignoring the occasional grumble which is generally regarded as 'fashionable'. Children's food problems are to a large extent sorted out when they stay at school for dinner, those that disappear in the group situation probably representing a form of self-assertion against the mother, while the more deep-seated aversions and fastidiousness are often aggravated by the pressure (even if gentle) to eat what is offered. Dinner helpers are not always the best people to handle such problems. Some children are put off not by the food itself but by the way the meal is served, by its appearance or smell, or by the crowds, noise and sense of hurry. Others simply prefer their mothers' cooking and familiar menus. But others again enjoy the dinners and their only complaint (discounted for our purposes) may be that they don't get enough. A different reason for

c

preferring to go home for dinner, especially at the infant stage, is that some children find the unbroken school day too long, and the long after-dinner playtime too much of a strain; while for the extraverts this may be the best part of the day.

Examples

Boy 558, 7yr   'Was never keen on school food. A natural vegetarian who never wants large meals.' Allowed to come home for some months; then to stay again at own request. No further complaints until 10yr, when 'occasional refusal of foods disliked has caused adverse comments from teachers, who say "You must eat everything up",

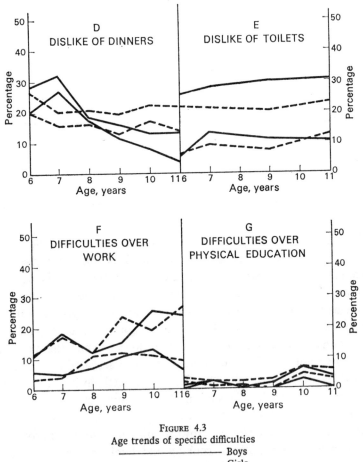

FIGURE 4.3

Age trends of specific difficulties

————————————— Boys

— — — — — — — — Girls

Upper lines—All difficulties

Lower lines—Excluding milder difficulties

and from dinner lady, who, when asked for a little, gives much and vice versa.' (Coded d.)

Boy 734, 7yr 'Doesn't like the way the meal is served, and some of the food. Table manners getting bad: clutches his plate—says he has to at school, or it disappears!' At 8yr and 9yr, 'Complains quite often, made to eat things he dislikes. But at other times, seems to prefer school cooking to mine.' (d.)

Girl 584, 7yr 'Strongly objected to being spoon-fed by teachers to hurry her along.' (d+.) As her manners were also becoming very bad, dinners at school were discontinued, but resumed later. At 11yr, 'complains that the serving ladies have favourites.' (d—.)

As some children alternated between periods of dining at school and at home, no estimate was made of the number actually receiving school dinners in any year. Percentage disturbance shown in figure 4.3D is based on the total sample, and would have been proportionately higher had home diners been excluded. Even so, complaints were recorded from nearly one-third of the boys at 7 yr, and from over one-quarter of the girls at 6 yr.

The sexes show different age trends. After a peak at 7, the boys' curve drops steadily. The girls' curve is nearly horizontal except for a slight drop from 6–7. The boys show the greater frequency of disturbance at 7, the girls thereafter. Explanation of these differences would require more detailed analysis. It may be that the significance of food in relation to emotional development differs for the two sexes. There was no significant social class difference.

E. *Dislike of school toilets.* This occurred with unexpected frequency in our records. The direct question 'Has he ever made a fuss about using the school toilet?' was put to all the mothers at 6, 7, 9 and 11 years, as a result of their spontaneous mention of the problem in many cases at the 5-yr interview, and earlier, at nursery school. Some children complained that the lavatories were dirty, wet or smelly; others resented the lack of privacy where the doors could not be secured; some would not go in a crowd at break, but were loth to ask permission during lessons, especially if they also had to ask for toilet paper. Not a few children refused to use the facilities, returning home in considerable discomfort at the end of every morning and afternoon; constipation or loss of bladder control occasionally resulted.

Examples

Boy 882, 7yr 'Won't use school toilets. He likes to have soap and water to wash his hands afterwards.' Mother visited the lavatories and found them filthy, in an otherwise good school. Trouble continued throughout. (Coded e+.)

Boy 508, 9yr   'Dislikes school toilets. Will only use them if absolutely necessary, because no privacy, no locks, and no toilet paper provided.' (e.) At 11yr: 'Lost control of bladder on way home twice.' Never otherwise enuretic. (e.)

Girl 718 11yr   'Dislikes W.C.s because doors are low enough for other children to look over the top. Won't use them if it can be helped; dashes home with a full bladder.' (e.)

Girl 660, 7yr   'Dislikes the toilets because they are not clean and she has to ask for paper.' (e.) At 8yr: 'Avoids them as much as possible; occasionally constipated as a result. No bolts; she wants privacy.' (e+.) Still troubled at 11yr.

Girl 892, 6yr   'Wets pants periodically, only at school, because afraid to ask to leave classroom. Dislikes being conspicuous in any way.' Trouble continued to 6½yr; improved when Mother obtained teacher's permission for child to leave the room without asking. (e.)

In figure 4.3E the incidence of complaints is plotted only for the four ages at which the direct question was asked. Coding was conservative; fussing 'rarely' or 'sometimes' was scored minus and the lower curves include only frequent complaints with or without avoidance. It will be seen that the proportion of children complaining remains roughly constant, rising a little with age, about one 11-year-old in four protesting at times and between 10 and 12 per cent experiencing a real problem.

Although neither sex nor social class differences were significant in this area, their direction is interesting. In each class, boys made more complaints than girls; and working-class children of both sexes complained more than those from professional homes. The mean score for working-class boys was 7·0; for professional-class girls, 1·92. This was contrary to expectation, but may reflect poorer facilities in underprivileged areas.

This is a problem that could be remedied relatively simply on Head Teachers' initiative, even in old accommodation, by the provision of a coat of paint, some sweet-smelling disinfectant, simple bolts for the doors, and a cleanliness campaign, which, it seems, would receive the enthusiastic support of many children.

F. *Difficulties relating to work.* No specific question was asked concerning work, which usually came up in connection with the child's response to teachers or general adjustment at school. Codings were entered only where the child himself expressed worry or marked distaste concerning one or more subjects or aspects of the work; not for back-wardness as such, nor for failure to worry where adults felt it would be appropriate to do so. There is inevitably some overlap between difficulties with work and those relating to the teacher. Liking and dislike of a specific subject often fluctuate according to the particular presentation. In the primary school, because all but the specialized subjects are usually taught by the class teacher, a child's relationship to this teacher can colour his whole attitude to work for an entire year.

Even though he likes the teacher, a child in a large class may plod on for a long time without understanding the processes he is supposed to be mastering, refusing to ask for help not so much out of fear of consequences as out of reluctance to admit ignorance, and sometimes a fear of ridicule by classmates.

Marks and class places cause worry and distress to some children, whose parents, far from exhorting them, generally find themselves trying to lower the child's perfectionist standards. Others may take the daily work in their stride but dread examinations or tests of any kind. The bogey of the 'eleven-plus', however, is mentioned seldom as an ordeal in itself but very frequently as a cause of undue pressure, excessive homework and overwrought teachers in the last two years of junior school. As much as two hours' homework a night is sometimes expected of children of ten and eleven. When difficulties arise, parents find themselves in a quandary: to offer help is to interfere and perhaps to confuse; to withhold it may let fatigue and frustration make learning impossible; to call a halt and write to the teacher is a step often stoutly resisted by the child, who would rather fail than be made an exception.

Other difficulties reported include idiosyncratic problems such as slow working tempo, inability to concentrate and specific learning blocks. Finally, there are children who find the work too easy and get bored, especially if they have to go over it a second time—as do some who, reaching the top of the primary school before the official age for transfer, are compelled to repeat an entire year's work.

Examples

Boy 768, I.Q. 128   At 8yr, 'He was worried about being behind with reading owing to repeated absences; worry brought on his asthma; a vicious circle. I had to fight to get him to school, and then he would have an attack. It lasted 4 or 5 months, till at last he told me it was the reading. The teacher helped; now he reads well and likes it.' (Coded f+, a+.) At 10yr: 'He now has difficulty with sums, but is good at other subjects. He doesn't want me to help him; teacher is impatient and hits him with a ruler; so I will try to find an older child to help him in the holidays.' (f, b.)

Boy 560, I.Q. 132   At a private school. At 8yr, 'He likes but fears the teacher, and complains that they work far too hard.' Mother agreed there was too much homework—2 hours a night—'but I can't do anything about it. The teacher tends to frighten them into working. If he hasn't done his homework well enough he worries and cries about it.' (f+, b.)

Girl 698, I.Q. 114   At 8yr, 'She likes her new teacher and is keen to please her, but has become very anxious about homework and about sums at school; cries over the sums, even after getting them all right.' (f.) She gradually relaxed and became less over-anxious; but at 10yr: 'They are under pressure for the 11+. She is a slow worker and worries about subjects involving written answers; not arithmetic now. She is afraid of appearing stupid.' (f.)

Boy 542, I.Q. 129   Had always been extremely slow in everything he did, and given to daydreaming. He attended a private school. At 10yr, 'Headmaster intends to give him a speed test daily, and reward him with sixpence for good results. His work is accurate but very slow, and he worries when told he will not pass the 11+ unless quicker. Father helps him with arithmetic every evening—homework takes 1–2hr—but child can't concentrate on it and finishes in a furious temper in which he beats his own head.' (f+.)

Girl 924, I.Q. 118   On change from B to A stream at 8yr, 'Dislikes no longer being top of the class. If she can't get 20 out of 20 she is upset and cries: "I'm no good." Afraid to ask questions of the teacher, who shouts, until I went to see her. Teacher now encourages her, gives her stars, etc.' (f.)

Figure 4.3F records that the incidence of complaints about work rises, as would be expected with the gradual increase in pressure, reaching 25 per cent in boys at 10 and girls at 11; while definite disturbances in this sphere affect 10 per cent of this predominantly intelligent sample from 8–10 years. All these difficulties were spontaneously mentioned by the mothers; had a direct question been asked, the figures would certainly have been higher. Boys and girls are affected about equally, and although professional-class children score highest, class differences do not reach significance.

G. *Difficulties relating to physical education.* These were not elicited by any direct question. They occasionally arise from a distaste for physical exertion, usually in overweight children; more often from fear of getting hurt, or fear of water when taken swimming; from a feeling of awkwardness or inability; or from dislike of the teacher. But the commonest complaint is dislike of undressing. This is sometimes attributed to cold, sometimes to modesty; and younger children may have trouble in tying ties and shoelaces or getting ready in the time allowed. Perhaps too, taking off clothes, which brings to confident children a sense of freedom and wellbeing, amounts to shedding the armour without which a more anxious child feels defenceless.

Examples

Boy 850, 7yr   'Dislikes P.E. though active and athletic. Partly due to the teacher, but also (8yr) dislikes taking off his vest.' (Coded g.)

Girl 704, 10yr 'Disliked P.E. as she didn't want to undress down to vest and knickers. Allowed to do it with dress on after an illness, and has continued since.' (g.) At 11yr, 'No complaints about undressing since swimming began—her favourite activity.'

Girl 674, 11yr 'Asks to be excused from sports. Hates being pushed around or hurt in any way.' (g.)

Girl 878, 6yr   'Dislikes P.E. because she cannot easily fasten her shoe.' (g.) But at every subsequent interview she was said to dislike undressing.

As figure 4.3G shows, spontaneous complaints connected with physical education are few—under 5 per cent up to 9 years, with 7 per cent as a maximum at 10. This speaks well for the teaching, as well as reflecting most children's healthy pleasure in games and exercise. The girls' curves are consistently a little higher than the boys', but incidence is too low to yield significant sex or class differences.

H. *Miscellaneous problems*. Difficulties which did not fit into one of the seven areas already discussed were too few to graph, affecting only 1 per cent of children. Examples follow:

Boy 634, 6–7yr   Eight teachers in two years. 'Child confused; doesn't seem to learn.' (f, h.)

Boy 810, 10yr   'Dislikes school buildings.' (h—.)

Boy 756, 10–11yr 'Hates violin lessons and school orchestra', though musical and learning guitar for pleasure. Headmistress insisted he continue with the violin, and Father agreed they should not 'give in'; but lessons were finally abandoned because of battles over practising and no progress. (h.)

Boy 724, 7yr   On transfer from a school where he had seen his siblings at playtime, 'felt lonely and lost when separated from them at new school. Settled after two weeks.' (h—.)

3. *Persistence of difficulties*

The longitudinal nature of the study makes it possible to determine how persistent various difficulties tend to be. Taking only the 128 children with complete records for the six years, table 4.6 shows, for each area of disturbance, the number complaining on varying numbers of occasions from none to six. All degrees of severity are included.

Combining the figures for the two sexes, we have a total of 520 problems reported. Of these, as shown in the last column, 41 per cent were mentioned once only. One-third cropped up three or more times, including 35 problems which were reported in five or all six interviews. Twenty-three of these very persistent problems concerned a general dislike of school or reluctance to go (Area A), which in this sample of 128 indicates some degree of chronic aversion from school in every fifth or sixth child.

The bottom row of the table shows the average number of times per child that difficulties are mentioned in each area. After the general attitude of reluctance, difficulty with teachers is the next most recurrent problem, but in some cases this amounted only to a temporary difficulty of adaptation to each fresh teacher. Conversely, the infrequency of persistent problems relating to other children may be attributed to the fact that the majority pass through primary school in the same group, or with only one change on transfer from infant to junior school, and become accepted by their classmates. Dinners and lavatories can be constant or recurrent sources of conflict and emotional discomfort, partly no doubt because they involve the deepest levels of feeling, stemming from early infancy and nearer the surface in childhood than in later life. Difficulties with work might have been expected to recur every year for some children; that only one was reported more than four times may be due to our failure to enquire specifically at each interview.

The figures in the lower right-hand corner provide an overall estimate for the whole period: over all six interviews, 8·88 mentions of difficulty occurred in relation to the average child, and the average problem was mentioned rather more than twice.

Discussion

1. *Validity*

Some aspects of the validity of these data have already been discussed.

TABLE 4.6

RECURRENCE OF DIFFICULTIES: NUMBERS OF CASES

Sample: all cases completing 6 interviews. 67 boys and 61 girls = 128

Number of times reported	A Reluctance B	A Reluctance G	B Teachers B	B Teachers G	C Children B	C Children G	D Dinners B	D Dinners G	E Toilets B	E Toilets G	F Work B	F Work G	G Phys. Educ. B	G Phys. Educ. G	H Miscellaneous B	H Miscellaneous G	ALL AREAS Boys	ALL AREAS Girls	ALL AREAS Total	% of all problems
0	3	7	14	13	86	42	20	21	31	40	29	26	57	48	59	59	—	—	—	—
1	15	9	21	20	20	15	19	18	10	8	16	15	7	12	6	2	114	99	213	41·0
2	8	21	16	14	7	4	18	9	8	4	12	9	3	0	1	0	73	61	134	25·8
3	12	11	13	8	3	0	6	6	6	3	8	8	0	0	0	0	48	36	84	16·1
4	11	8	3	5	1	0	3	5	9	4	2	3	0	0	0	0	29	25	54	10·4
5	10	3	1	1	0	0	1	1	2	2	1	0	0	1	0	0	15	8	23	4·4
6	8	2	0	0	0	0	0	1	1	0	0	0	0	0	0	0	9	3	12	2·3
Total number of times mentioned	209	143	109	97	47	23	90	85	96	51	77	69	13	17	8	2	288	232 Problems	520	100
Total (both sexes)	352		206		70		175		147		146		30		10				1,136 mentions	
Average number per child	2·75		1·61		0·55		1·37		1·15		1·14		0·23		0·08		8·88 mentions per child		2·18 mentions per problem	

It must be borne in mind that the evidence is based not on verified happenings but on the perceptions of children and parents. But perceptions determine attitudes and behaviour, and therefore are well worthy of consideration in their own right. Since parents' attitudes to school certainly affect those of their children, both merit study; but it is a weakness of the present material that the two cannot be unravelled. For this purpose children would also have had to be interviewed; this was not done before the age of twelve.

The mothers stood to gain nothing from deliberately exaggerating difficulties, since they knew that the research policy was never to intervene. Many of them, indeed, had a tendency to play down the child's problems rather than the reverse. It was for this reason that the questions asked were specifically about difficulties and dislikes, since it had been found that open questions of the form 'How does he like school?' tended in general to produce conventionally positive replies.

2. Origin and outcome of difficulties

As already noted, certain types of difficulty, especially reluctance to go to school where the child can give no specific reason, difficulty in mixing with other children and dislike of physical education, are characteristic of overdependent children. Overdependence is a sign of faulty family relationships, usually traceable to the failure of one or both parents to reach adequate emotional maturity (Levy, 1943). The origins of this failure have generally to be sought in their relationships with their own parents, and so on. This is the pattern very commonly discovered in cases of school refusal (Hersov, 1961a; Davidson, 1961; Frick, 1964) and confirmed in the histories of a number of our subjects.

But the vicious circle is not necessarily unbreakable. A wise teacher who takes a personal interest can often help an overdependent child to master his fears, thereby in some measure freeing him from his parents' neuroses. That this does happen is attested by some of the examples already given, and by these additional follow-ups:

Boy 522, whose intense fears were noted under headings A and C, was made Head Prefect in his last year of Junior School. At 11yr the psychologist commented: 'He seems to have received a real boost . . . which is reflected in his increased confidence, somewhat decreased fears and partially successful efforts to stop nail-biting. He still has marked anxiety beneath the surface', but took the transfer to secondary school in his stride. At 12yr, 'He loves the new school because the teachers treat them as grown-up, talk to them seriously but also joke. Likes the discipline. No trouble with other children.'

Girl 620, very dependent on her nervous and ailing mother, attached to each teacher in turn and upset by every change, rejected school dinners and found work difficult, but with considerable help from teaching staff she finished in the A-stream. Took to Secondary Modern school very well: at 12yr, 'really loves it, except the arithmetic.' Much more confident.

Boy 576 had a mother who found great difficulty in leaving him each morning at nursery school. On transfer to infant school she reported: 'He could not bear to leave me the first six weeks, but they said he cheered up as soon as I left. Then he decided he liked it. Finds the boys rough, but so is he. Very fond of his teacher, but worries about writing and spelling, and has started twitching his face, blinking and picking his nose.'

At 7yr, 'disliked the discipline and harder work imposed by a new teacher, and objected to going to school for 2 months. She won his confidence by giving him little jobs.' The next two teachers were less successful; he joined a tough gang and played truant four times. At 10yr he was put with a young, energetic male teacher who taught him to box and captured his interest in work. Truancy ceased, as did complaints except about writing lessons. At 11yr was working well, enjoying school and made Head Prefect. Took some time to adapt to a less distinguished role at Grammar School.

We have seen that children adapt progressively during the six years (figure 4.2A); yet 18 per cent never became thoroughly reconciled to school throughout this period. These were not all overdependent children. In some of the cases cited the school atmosphere was clearly not helpful.

It is possible to attribute some of the more specific difficulties to fussiness, over-sensitiveness, or contrariness in some of the children; or more generally, to the impossibility of catering for all tastes and personal idiosyncrasies. But there is no denying that many of the problems arise from faulty school organization, inappropriate attitudes in teachers, and underlying these a system of social pressures which make insufferable demands on both teachers and taught. Wall (1955) and other writers have maintained that much maladjustment can be avoided, and Burt and Howard (1952) have shown that existing maladjustments can sometimes be eradicated, by adapting education to the child's needs.

3. Significance

Yet should such stress be laid on the needs and difficulties of the individual child? Since frustrations cannot be eradicated from life, should children not learn to face them in school as a part of the educative process? The best brief examination of this familiar argument that I have encountered comes from Tibble (1959). He shows how maladjustment in some sense is an inevitable concomitant of change, and therefore essential to the continuation of society. Every child today has enough to cope with in finding some sort of adjustment amid the conflicting attitudes of adults around him on most of the major issues of life—war, aggression, sex, work, religion and so forth. Indeed, the more aware he is, the harder this becomes. Tibble concludes: 'It is our special task as educators to try to ensure that the maladjustments are as far as possible made serviceable.'

'Serviceable maladjustments' imply a resourceful and resilient personality. How can this best be developed? Neither by smoothing away all difficulties, nor by adding to them gratuitously, whether by a punitive attitude, destructive criticism, or the equating of work with imposition; rather by fortifying the child in the belief that he can indeed overcome difficulties and find solutions to the problems he meets both in work and in personal relationships.

Good teachers know this and practise it almost unconsciously as far as their conditions of work permit. Many schools nowadays are happy and exciting places to which children return eagerly day after day to find out, to master skills, and to be members of a purposefully active group. In such a school, as described by Hemming (1948), pupils and staff can perceive that their individual needs are not opposed to, but congruent with, those of the community. This is a great achievement; only it throws into deeper shadow the less happy school.

Children cannot learn effectively if they are frightened, angry, bewildered, or bored. Yet these states are too often produced and even condoned in the name of discipline or the exigencies of the syllabus. Nor are they likely to learn good manners and respect for others by being shouted at, slapped, or made the butt of sarcastic remarks— however one may sympathize with teachers who are faced with numbers and conditions that make their task well-nigh impossible. And what becomes of the attempt to awaken a response to the beauty of poetry, music or nature, if a child is then hustled off and put under pressure to eat food that (however unreasonably) he finds distasteful, or faced with the alternatives of visiting a lavatory which nauseates him or retaining the contents of his bowel or bladder for several hours?

The fastidiousness of children; their personal modesty, even at nursery school age, as shown in the desire for privacy in the toilet; and their sensitiveness to the opinions of others about their appearance, behaviour and work—any of these can become excessive, but in normal degree they are social assets which are too often ignored and trampled over because of adults' misconceptions.

4. Remedies

The first need is undeniably for the provision of the necessary basic conditions for sound education: classes small enough to allow of attention to individual needs, adequate space and equipment, class-rooms designed for sound absorption, improved dining facilities and pleasant indoor lavatories with simple bolts.

Equally important in the junior school is a reduction of the pressure that at present impinges in most areas from secondary selection procedures.

But even the best conditions would make little or no difference to a number of the most unsatisfactory situations reported here. For these arise from certain fundamental concepts of education, which determine teachers' approaches to their work.

Competition is taken for granted in the great majority of British schools as an indispensable motive for learning. It is fostered by the use of marks, grades or credit points, and sometimes by numbered positions in the class for specific subjects. All this does less than justice to children's natural thirst for knowledge; exalts the desire to beat one's neighbour at a time when the world's need is surely for practice in cooperation; and adds gratuitously to the problems of those children whose sense of personal worth is insecure. Four groups clearly suffer: those at the bottom, saddled with the dead weight of repeated failure; those at the top, tempted to intellectual snobbery; those pressed too hard, whether by teachers, parents or their own anxiety, whose distress we have glimpsed in a few of our examples; and those who care too little—sometimes as a defence against caring too much—who are the despair of every teacher.

Gardner (1942, 1950, 1965) has demonstrated that activity methods, which stress cooperation rather than competition and render marks largely irrelevant, produce results in many ways superior to the traditional teacher-directed approach. But even with a direct approach, which suits some teachers and probably some types of material better, competitive marking might well be replaced by one or another form of self-pacing. There is scope here for experiment by individual teachers. Grimes and Allinson (1961) have shown how different children respond best to teaching situations of varying degrees of structure, depending on their tendencies to anxiety and to compulsiveness. While it is not yet possible to arrange children in separate classes according to these traits, it may be possible for a teacher, given this knowledge plus sufficient flexibility of classroom organization, to vary his methods deliberately to suit different groups of children at different times.

Finally, what distinguishes a good teacher? Taylor's (1962) eleven-year-olds selected as his most important qualities: ability to help, explain and encourage, knowledge of his subject, firmness in keeping order, fairness, good manners, patience and kindly understanding. This boils down essentially to teaching ability plus a combination of firmness and respect for the child as an individual. Our own studies amply confirm how these qualities, or their lack, can make or mar a child's happiness and progress. How far can we hope to find them in the many thousand teachers that must be trained in this country during the next few years? To what extent can they be developed by training? At present teacher training is often felt to offer a counsel of perfection with inadequate guidance in adapting it to reality. The difficulties encountered by young teachers in coming to terms with problems of authority are discussed by Herbert (1955). Popper (1952) illustrates the pitfalls of excessive unconscious identification with a difficult child. A conference at Keele (Halmos, 1958) discussed the impact of courses in personality development on student teachers, and the implications for those who train them. The inevitable difficulties of the early years of teaching might be reduced by group discussion, perhaps organized by the schools psychologist. Psycho-drama might occasionally prove useful. Head teachers, as a separate group, might also appreciate an occasional opportunity to discuss ways of supporting their junior staff through the first awkward years. For in a time of increasing mechanization there is a greater need than ever to foster the variety that can only come through the development of individual contributions from teachers and pupils alike.

BIRCH, L. B.

5. The Incidence of Nail-Biting among School Children

Introduction

At a psychology class, attended by practising teachers, the writer of this account was approached by the head master of a junior school, who said he was very worried to find that almost half of the children in his top class bit their nails, a few severely enough to cause considerable discomfort and even bleeding. Most of the other teachers present said that they, too, had noticed that many of the children in their classes bit their nails, though they had not actually counted the number. They undertook to do so for the next meeting of the class, and the writer promised to find out in the meantime whether there had been any recent surveys carried out on normal school populations which could be used for comparison. He was unable to find anything and when, at the next meeting, all the teachers reported a high proportion of nail-biters among the children they taught, he decided to approach Professor Valentine (then Professor of Education at the University of Birmingham—ed.) to see whether he knew of any surveys on the topic. Before he had done this, however, he received a letter from Professor Valentine which really began the enquiry which is reported below.

It so happened that Professor Valentine had himself become interested in the incidence of nail-biting among children and had searched the literature for results of large-scale surveys which he could use to illustrate a section in his latest book. Having discovered that about 60 per cent of the boys and rather less than 60 per cent of the girls between the ages of 8 and 11 in Chicago, were reported to be nail-biters, he had, in the absence of any recent English work, begun an enquiry in this country. His first data, from rather small numbers, seemed to

Birch, L. B. (1955) 'The incidence of nail-biting among school children.' *British Journal of Educational Psychology*, 25, 2, 123–8.

indicate that the incidence here was probably not very different from that in the American survey and his letter to the writer was a request for help in the collecting of data from a larger sample in order to verify this indication. When this request was made known to the group of teachers who had raised the question with the writer they at once offered to help, as did members of several other classes when they heard about it. It was clear that results from a reasonably large number of children could be collected fairly easily and when Professor Valentine heard of this he was pleased to leave the enquiry to the writer and, in addition to suggesting a scale for use in recording the degree of nail-biting of the children, he also made available the data which had already been collected for him by a number of teachers. These data have not been included with those collected for the writer though they are referred to in other places.

Method of the Enquiry

As has been indicated, the data for this enquiry were mostly collected by teacher volunteers who were attending part-time courses of various kinds in the University of Sheffield Institute of Education. One of the courses at the time was on elementary statistics and, because nearly all the members of this class were men and because this class provided a large number of volunteers, there are rather more boys than girls in the final sample of children.

Altogether, seventy-eight teachers from thirty-nine schools took part in the enquiry; some reported upon only one class, others on more than one and a few on a whole school. They were not selected specially for the task, but, having volunteered, were carefully instructed upon how to scale and record their results. Each teacher was given a printed sheet, giving the following details for scoring:

Score   *Degree of fingernail-biting*
0   No finger bitten—Free margin of nail beyond soft tissue intact on all fingers.
1+Mildly bitten—Free margin of one or more nails irregular parts bitten (if any doubt, question child).
2+Moderately bitten—Free margin of nail absent, i.e. fingernail bitten to the soft tissue.
3+Severely bitten—Nail bitten *beyond* the free edge; nail margin now below the soft tissue border.

Below this schedule were drawings showing exactly what was meant by each of the four degrees of nail-biting. Teachers were asked to assess

TABLE 5.1

SURVEY OF NAIL-BITING AMONG CHILDREN

| Age of Children | Numbers of Children at each age | | | PERCENTAGE OF CHILDREN IN EACH CATEGORY | | | | | | | | | | | |
| | | | | 0 (No finger bitten) | | | 1 (Mildly bitten) | | | 2 (Moderately bitten) | | | 3 (Severely bitten) | | |
	Boys	Girls	Total	Boys	Girls	Boys and Girls together	Boys	Girls	Boys and Girls together	Boys	Girls	Boys and Girls together	Boys	Girls	Boys and Girls together
16+	50	42	92	70	68	69	12	14	13	14	9	13	4	9	5
15+	187	158	345	45	71	55	28	10	20	17	12	15	10	7	9
14+	287	243	530	44	53	48	21	22	21	16	11	14	21	13	17
13+	284	232	516	43	53	47	19	15	17	18	18	18	22	15	18
12+	315	231	546	38	52	43	21	15	19	18	18	18	22	16	20
11+	310	262	572	48	49	48	21	19	23	13	16	14	18	16	17
10+	256	122	378	40	53	44	20	16	19	19	14	18	20	17	19
9+	263	107	370	44	62	48	20	14	18	18	9	15	19	15	18
8+	176	61	237	43	52	46	30	8	23	13	18	14	16	21	17
7+	193	83	276	51	61	54	25	18	23	12	10	12	11	12	11
6+	153	106	259	59	51	56	19	18	19	9	16	12	13	15	14
5+	57	45	102	74	51	64	9	18	13	5	25	14	12	7	10
Totals	2,531	1,692	4,223	46	54	49	21	16	19	16	15	15	18	15	17

FIGURE 5.1
Percentage distribution of nail-biters (boys and girls together)

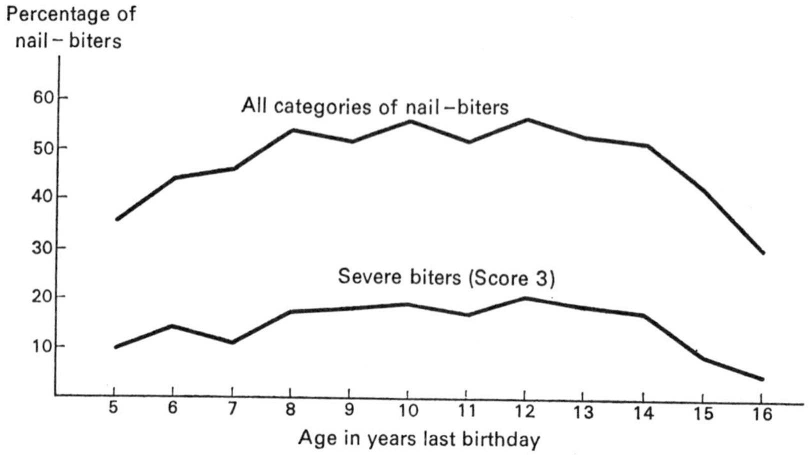

Percentage of nail – biters

All categories of nail – biters

Severe biters (Score 3)

Age in years last birthday

all the children in any particular class, but were told not to try to obtain the scores of children who were absent. Printed record forms were provided for recording each child's sex, age last birthday, type of school, and nail-biting score. A small group of teachers also agreed to ask all the nail-biters in their classes when and under what circumstances the children actually indulged in the biting.

Results

(a) In general

Table 5.1 gives the percentage frequency of nail-biting at various ages of boys, girls and boys and girls taken together. It will be seen that, in the whole sample, roughly half of the children bite their nails to some extent, there being 51 per cent biters and 49 per cent non-biters (S.E. = 0·77). On the whole, boys are more frequently biters than girls, the difference between the 54 per cent for boys and 46 per cent for girls being highly significant. This difference is apparent in the figures for all ages between 7 and 15 though, in many cases, the difference is not statistically significant. Below the age of 7, the results seem to show that boys are less frequently nail-biters than are girls; unfortunately the numbers here are too small to establish significance. When the results are set out in graphical form, they seem to show a steady increase in the number of nail-biters up to the age of 8, followed by a period up to the age of 14 when the numbers remain fairly constant. In fact, the most noticeable feature is the absence of marked peak periods at particular ages, even that at the age of twelve is hardly significantly higher than the percentage found for the whole population.

When graphed separately for the sexes, as in figure 5.2, it will be seen that there is one marked peak period for nail-biting among boys, at the age of 12. The incidence at this age is significantly higher than the percentage found for the whole male population. In view of the connection which some writers hold to exist between anxiety and nail-biting, it is interesting to note that there is so little evidence for an increase in the incidence of nail-biting at the time of the special place examinations at the age of 10.

When the numbers of children biting their nails are broken down into the three categories of 'slight', 'moderate' and 'severe' biting, it is found that they are fairly evenly distributed among the three categories.

(b) Nail-biting in different types of school

At the secondary age there were, in the sample, children from most types of secondary school, though some, such as those from secondary technical, private and special schools were too few in number to make comparisons worth while. In table 5.2 a comparison is made between

FIGURE 5.2
Percentage distribution of nail-biters (boys and girls separately)

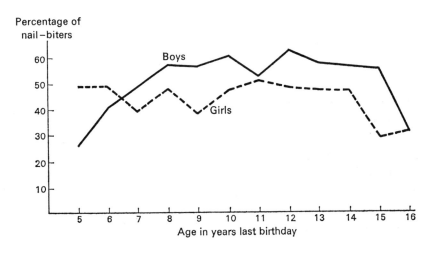

the results obtained for grammar school and secondary modern school children between the ages of 11 and 15.

TABLE 5.2

PERCENTAGE OF NAIL-BITERS AMONG CHILDREN AGED 11 TO 15 YEARS IN SECONDARY GRAMMAR AND SECONDARY MODERN SCHOOLS

Type of School	Boys	Girls	Boys and Girls together
Grammar	50 (N = 392)	38 (N = 413)	44 (N = 805)
Secondary Modern	56 (N = 413)	49 (N = 595)	53 (N = 1461)

It will be seen that the grammar school children are less frequently nail-biters than are secondary-modern children and when the boys and girls are considered together, the difference is almost three times the standard error and so can be regarded as statistically significant.

Results were obtained from 156 boys, aged 11 to 15, in three special (E.S.N.) schools, and also from 196 men and 383 women students, aged 18 and 19, from four teacher-training colleges. 47 per cent of the special school children were nail-biters, a smaller proportion than was found among grammar school boys of similar age. The difference is not, however, significant.

Of the training college students, 46 per cent of the men and 35 per cent of the women students were found to be nail-biters, a figure very similar to that found for grammar school children, though here again the standard error with such small numbers is so large that confident conclusions cannot be drawn.

An interesting feature of the results from the training college students was that very few of them scored 3 on the schedule, there being less than 1 per cent of the women and less than 3 per cent of the men in this category of 'severe biters'.

(c) *When do children bite their nails?*

473 nail-biters of both sexes, aged between 8 and 10, and coming from five junior schools, were asked personally under what circumstances they bit their nails. Of these more than half (54 per cent) either said that they did not know when they bit their nails or said they bit them at no special times. 23 per cent of them said they bit theirs most frequently at the pictures or when watching television; 8 per cent when reading an exciting book, hearing an exciting story, or seeing an

exciting incident shown as a film or on television. 11 per cent said that they tended to bite when they were concentrating at school, especially when doing arithmetic ('hard sums'). 5 per cent seemed to bite their nails chiefly when they were bored, about half of this group referring to biting in bed. One boy in this group said that he quite often bit his toe nails too. A small group (2 per cent) referred to worry or 'being grumbled at' as factors connected with their biting.

A similar range of reasons was given to one of Professor Valentine's teachers who collected her data from a large rural school in Worcestershire.

Conclusions

The sample of children used in this enquiry was probably not a random one, even for the industrial area of South Yorkshire, in which all the schools taking part were situated. On the other hand, it seems unlikely that there were any factors systematically influencing the results with reference to the trait being considered. It is probable, therefore, that the figure of 51 per cent (S.E. $= 0.77$) of all children being nail-biters in some degree is reasonably representative of the district. It should, of course, be remembered that the results do not show how many children give up biting, their numbers being made up by others who start biting late in their school life. If these were taken into consideration, it seems possible that the number of children who bite their nails at some time or other may be considerably above the half which was found in this survey. Further, as a number of teachers pointed out, there are children who, while not being nail-biters, do bite their hands somewhere else, e.g. the backs of their hands or the skin round their nails. There are also others having the appearance of nail-biters whose nails are torn off by hand rather than by biting. In fact, one teacher in a large, boys' secondary-modern school reported that all but three children in the four classes he taught had some habit of chewing or 'picking' the nails or the skin on the fingers.

No attempt was made in this enquiry to assess the causes of nail-biting. Some writers have viewed the condition gravely, regarding it variously as an expression of repressed aggression, emotional maladjustment, or anxiety. Hadfield (1950), for example writes: 'The child who cannot let off its aggression against others, lets off its aggression by biting its own nails.' English and Pearson (1947) write: '. . . despite the prevalence in the population we must regard it as a sign of poor emotional adjustment.' On the other hand, Barton Hall (1947), while agreeing that there are cases 'in which there is a pronounced element of anxiety and frustration and in which the nails are unusually very severely bitten,' considers that in the majority of cases the nail-biting '. . . is an habitual reaction and is otherwise of no particular significance except perhaps for the fact that children with this habit are often of overactive, energetic, restless nature.'

Since roughly half the children in our schools and a good proportion of the students in some of our training colleges seem to bite their nails, there is obviously a need to find out to what extent there is a connection between nail-biting and maladjustment.

Identification of Maladjusted Behaviour

Introduction

This section is concerned with the identification of children's behaviour problems. The first article deals with a questionnaire which in the last two or three years has gained wide acceptance as an instrument for rapidly assessing children's behaviour in school. It is interesting in that it not only provides teachers with a very quick and easy measure of the extent of perceived maladjustment or disturbed behaviour which children show, but it also gives an indication of the extent to which behaviour is weighted in the direction of 'neurotic' behaviour on the one hand, or 'antisocial' behaviour on the other.

Rutter's classification of disturbed behaviour into 'neurotic' and 'antisocial' categories is a classification based on a clinical approach. It is interesting to compare it with the classification proposed by Burt and Howard (see article 9), which is based on a statistical approach.

The next paper in this section illustrates the use of a similar kind of questionnaire in a study which examines the way in which children's behaviour at home and at school differs. It illustrates the principle that 'maladjustment' is 'situation-specific', that is, the child who exhibits a particular form of behaviour in school may not necessarily show the same characteristics in the home situation, and vice versa.

In the final paper in this section, Tizard indicates some of the dangers which are inherent in using questionnaire measures of maladjustment, but emphasizes the value of these techniques as screening devices which are easily and rapidly used by teachers in school.

RUTTER, M.

6. A Children's Behaviour Questionnaire for Completion by Teachers: Preliminary Findings

Introduction

An overall psychiatric assessment of the child requires the combination of several different approaches to the measurement of the child's behaviour (Rutter and Graham, 1966), but as a first step in the evaluation, questionnaires have an important place, especially for screening or survey purposes. Because school teachers have the opportunity of observing and comparing large numbers of children and because of the practical importance of the child's behaviour in school, questionnaires completed by teachers are particularly useful screening devices. Unfortunately, as with other measures of child behaviour there are few adequately developed instruments (Pritchard, 1963). The present paper reports the development of a simple behavioural questionnaire for completion by teachers.

Wickman (1928) was the first to make a systematic attempt to measure children's behaviour in the classroom, and revisions of his scales by Haggerty (1952) and Olson (1930) were shown by them to have good reliability and validity. Among the more recent scales of general applicability for which there are some published details on reliability and validity are those described by Eisenberg *et al.* (1962), Mulligan (Mulligan, 1963; Mulligan *et al.*, 1963), Ross *et al.* (1965), and Stott (1958). Although excellent in many ways all the scales have important disadvantages (e.g. lack of diagnostic distinction within the overall concept of maladjustment, lack of recent validation, too great a length for a teacher to complete the scale on a whole class of children, unsuitability for pre-adolescent children etc.).

It appeared that there was a need for a reliable and valid short

Rutter, M. (1967) 'A children's behaviour questionnaire for completion by teachers: preliminary findings.' *Journal of Child Psychology and Psychiatry, 8*, 1–11.

questionnaire suitable to be used with children in the middle age-range, which teachers could complete fairly quickly (so that they might reasonably be expected to fill in the scale for a whole class of children for survey or other purposes), which concerned behaviour occurring in a school situation, and which could be used to discriminate between different types of behavioural or emotional disorder, as well as discriminating between children who show disorder and those who do not. The present paper reports preliminary findings on a scale which attempts to fill this need.

Development of the Scale

During the development of the scale, teachers in several classes in eight different schools completed the scale for 7- to 13-year-old children in classes of mixed sex. Where possible, two or more teachers completed the scale on the same children. Afterwards, the teachers were interviewed; usually the teachers in each school were seen together for a group discussion. They were asked to describe the children they had rated, to outline the behaviour which had led to positive ratings, and to say what behaviours they considered relevant for each item on the scale. Samples of children who had been rated were also observed by the author.

By this means ambiguous or misunderstood items were revised or omitted. Most items requiring much inference on the part of the teacher were found unreliable and were dropped. Similarly, items referring to rare abnormalities (e.g. obsessional phenomena) were often interpreted in widely divergent ways, especially by teachers who had not encountered the behaviour in question, and these items also had to be omitted. Altogether, ten items used in earlier versions were omitted from the scale when it was finalized. Only one item (No. 6, 'not much liked by other children') was retained in a negative form. In earlier versions the term 'unpopular' had been used in this item but this was taken by some teachers to include only *active* dislike of the child by other children, and it was found necessary to use the phrase 'not much liked by other children' if socially isolated or rejected children were to be identified, as well as those actually hated or tormented by others.

Two-point scales (yes or no) were found to be unnecessarily crude, and also to lead to large differences between teachers in the way they rated slightly deviant behaviour. On the other hand, some teachers (especially those in secondary schools who often had less intimate contact with the children) felt unable to make the discriminations required for four- or five-point scales. Thus, three-point scales were selected as those which all teachers felt able to use.

With all behavioural questionnaires there has been the problem of what criterion of disorder to use to assess the validity of the instrument being developed. As a first step it was decided to use children attending a psychiatric clinic as a criterion group of 'abnormal' children. While it was realized that this group was likely to be a special population of children with emotional or behavioural disorders, clinic groups had been used in the development of other scales and it was felt that if the scale were to have any usefulness it should at least be able to differentiate children attending psychiatric clinics. By comparing the total scores on the questionnaire (see below for details of scoring method) of samples of clinic and non-clinic children it was found that a score of 9 or more produced the best differentiation between the groups. As a further test of validity, another study was undertaken in which psychiatric interview rating of those scoring above and below the cut-off point (a score of 9) were compared. More detailed information from teachers and from parents would also be necessary to assess validity adequately. Some preliminary findings on the relationship between different measures of behaviour have already been reported as part of a survey of 10- and 11-year-old children (Rutter and Graham, 1966).

In using the scale to select diagnostic sub-groups there were two main alternatives. Either the sub-groups could be derived from data obtained with the scale (e.g. by factor analysis) or the scale could be scored to discriminate between already established clinical diagnostic sub-groups. The latter course was taken, as there are known and important differences in family background, response to treatment, and prognosis between the two largest clinical diagnostic categories: neurotic disorders and antisocial disorders (Rutter, 1965). Finer diagnostic distinctions with the scale were not found possible at this stage in its development (a different type of scale had to be developed to select children with certain rarer disorders such as child psychosis and the hyperkinetic syndrome). Neurotic and antisocial sub-scores were then derived by comparing the items scored positively for neurotic clinic children and for antisocial clinic children (the clinic diagnoses being based on clinic case records).

The results reported later in this paper refer to the study of samples obtained after the method of scoring the questionnaire in its final form had already been worked out from these earlier pilot investigations.

Description of the Scale

The scale consists of twenty-six brief statements concerning the child's behaviour (see page 94) to which the teacher has to check whether the statement 'certainly applies', 'applies somewhat' or 'doesn't apply' to the child in question. These are given a weight of '2', '1', and '0' respectively to produce a total score with a range of 0–52 by summation of the scores of the twenty-six items. A 'neurotic' sub-score is obtained by summing the scores of items, 7, 10, 17 and 23 ('often worried, worries about many things'; 'often appears miserable, unhappy, tearful or distressed'; 'tends to be fearful or afraid of new things or new situations'; 'has had tears on arrival at school *or* has refused to come into the building this year'). An 'antisocial' sub-score is obtained by summing the scores of items 4, 5, 15, 19, 20 and 26 ('often destroys own or others' belongings'; 'frequently fights with other children'; 'is often disobedient'; 'often tells lies'; 'has stolen things on one or more occasions'; 'bullies other children').

The selection of children with neurotic or antisocial disorders by means of the scale is a two-stage procedure: (1) children with a total score of 9 or more are designated as showing some disorder; (2) of these children, those with a neurotic score exceeding the antisocial score are designated 'neurotic', and those with an antisocial score exceeding the neurotic score are designated 'antisocial'. The children with equal neurotic and antisocial sub-scores remain undifferentiated.

Method and Results

(1) *Re-test reliability* was tested by getting four teachers to rate eighty 7-year-old children (forty boys and forty girls) in one school twice, with a 2-month interval between ratings. The ratings were made in different school terms and on the first occasion the teachers were not told that they would have to rate the children again the next term. The product-moment correlation between the total scores on the two occasions was $+0\cdot89$.

(2) *Inter-rater reliability* was tested by getting four teachers to rate seventy children (thirty-five boys and thirty-five girls) in the last term

of infant school and four other teachers to rate the same children 2–3 months later in the children's first term in junior school. The product-moment correlation between the total scores on the two occasions (with ratings made by different teachers) was +0·72.

(3) *The discriminative power* of the scale was tested by comparing the scores of children in the general population with the scores of children attending psychiatric clinics for emotional or behavioural disorders. The general population sample consisted of a random sample of fifty-five boys and thirty-one girls aged 9–13 years resident in the city of Aberdeen. Two clinic samples were studied. The first consisted of the twenty-two boys and twelve girls in the same age-range who, at the time the questionnaires were completed, were currently attending the psychiatric clinic at the Hospital for Sick Children, Aberdeen, for emotional or behavioural disorders (children attending for uncomplicated mental retardation or educational disorders only were excluded). The questionnaires were obtained as part of a total population survey and in many cases the teachers will have been unaware that the child was attending a psychiatric clinic. The second sample consisted of a similarly selected group of children attending the Maudsley Hospital. The questionnaires were sent out individually and the teachers knew that the child was attending the hospital.

In line with the results of the pilot investigations, it was found that the best discrimination between clinic and non-clinic children was obtained with a total score of 9 or more. About 11 per cent of boys and 3½ per cent of girls in the general population obtained scores of 9 or greater compared with about 80 per cent of the boys and 60 per cent of the girls in the clinic samples (see table 6.1).

Very similar results were obtained in further samples obtained for cross-validation (table 6.1). It was concluded that the scale was reasonably efficient in differentiating children attending psychiatric clinics. Both antisocial and neurotic children were differentiated but a slightly higher proportion of antisocial children than neurotic children were picked out by means of the scale.

(4) *Discrimination between neurotic children and antisocial children.* It could be argued that the discrimination between clinic and non-clinic children may have been partly due to the teachers' knowledge of the child's clinic attendance. This is unlikely to have been a major factor in that the discrimination of clinic children in Aberdeen (where many or most of the teachers were unaware of the child's clinic attendance)

was nearly as good as for Maudsley Hospital children. Nevertheless, a harsher test of validity is the scale's power of discrimination between neurotic children and antisocial children.

The case notes of all new referrals to the Maudsley Hospital Children's Department were examined and a diagnosis of neurotic disorder, antisocial disorder, or other condition was made. Teachers were asked to complete scales on all children diagnosed as having a neurotic disorder or antisocial disorder. The diagnoses based on the scale sub-scores were then compared with the clinical diagnoses made previously from the case notes for all children scoring 9 or more on the scale. In about 90 per cent of antisocial children and 80 per cent of neurotic children the questionnaire diagnoses and the clinical diagnoses were in agreement (table 6.2).

The findings were cross-validated using further samples of thirty-nine antisocial children and sixteen neurotic children with total questionnaire scores of 9 or more. The results were closely similar (table 6.2).

The items used to produce the neurotic and antisocial sub-scores were based on the proportion of neurotic, antisocial and control children scoring 1 or 2 on each item during a pilot study undertaken during the development of the scale. The results for the study proper are given in table 6.3 which shows the proportion of children in each of the groups scoring 1 or 2 on each item, with the pooled first and cross-validation samples. Table 6.4 shows which items discriminate between the groups at a significance level of 5 per cent or better. The items used to produce the sub-scores all reliably discriminate between neurotic and antisocial children of both sexes, except item 23 where the discrimination falls just short of the 5 per cent level for boys. No other items significantly discriminate between the groups for both boys and girls.

(5) *Relationship between questionnaire scores and ratings based on a standardized psychiatric interview with the child.* Children aged 9, 10 and 11 years were interviewed for approximately ½ hr by child psychiatrists, as part of a survey on the Isle of Wight, using a standardized technique of known and satisfactory reliability (Rutter and Graham, 1966). On the basis of the interview a rating of definite psychiatric disorder, uncertain, or no psychiatric disorder was made. Teachers had previously completed behavioural scales on all children in the age group, so that it was possible to compare the psychiatric ratings for those children with a score below 9 and those with a score of 9 or more on

TABLE 6.1

CHILDREN WITH A TOTAL SCORE OF 9 OR MORE

			% scoring 9 or more	Total number
1st Sample				
	Boys	General population—Aberdeen	10·9	55
		Aberdeen psychiatric clinic	77·3	22
		Maudsley Hospital	87·7	46
	Girls	General population—Aberdeen	3·2	31
		Aberdeen psychiatric clinic	50·0	12
		Maudsley Hospital	72·1	29
2nd Sample				
	Boys	General population—Aberdeen	9·0	100
		Maudsley Hospital	68·8	45
	Girls	General population—Aberdeen	5·0	100
		Maudsley Hospital	69·1	39
TOTAL (1st and 2nd samples)				
(a) By Sex				
	Boys	General population	9·7	155
		Clinic	77·9	113
(b) Girls		General population	4·6	131
		Clinic	67·5	80
(b) By diagnosis and sex				
	Antisocial boys (clinic)		85·7	63
	Neurotic boys (clinic)		80·0	30
	Antisocial girls (clinic)		70·0	40
	Neurotic girls (clinic)		64·5	31

TABLE 6.2

DISCRIMINATION BETWEEN NEUROTIC CHILDREN AND ANTISOCIAL CHILDREN[*]
(WITHIN CLINIC SAMPLE)

	Agreement between clinic diagnosis and scale diagnoses			Clinic diagnosis
	No. agreement	Total No.	%	
1st sample				
	26	30	86·6	Antisocial boys
	11	15	73·3	Neurotic boys
	11	12	91·7	Antisocial girls
	9	10	90·0	Neurotic girls
2nd sample				
	17	21	80·9	Antisocial boys
	6	8	75·0	Neurotic boys
	13	18	72·2	Antisocial girls
	7	8	88·0	Neurotic girls

[*] N.B. Only children with total score of 9 or more included

TABLE 6.3

CHILDREN IN ANTISOCIAL, NEUROTIC, AND CONTROL GROUPS SCORING 1 OR 2 ON INDIVIDUAL ITEMS

Item No.	Antisocial boys		Antisocial girls		Neurotic boys		Neurotic girls		Control boys		Control girls	
	No.	%	No.	%	No.	%	No.	%	No.	%	No.	%
1	42	66·67	20	50·00	16	53·33	7	22·58	24	15·48	21	16·03
2	22	34·92	16	40·00	5	16·67	7	22·58	5	3·23	1	0·76
3	34	53·97	16	40·00	20	66·67	10	32·26	33·	21·29	24	18·32
4	21	33·33	8	20·00	3	10·00	1	3·23	6	3·87	1	0·76
5	39	61·90	20	50·00	9	30·00	1	3·23	20	12·90	9	6·87
6	35	55·56	23	57·50	21	70·00	15	48·39	17	10·97	24	18·32
7	26	41·27	18	45·00	24	80·00	26	83·87	24	15·48	17	12·98
8	32	50·79	18	45·00	22	73·33	17	54·84	22	14·19	13	9·92
9	32	50·79	24	60·00	19	63·33	7	22·58	15	9·68	7	5·34
10	19	30·16	15	37·50	20	66·67	21	67·74	21	13·55	6	4·58
11	9	14·29	8	20·00	9	30·00	7	22·58	11	7·09	3	2·29
12	4	6·35	2	5·00	6	20·00	1	3·23	4	2·58	10	7·63
13	11	17·46	14	35·00	5	16·67	7	22·58	39	25·16	32	24·43
14	14	22·22	9	22·50	9	30·00	16	51·61	8	5·16	0	—
15	45	71·43	24	60·00	7	23·33	8	25·81	20	12·90	9	6·87
16	54	85·71	27	67·50	22	73·33	16	51·61	58	37·42	33	25·19
17	16	25·39	16	40·00	19	63·33	20	64·52	24	15·48	23	17·56
18	3	4·76	17	42·50	12	40·00	15	48·39	9	5·81	6	4·58
19	44	69·84	24	60·00	10	33·33	4	12·90	12	7·74	2	1·53
20	26	41·27	16	40·00	1	3·23	0	—	4	2·58	1	0·76
21	6	9·52	2	5·00	3	10·00	1	3·23	0	—	2	1·53
22	8	12·69	16	40·00	6	20·00	18	58·06	3	1·94	4	3·05
23	8	12·69	6	15·00	8	26·67	12	38·71	3	1·94	0	—
24	8	12·69	3	7·50	5	16·67	1	3·23	7	4·52	0	—
25	14	22·22	2	5·00	1	3·33	3	9·68	11	7·09	0	—
26	33	52·38	18	45·00	6	20·00	0	—	8	5·16	3	2·29
TOTAL	63		40		30		31		155		131	

the scale. The psychiatrist who saw the child was told only the child's name and age and was unaware of the scale score or any other information about the child.

In a 5 per cent random sample of 147 children[1] there were 133 who scored 8 or less on the scale. Only three (2·3 per cent) received a rating of definite disorder on the psychiatric interview with the child, while thirty-two (24·1 per cent) were rated as showing possible disorder; 73·7 per cent were rated normal. Of the total population of 10- and 11-year-old children resident on the Isle of Wight, there were 7·2 per cent (157) children with scores of 9 or more. Of these, 20 per cent were rated as definitely abnormal (over eight times as many as among

TABLE 6.4

DISCRIMINATIVE POWER OF INDIVIDUAL ITEMS OF SCALE FOR BOYS

Item	Total 'disturbed' vs. control	Neurotic vs. control	Antisocial vs. control	Neurotic vs. antisocial
1	D	N	A	
2	D	N	A	
3	D	N	A	
4	D		A	A
5	D	N	A	A
6	D	N	A	
7	D	N	A	N
8	D	N	A	N
9	D	N	A	
10	D	N	A	N
11	D	N		
12	D	N		
13				
14	D	N	A	
15	D		A	A
16	D	N	A	
17	D	N		N
18	D	N		N
19	D	N	A	A
20	D		A	A
21	D	N	A	
22	D	N	A	
23	D	N	A	
24	D	N	A	
25	D		A	A
26	D		A	A

In each cell a letter indicates that there is a significant difference between the groups (using the critical ratio for a difference between proportions). The letter used indicates the group with the higher proportion of children scoring 1 or 2 on that item (N = neurotic, A = antisocial, C = control, D = Total 'disturbed').

those scoring less than 9 on the questionnaire), 48 per cent as possibly abnormal and only 32 per cent as normal. Thus, as judged from a psychiatric examination of the child, children scoring 9 or more on the questionnaire included a considerably higher proportion of psychiatrically abnormal children than that found in children scoring less than 9 on the scale.

However, the validity of the psychiatric interview has still to be established, and it appears that an interview with the child is less efficient in the differentiation of antisocial behaviour than it is in the differentiation of neurotic disorders (Rutter and Graham, 1968). A better evaluation of the psychiatric state of children scoring 9 or more on the scale is provided by an assessment based on an intensive interview with the child's parent, and detailed information from the school,[2] as well as a psychiatric examination. On this total assessment 43 per cent

TABLE 6.5

DISCRIMINATIVE POWER OF INDIVIDUAL ITEMS OF SCALE FOR GIRLS

Item	Total 'disturbed' vs. control	Neurotic vs. control	Antisocial vs. control	Neurotic vs. antisocial
1	D		A	A
2	D	N	A	
3	D		A	
4	D		A	A
5	D		A	A
6	D	N	A	
7	D	N	A	N
8	D	N	A	
9	D	N	A	N
10	D	N	A	N
11	D	N	A	
12				
13				
14	D	N	A	N
15	D	N	A	A
16	D	N	A	
17	D	N	A	N
18	D	N	A	
19	D	N	A	A
20	D		A	A
21				
22	D	N	A	
23	D	N	A	N
24	D		A	
25	D	N		
26	D		A	A

Notations as in table 6.4.

of children scoring 9 or more on the scale are rated as having a definite psychiatric disorder compared with 6·3 per cent in the population as a whole (Rutter and Graham, 1966).

Discussion

It has been shown that the scale has satisfactory re-test and inter-rater reliability, and that it is reasonably efficient in differentiating children with neurotic or antisocial disorders. Similar findings were reported by Richman (1964), using a slightly modified version of the scale with a group of epileptic children at a special school. She found that the re-test reliability over a 13-week period was + 0·85 (N = 91) and the correlation between the ratings of a class teacher and a special subject teacher was + 0·70 (N = 73). She also found a high level of agreement between questionnaire scores and the ratings on a 'blind' psychiatric interview with the child (agreement in 76·7 per cent of cases, N = 60, χ^2 = 17·51, $p < 0·001$). Thus, Richman's findings confirm those reported here that the scale is reliable and is efficient in differentiating children with psychiatric disorder.

The scale requires only a short time to complete and is easy to score. The findings suggest that the questionnaire may usefully be employed as a screening instrument to select children likely to show some emotional or behavioural disorder. As the scale differentiates neurotic and antisocial disorders it may also be used as a standardized means of describing a child's disorder, and it has been found to form a useful part of the school report routinely obtained for children referred to the Maudsley Hospital. Similarly it has been used as one measure of behaviour in several therapeutic trials currently being conducted, but its value in the assessment of changes in behaviour has yet to be demonstrated.

Although the questionnaire has been shown to be a very useful measure of the child's behaviour in the school situation, certain limitations need to be emphasized. Firstly, it is a simple and crude measure and for clinical purposes it needs to be supplemented by other information from the teacher. Secondly, as scored in the way described, it cannot be used to pick out children with monosymptomatic disorders. Thirdly, it is less efficient in differentiating children with certain less common disorders of a circumscribed kind such as anorexia nervosa, conversion hysteria and some obsessional disorders. Necessarily, it will

CHILD SCALE B

TO BE COMPLETED BY TEACHERS

Below are a series of descriptions of behaviour often shown by children. After each statement are three columns: 'Doesn't Apply', 'Applies Somewhat', and 'Certainly Applies'. If the child definitely shows the behaviour described by the statement place a cross in the box under 'Certainly Applies'. If the child shows the behaviour described by the statement but to a lesser degree or less often place a cross in the box under 'Applies Somewhat'. If, *as far as you are aware*, the child does not show the behaviour place a cross in the box under 'Doesn't Apply'.

1. Please put ONE cross against EACH statement. Thank you.

Statement	Doesn't Apply	Applies Somewhat	Certainly Applies	FOR OFFICE USE ONLY
1. Very restless. Often running about or jumping up and down. Hardly ever still ...	☐	☐	☐	☐
2. Truants from school ...	☐	☐	☐	☐
3. Squirmy, fidgety child ...	☐	☐	☐	☐
4. Often destroys own or others' belongings	☐	☐	☐	☐
5. Frequently fights with other children ...	☐	☐	☐	☐
6. Not much liked by other children ...	☐	☐	☐	☐
7. Often worried, worries about many things	☐	☐	☐	
8. Tends to do things on his own—rather solitary ...	☐	☐	☐	☐
9. Irritable. Is quick to 'fly off the handle'	☐	☐	☐	☐
10. Often appears miserable, unhappy, tearful or distressed ...	☐	☐	☐	☐
11. Has twitches, mannerisms or tics of the face or body ...	☐	☐	☐	☐
12. Frequently sucks thumb or finger ...	☐	☐	☐	☐
13. Frequently bites nails or fingers ...	☐	☐	☐	☐
14. Tends to be absent from school for trivial reasons ...	☐	☐	☐	☐
15. Is often disobedient ...	☐	☐	☐	☐
16. Has poor concentration or short attention span ...	☐	☐	☐	☐
17. Tends to be fearful or afraid of new things or new situations ...	☐	☐	☐	☐
18. Fussy or over-particular child ...	☐	☐	☐	☐
19. Often tells lies ...	☐	☐	☐	☐
20. Has stolen things on one or more occasions	☐	☐	☐	☐
21. Has wet or soiled self at school this year	☐	☐	☐	☐
22. Often complains of pains or aches ...	☐	☐	☐	☐
23. Has had tears on arrival at school *or* has refused to come into the building this year	☐	☐	☐	☐
24. Has a stutter or stammer ...	☐	☐	☐	☐
25. Has other speech difficulty ...	☐	☐	☐	☐
26. Bullies other children ...	☐	☐	☐	☐

Are there any other problems of behaviour?

....

....

Signature: Mr/Mrs/Miss..   ☐

How well do you know this child?   Very well ☐

Moderately well ☐   Not very well ☐   ☐

THANK YOU VERY MUCH FOR YOUR HELP

not select children with symptoms only manifest outside the school situation (e.g. nocturnal enuresis and sleep disorders). An earlier study (Rutter and Graham, 1966) has suggested that the overlap between disorders perceived by teachers and those perceived by parents is surprisingly small, but the reasons for this await further investigation. Lastly, the value of any scale for completion by teachers depends on the skill of the teacher as an observer, and on the opportunities for the teacher to observe the child in varied situations. The scales probably convey a more valid picture of the child's behaviour when the teacher has seen the child at play and at mealtimes as well as in the classroom situation. Such opportunities are often more freely available in primary than secondary schools.

Notes

1 The random sample obtained actually consisted of 159 children, but owing to refusals and emigration from the Isle of Wight during the interval between selection and testing, only 147 children were seen.
2 All the children had moved class and half had moved school since the teachers' questionnaire had been obtained. Thus, in all cases the more detailed information was provided by a different teacher from the one who completed the scale.

MITCHELL, S. and SHEPHERD, M.

7. A Comparative Study of Children's Behaviour at Home and at School

Introduction

For many years there has been considerable speculation about the extent to which 'behaviour problems', 'maladjustment', or 'emotional disorders' exist among the child population as a whole. Many studies designed to investigate this problem have been carried out in the school situation, including those of Olson (1930), McFie (1934), Rogers (1942), Cummings (1944), Ullman (1952), Bower (1958) and Stott (1958). All these studies imply that the existence of 'maladjusted' or 'problem' behaviour in school is a reflection of a general emotional disturbance which will also be apparent in other aspects of the child's life. Few studies have attempted to estimate the association between the child's behaviour in the two environments though Schonell (1952) has epitomized common knowledge with his remark that 'It must always be borne in mind that some children present a form of dual personality in respect to home and school.' In the main, this deficiency may be due to the greater administrative difficulties involved in obtaining information from a representative group of parents and to the mistaken belief that parents would prove less cooperative than teachers and less reliable in their reports. Most workers who have obtained a great deal of information from a sample of mothers (MacFarlane, Allen and Honzik, 1954; Lapouse and Monk, 1958) have not obtained comparative data from schools. Those studies which have attempted to relate adjustment at home and at school show some disagreement in their findings. Douglas (1964), for example, dealing with a national sample of children, found that teachers rated as 'highly strung' a high proportion of 11-year-old children whose mothers reported them to be suffering

Mitchell, S. and Shepherd, M. (1966) 'A comparative study of children's behaviour at home and at school.' *British Journal of Educational Psychology, 36*, 3, 248–54.

from one or more of the following 'symptoms': bedwetting; night-mares; abdominal pain or recurrent vomiting; nail-biting; thumbsucking or other such habits. Children with such behaviour problems were also found to show poor attainment and concentration at school. Glidewell *et al.* (1963) in St Louis, also found in a sample of 830 third-grade children that the number of 'symptoms' reported by the mother showed a positive relationship to the degree of maladjustment reported by the teacher. The pilot investigation carried out in Birmingham for the Underwood Committee (Ministry of Education, 1955) found that psychologists' clinical ratings of the questionnaires completed by parents and teachers agreed in 60–65 per cent of cases. Nevertheless, the same investigation showed that, of sixteen children later seen by a psychiatrist at their parents' request, eleven had been rated free of maladjustment on the basis of their teachers' reports. Similar disagreement is revealed in a small-scale clinical enquiry carried out by Piltzer (1952) who found that fifteen out of forty children selected as well-adjusted by teachers, did not appear so on Rorschach testing and that eight of these were found to show maladjusted behaviour at home.

Methods of Investigation

In 1961, questionnaires dealing with behaviour, health and family background were sent to the parents of a one-in-ten random sample of children aged between 5 and 15 years, who were attending local authority schools in Buckinghamshire: approximately 6,300 question-naires (93 per cent) were returned, completed. At the same time, separate questionnaires were also sent to the child's school to be completed by his, or her, class teacher. In this case, approximately 6,600 (97 per cent) were received back. Completed questionnaires from both teachers and parents were available for 6,077 children, com-prising 1,870 boys and 1,735 girls, aged 5 to 10 years, and 1,206 boys and 1,266 girls aged 11 to 15 years.

The information sought from parents about their children's behaviour was of two main types. (1) A series of twenty-two triple choice questions on behaviour traits as measured by the parent's estimate of *intensity* of behaviour (extreme, moderate, absent), e.g. afraid of the dark when in bed at night—a little uneasy without a light—not at all afraid of the dark. Of these items, fourteen were adapted from the fifty-three triple-choice items used by Cattell and Coan (1957) in their study of personality variables. (2) Fifteen items in which the parent had to record an impression of the *frequency* of certain kinds of behaviour (for instance, crying, nail-biting, headaches) on an eight-point scale ranging from 'Never or less than once a year' to 'Every day or nearly every day'. (See article 13—ed.)

The items of behaviour included are described in detail elsewhere (Mitchell, 1965). They covered most of the behaviour problems described in the standard works on child psychiatry as occurring in clinic-attending, and therefore, presumably maladjusted, children of school age. The items *excluded* were: (i) the more bizarre forms of abnormal behaviour, e.g. autism, hallucinations, obsessional behaviour; (ii) sexual problems; and (iii) certain kinds of blatantly delinquent behaviour like arson. Such types of behaviour appeared to be rare even in child guidance samples and it was felt that the inclusion of questions about 'wicked' or 'mad' behaviour might worry or antagonize parents and so diminish the response rate. All the items included in the form had previously been piloted for intelligibility and lack of ambiguity by interview with mothers throughout the county.

The teachers' form covered attendance, attainment and physical disabilities as well as the presence of behaviour 'problems' in school.

In attempting to relate the children's behaviour at home to other aspects of their life, we felt it desirable to obtain some overall index of disturbance. Originally, it was intended to use for this purpose the child's total problem score, obtained by adding together the total number of extreme items underlined by the mother. This crude score would have given each 'problem' the same weight without regard to the frequency with which it occurred. Information gained in the survey about the distribution of each behaviour trait showed clearly, however, that some types of 'problem' behaviour were very much more common than others. For instance, about 20 per cent of girls were described by their mothers as having food fads. Where behaviour was reported as occurring at such a high frequency, it was felt that it was scarcely justifiable to consider it as contributing to an index of abnormality. Furthermore, it was felt necessary to make some adjustment for the changing incidence of various types of behaviour at different ages: for instance, 25 per cent of 6-year-old boys were found to cry at least two or three times a week compared with 1 per cent of those aged 14 years. Clearly, therefore, such crying should be given different weight in the two age groups.

In order to allow for these factors, it was decided to adopt a concept of 'deviant behaviour' framed in terms of a 10 per cent limit. If any type of behaviour was reported to have occurred at an intensity or frequency found in 10 per cent or less of any age (yearly) or sex group, then it was considered as deviant for that age and for that sex. If it occurred in more than 10 per cent of children of that age and sex then it was discounted. Thus, in the example already given, crying two or three times a week would be considered as deviant behaviour in a 14-year-old boy, but not in a 6-year-old. An overall index of 'deviance' was then constructed by summing the number of deviant items scored for each child. This score, then, indicated the number of types of behaviour shown by any child which were atypical of his age and sex group.

An analysis of the teachers' questionnaires revealed that only one type of behaviour, 'Very quiet or withdrawn' among girls, was recorded as occurring in more than 10 per cent of any age-sex group. The concept of deviance was not, therefore, applied to these items and the overall index of disturbance in school has merely been taken as the number of behavioural items underlined by the teacher in the questionnaire (see Appendix for list of items included).

Results

TABLE 7.1

THE RELATIONSHIP BETWEEN THE NUMBER OF DEVIANT BEHAVIOUR ITEMS UNDERLINED BY PARENTS AND THE NUMBER OF BEHAVIOUR PROBLEMS UNDERLINED BY TEACHERS

Number of Problems Underlined by Teachers	Number of Deviant Items Underlined by Parents							
	Boys				Girls			
	None	1–3	4–6	7+	None	1–3	4–6	7+
None (No.)	740	846	108	35	817	847	135	47
(%)	62%	55%	41%	43%	65%	61%	53%	45%
1 (No.)	259	387	62	20	283	308	68	29
(%)	22%	25%	24%	24%	22%	22%	27%	28%
2 (No.)	115	158	43	10	107	127	24	13
(%)	9%	10%	16%	12%	8%	9%	9%	12%
3 or (No.)	85	142	49	17	55	98	27	16
more (%)	7%	9%	19%	21%	4%	7%	11%	15%
Total (No.)	1,199	1,533	262	82	1,262	1,380	254	105

Significance of Association	Chi-squared = 73; 9 degrees of freedom; $p < 0.001$	Chi-squared = 46; 9 degrees of freedom; $p < 0.001$

Table 7.1 shows that there was a significant degree of association between the presence of deviant behaviour items at home and the reporting of problems of behaviour in school. Thus, children whose parents reported that they were free of deviant behaviour were also the most problem-free group at school. Similarly, at the other end of the scale, children whose parents reported many deviant items were three times as likely to have multiple (three or more) problems recorded at school as were those who were deviance-free at home. This relationship, however, was by no means comprehensive. Thus, table 7.1 demonstrates that more than a third of the children who were reported free of deviant behaviour at home nevertheless exhibited at least one problem in school, and that nearly half of the children whose parents underlined seven or more deviant traits were apparently problem-free at school.

As for specific types of behaviour at school, there was no overall pattern which distinguished children with many deviant items underlined by their parents from those with few. The school problems of those children who were markedly deviant at home varied with age and sex.

Among the boys at all ages, those with four or more items of deviant behaviour marked by their parents were significantly more likely than the remainder to have been assessed by their teachers as very easily frightened (11 per cent of deviants: 5 per cent of others aged 5 to 10 years; 5 per cent of deviants: 2 per cent of others aged 11 to 15 years), to have been found disinterested in school work (12 per cent: 6 per cent at 5 to 10 years; 17 per cent: 5 per cent at 11 to 15 years) and to have been recorded as having stolen on one or more occasion (4 per cent: 1 per cent for all ages). Among boys in the 5 to 10 years age group, but not among the older boys, those with four or more deviant items marked by their parents were significantly more likely to have been reported as sucking their thumbs (7 per cent: 3 per cent), wetting or soiling themselves at school during the current school year (5 per cent: 1 per cent) and as being quiet and withdrawn (17 per cent: 10 per cent). Among the boys of 11 or older, on the other hand, the deviant group were more likely than their fellows, to have been marked as uncooperative in class (9 per cent: 2 per cent), often telling lies (12 per cent: 1 per cent), very irritable (8 per cent: 3 per cent), aggressive towards other children (8 per cent: 3 per cent) and worrying more than other children (8 per cent: 3 per cent).

Among the girls the only teachers' item which differentiated the

TABLE 7.2

THE RELATIONSHIP BETWEEN THE NUMBER OF DEVIANT BEHAVIOUR ITEMS UNDERLINED
BY PARENTS AND THE CHILD'S GENERAL ATTAINMENT LEVEL AT SCHOOL

General attainment level relative to others of the same age at the same type of school		Number of Deviant Items Underlined by Parents							
		Boys				Girls			
		None	1–3	4–6	7+	None	1–3	4–6	7+
Above Average	(No.)	264	279	25	3	335	279	36	7
	(%)	23%	19%.	10%	4%	30%	21%	15%	7%
Average	(No.)	565	684	110	38	649	715	127	58
	(%)	49%	46%	43%	49%	58%	53%	52%	58%
Below Average	(No.)	331	522	122	37	132	342	80	35
	(%)	28%	35%	47%	47%	12%	26%	33%	35%
Significance of Association		Chi-squared = 40; 6 degrees of freedom; $p < 0.001$				Chi-squared = 85; 6 degrees of freedom; $p < 0.001$			

deviant group at all ages was 'Often tells lies' (4 per cent: 1 per cent in each age group). Among the older girls, those with four or more deviant items marked by their parents were also more likely to have been described as 'Not interested in school work' (12 per cent: 4 per cent) but this was the only item which distinguished them from the rest of the girls in their age group. Among the younger girls, on the other hand, the deviant children were more likely to be reported as very restless (11 per cent: 4 per cent), very irritable (6 per cent: 3 per cent) and easily frightened (9 per cent: 5 per cent) in school.

Academic success in school was found to be negatively associated with deviant behaviour in the home. Table 7.2 shows that the chance of achieving an above-average rating in general attainment at school was more than five times as great for boys, and four times as great for girls, who were free of deviant behaviour at home as it was for those who showed seven or more deviant items of behaviour, and about twice as great as for children with four or more items noted by their parents.

A similar pattern emerged with respect to the children's position in their immediate teaching group (see table 7.3) where the proportion of children with four or more items of deviant behaviour marked by their parents was about twice as great among those in the bottom quarter of the class as among those near the top.

TABLE 7.3

THE RELATIONSHIP BETWEEN THE NUMBER OF DEVIANT BEHAVIOUR ITEMS UNDERLINED
BY PARENTS AND THE CHILD'S USUAL POSITION IN THE IMMEDIATE TEACHING GROUP

Number of deviant Behaviour Items Marked by Parent		Position in the Teaching Group					
		Boys			Girls		
		In top 25%	In middle 50%	In bottom 25%	In top 25%	In middle 50%	In bottom 25%
None	(No.)	352	555	250	441	566	220
	(%)	43%	40%	32%	48%	41%	37%
1–3	(No.)	405	688	400	402	657	276
	(%)	50%	49%	51%	43%	47%	47%
4–6	(No.)	41	123	95	68	116	65
	(%)	5%	9%	12%	7%	8%	11%
7 or more	(No.)	13	33	35	17	56	30
	(%)	2%	2%	4%	2%	4%	5%
Significance of Association ...		Chi-squared = 40; 6 degrees of freedom; $p < 0.001$			Chi-squared = 42; 6 degrees of freedom; $p < 0.001$		

Discussion

The relationship between poor school attainment and the presence of behaviour disorders in the school setting has been discussed in several previous studies, including Burt (1937), Stott (1958) and Chazan (1958). The present study indicates that such a relationship also exists between behaviour at home and school conduct and attainment. From the information available, however, it is not possible to postulate any causal relationship. Burt and Howard (1952) found that maladjustment, defined in terms of referral for psychological investigation, was correlated with the child's exposure to too high a standard of work or to contact with an uncongenial teacher among other factors. On the other hand, Pearson (1952) suggested that emotional strains rooted in the home were often the cause of poor performance and lack of concentration at school. It is also possible that some underlying factor in the child, such as slow maturation, slight brain damage or neurological defect, may affect performance both at home and at school without there being any corresponding deficiency in either environment. Unravelling such complex interactions would require more detailed personal investigation than was possible in a large-scale statistical enquiry of the present kind. The types of behaviour which characterized the deviant children in their school setting, however, support the notion of emotional rather than organic causation. Thus, in three out of the four age-sex groups, the children who were most deviant at home were distinguished from the others by a greater tendency to be uninterested in school work, to be easily frightened and to tell lies.

It should also be emphasized that though there is a significant relationship between deviant behaviour at home and the existence of problems of behaviour in school there is still considerable divergence between the two areas of conduct. Thus, the teachers' questionnaire identified 10 per cent of children as exhibiting three or more behaviour problems in the school setting; the same proportion had four or more deviant items recorded on the parents' questionnaire. It might be considered justifiable to pick either of these groups of children as consisting of those who were most likely to be maladjusted. Unfortunately, however, the individuals picked by the two methods are not the same: only about one child in five picked as in the worst 10 per cent by one questionnaire was also picked by the other. This fact is important in any attempt to screen the child population to obtain a general estimate of the incidence of maladjustment. At present it is impossible to say how far the difference lies in the child's actual behaviour and how far in variation in the powers of observation and frames of reference of the persons reporting the behaviour. Clearly, however, it seems very necessary that any comprehensive screening device must study the child in both of his principal environments, the home and the school.

Appendix

Behaviour Items Included in the Teachers' Questionnaire

Please underline, in the list below, any items which describe this child as he often is:

(a) Very restless, can't sit still for a moment.
(b) Cries more than most children.
(c) Has a stammer.
(d) Has other speech difficulty.
(e) Often tells lies.
(f) Has stolen things on one or more occasions.
(g) Is very easily frightened.
(h) Bites fingernails.
(i) Sucks thumb or finger.

(j)   Very irritable, easily becomes cross or annoyed.

(k)   Has had one or more temper tantrums at school during this year.

(l)   Is unco-operative in class.

(m) Very shy, finds it difficult to mix with other children.

(n)   Has wet or soiled self at school during last year.

(o)   Has noticeable twitch of face or body.

(p)   Worries more than other children.

(q)   Aggressive towards other children.

(r)   Very quiet or withdrawn.

(s)   Very moody—on top of world one minute, down the next.

(t)   Not interested in school work.

(u)   Has on one or more occasions during this school year shown fear of school—that is, tears on arrival or refusal to come into the building.

8. Questionnaire Measures of Maladjustment

The Underwood Committee (1955) and the Scottish Education Department's *Committee on the Ascertainment of Maladjusted Children* (1964) found it impossible to estimate either the prevalence of maladjustment in school children or the unmet needs for services. But without guide-lines as to numbers, any rational planning of services is impossible (Tizard, 1966). It is good, therefore, that psychologists and psychiatrists are again taking up the study of epidemiological problems of mental ill-health in children—problems first explored in this country by Sir Cyril Burt (1933).

Among the questions raised in the discussion of the papers presented to the Cambridge Symposium (a symposium on maladjustment held at the 1967 conference of the Education Section of the British Psychological Society—ed.), three have been singled out for comment:

(1) How should we classify the psychiatric disorders of childhood? Stott's classification appeared to most of the participants in the Symposium to have no advantages over the more widely used child guidance classification (Ministry of Education, 1955) or the empirically-based classification outlined by Rutter (1965). The introduction of terms such as 'unsettled', 'inconsequential', 'restless' etc., implies that certain reported symptoms constitute a syndrome which is in some way different from or more precisely defined than the types of behaviour described under such terms as 'sthenic neurosis' (Burt, 1933), 'conduct disturbance' (Beller, 1962; Cameron, 1955), 'acting out behaviour' (U.S. literature, *passim*), or 'behaviour disorder' (usual child guidance classification). This has not been established and the mere proliferation of terms has nothing to recommend it.

(2) Do the *Bristol Social Adjustment Guides* offer advantages over other inventories? The Guides are widely used, and are said to be liked

Tizard, J. (1968) 'Questionnaire measures of maladjustment.' *British Journal of Educational Psychology, 38*, 1, 9–13.

by teachers. On the other hand, they are expensive to buy and tedious to score in large numbers. Vernon (1964) has given a balanced appraisal of their usefulness and limitations: 'To the psychometrist, Stott's instruments are likely to seem distressingly amateurish; but their virtue lies in their simplicity—that they use terms to describe deviant patterns which lay observers can readily apply, and that the psychologist or psychiatrist is presented with an overview, only roughly categorised, so that he can further explore particular symptoms. No doubt the categories overlap a good deal, and might be purified by more thorough statistical analysis. Doubtless also, despite Stott's claim for high inter-rater agreement, there is still a good deal of subjectivity and halo in a typical record as filled in by, say, a teacher.'*

As there is virtually no information about the comparative advantages of any one of the currently used questionnaires and inventories over any other, psychologists looking for a screening measure might do well to consider whether their needs might not be equally well served by inventories which have not been copyrighted. Among these are Bowlby's (1956), Mulligan's (1964) and Rutter's (1966).

(3) How valid are inventories anyway as screening devices? This is the central question. It has been little studied. However, both Mulligan and Douglas (1963) and Rutter and his colleagues (Rutter and Graham, 1966; Yule and Rutter, 1968; Graham and Rutter, personal communication) have provided data bearing on this question, and for the record, their findings are summarized below.

Mulligan and his colleagues had teachers complete questionnaires in respect of 13-year-old children who were attending child guidance clinics, and who had been diagnosed by psychiatrists as suffering from an aggressive and troublesome disorder, or a nervous or neurotic disorder. They compared the findings obtained on these children with those obtained when the same teachers were asked to report on matched controls. The findings are summarized in table 8.1.

About a quarter (24 per cent) of the maladjusted children were wrongly classified as normal on the basis of the inventory data, while 29 per cent of normal children were wrongly classified as maladjusted. As maladjusted children constitute only 5–10 per cent of the general population, the screening power of this inventory still leaves a good

---

* The *Bristol Social Adjustment Guides* have been extensively revised since Vernon made this appraisal (see D. H. Stott, *The Social Adjustment of Children*, 5th edition, 1974. London: Hodder and Stoughton)—ed.

TABLE 8.1

MALADJUSTMENT CLASSIFICATION—BASED ON TEACHER RATINGS—OF MALE CHILD
GUIDANCE CHILDREN AND THEIR CONTROLS. RESULTS IN PERCENTAGES

Classification based on teacher ratings	Child Guidance Children			Controls
	Nervous N = 50 %	Aggressive N = 40 %	Total N = 96 %	N = 96 %
Nervous	56	6	32	18
Aggressive	4	63	32	9
Mixed	14	9	12	2
Normal	26	22	24	71

deal to be desired. Let us, for example, assume (a) that 6·6 per cent of children are maladjusted; (b) that 75 per cent of these will be correctly identified on the basis of information obtained from Mulligan's inventory; (c) that 30 per cent of normal children are misclassified as maladjusted on the basis of inventory scores. The results which would be obtained, if 1,000 children were screened with the help of this inventory, are as in table 8.2.

TABLE 8.2

Inventory Diagnosis		Final Diagnosis	
		Normal	Maladjusted
Normal	670	654	16
Maladjusted	330	280	50
Total	1,000	934	66

In correctly identifying fifty maladjusted children (and missing sixteen) one would also classify as maladjusted 280 normal children.

The Isle of Wight findings, if only because they are epidemiologically based and because they do not rely on clinic cases for the validation data, give information which bears more directly on our question. Of 2,193 children screened by both parent questionnaire and teacher questionnaire, both of which had been previously piloted extensively (Rutter, 1967), 157 were selected as 'maladjusted' on the basis of the teacher questionnaire, and 133 were selected as 'maladjusted' on the basis of the parent questionnaire. Only nineteen children were selected on the basis of both teacher and parent questionnaires. Virtually all of these selected children were seen individually by a child psychiatrist, and much additional information about them and their families was obtained through records and home interviews with parents (Rutter and Graham, 1966; Yule and Rutter, 1968). On the basis of all the available information, a *final diagnosis* was arrived at in respect of each child.

Of the 157 children selected on the basis of the teacher questionnaire, sixty-four were finally diagnosed as maladjusted. The corresponding figures for the other groups were: parent questionnaire, 133 selected, sixty-six finally diagnosed; both questionnaires, nineteen and fourteen.

Assuming the final diagnosis to be valid, these data give us both the numbers of maladjusted children who were correctly identified as such by each questionnaire ('true positives'), and the numbers of children finally diagnosed as normal who were *incorrectly* judged to be maladjusted on the questionnaires ('false positives').

An estimate was also made of the number of 'false negatives'—that is, the numbers of maladjusted children in the population who were not identified as such on either questionnaire. A group of 108 physically handicapped children in the same age group served as the validation group for this purpose. These children were selected for special study on physical grounds (through school medical records, hospital records, etc.), and were also studied by questionnaire and by psychiatric examination in virtually the same way as were the other selected children. There were twenty-four who were finally diagnosed as maladjusted, and for twenty of these twenty-four there was questionnaire information available on both teacher and parent inventories. In sixteen cases (80 per cent) the inventory scores were above the maladjustment cut-off point on one or other of the questionnaires. Thus, the proportion of false negatives was 20 per cent, or to put it another way, for every sixteen children correctly identified by inventory, four children were missed.

In table 8.3 the data are expressed as rates per thousand, as was done in table 8.2. The prevalence of maladjustment is once again presumed to be 6·6 per cent.

Assuming the 'final diagnosis' to be valid, the table shows (a) that both the teacher inventory and the parent inventory select about equal numbers of maladjusted children (true positives). The teacher inventory selects forty-two false positives for every twenty-nine true positives, and the parent inventory selects thirty-one false positives for every thirty true positives; (b) that each questionnaire taken by itself selects under half the total number of maladjusted children in the community: (c) since, however, each questionnaire picks out different children

TABLE 8.3

Inventory Diagnosis		Final Diagnosis	
		Normal	Maladjusted
Normal	876	863	13
Maladjusted:			
(i) on Teacher Inventory	71	42	29
(ii) on Parent Inventory	61	31	30
(iii) on *both* Inventories	8	2	6
(iv) on *either* Inventory	124	71	53
Total (Normal + those selected on either inventory)	1,000	934	66

(the overlap is surprisingly small), when used in combination they pick out four-fifths of the true positives (fifty-three out of an estimated sixty-six) together with one-and-a-third times as many false positives (seventy-one in the present instance compared with fifty-three true positives).

Conclusion

It has yet to be established that any other screening devices will be more efficient than these, and the data from the Isle of Wight study and from Mulligan's both indicate that teacher questionnaires alone cannot be regarded as valid indices of maladjustment. However, teacher questionnaires and parent questionnaires, used in combination to select children for special examination, can cut down very markedly the numbers requiring to be seen. If such questionnaires have been carefully piloted, *and if correct cut-off points are used* (Meehl, 1955) rather few 'cases' need be missed, though large numbers of false positives will be obtained. The evidence thus indicates that inventories can be used very effectively as screening devices but that they are not in themselves sufficient for epidemiological or clinical work.

Causes of Maladjustment

Introduction

This section is concerned with causation of behaviour difficulties in school children. The first article reports a classical study of maladjustment among children in the London area. It is interesting for Burt and Howard's attempt first to establish the concept of maladjustment before using it. They then employ careful statistical techniques to study objectively the ways in which maladjustment can be classified. Having used factor analysis to provide a workable classification of maladjustment, they proceed to compare the characteristics of maladjusted and non-maladjusted children. Throughout the article it is clear that the authors find the school situation to be an important determinant of the difficulties which the children of their study show. However, it is important to remember that the population with which they were working consisted of children who had been referred to a service based on an education department. Consequently school-based problems might be expected to figure prominently in the children's difficulties. It is also interesting to note that Cyril Burt's great concern lest we forget the impact of heredity on developmental characteristics of children appears in this paper (page 137) as in so many of his other writings.

The second two articles in this section deal with one aspect of the causation of maladjustment, that is, separation. In the first of the two articles, Pringle and Bossio are concerned to examine the extent to which maladjustment in the educational context appears in children who have experienced prolonged separations. They make the point that separation by itself does not necessarily lead to maladjustment, but that it is the rejection implied in some separations which is the most important determinant of the behaviour difficulties observed.

In the final article in this section, Goldenberg and Goldenberg consider one specific problem which is often associated with distress at separation from mother: 'school phobia'. They present two alternative models for explaining school phobia. One could be described as an analytical model, whereas the other can be described as the behaviour therapy model. It is with the alternative approaches to treatment based on these two models that the final section of this book is concerned.

BURT, C. and HOWARD, M.

9. The Nature and Causes of Maladjustment among Children of School Age

Maladjustment as a Psychological Category

The classification of handicapped children

Both psychologists and educationists frequently refer to what they call 'the maladjusted child' as though such children formed a separate type or class. Nearly all textbooks on educational psychology make at least a passing mention of this group. But few indicate how it is related to other groups.

Perhaps the clearest classification is that given by Sandiford (1938) in what for long was one of the best-known textbooks on educational psychology. In his discussion of individual differences he distinguishes five main groups: (i) 'a homogeneous central group' consisting of average pupils; (ii) towards the upper end of the scale, the 'intellectually gifted'; (iii) towards the other end (*a*) those who are defective in special intellectual capacities, of whom the most easily recognized are the partially blind, the partially deaf, and those exhibiting defects of speech; (*b*) the intellectually defective or 'feebleminded'; and (*c*) the 'maladjusted'. Among these last three groups the first, as he points out, is plainly composite. As to the second, it had often been alleged that the 'mentally defective form as mixed a group as the physically defective'; but 'correlation studies' have established the existence of an 'innate factor of general intelligence', in terms of which the intellectually defective could be described. The 'maladjusted group', however, are, as he admits, 'much less well defined'; and neither Professor Sandiford, nor, so far as we are aware, any other writer, has succeeded in producing first-hand evidence to support the notion that they form a distinct or relatively homogeneous psychological type.

Burt, C. and Howard, M. (1952) 'The nature and causes of maladjustment among children of school age.' *British Journal of Psychology (Statistical Section)*, V, 39–60.

Reports of education authorities and child guidance clinics often tabulate cases of 'maladjustment' as distinct from those of 'mental deficiency', 'educational backwardness', 'psychoneurosis', and the like. But their implicit interpretations of the word vary widely. As their figures and cases show, with some writers the 'maladjusted' consist mainly of 'delinquents' and 'neurotics', while with others both these sub-groups are placed in separate categories of their own. Most psychiatric writers who use the term appear to give it a different meaning from that previously adopted by psychologists; generally they treat it as *including* the 'educationally subnormal'.

The problem has recently acquired considerable practical importance. The Education Act of 1944 enumerates eleven categories of 'handicapped children'. If we leave on one side the various groups of physically defective pupils, and substitute the phrase 'educationally subnormal' for 'intellectually defective', the classification corresponds closely with that given by Sandiford and other educationists. For the first time in any statutory enactment 'the maladjusted' are specified as a separate class. The Act itself does not explain how the term is used. But, according to the Ministry's regulations (1945), such cases are to be distinguished from other forms of 'psychological disturbance' by the fact that they 'require special educational treatment in order to effect their personal, social, or educational readjustment'. But this merely tells us that the 'maladjusted' child is one who requires to be 'readjusted', which is not very informative.

The problems to which this enactment gives rise have, not unnaturally, led to numerous discussions. From these it seems clear that there are as yet no agreed conclusions about the probable number of such cases, or the causes responsible for such a condition, or even the precise definition of the term. It is partly on this account that we have been asked to summarize in more accessible form some of the relevant data collected during earlier surveys and hitherto available only in unpublished memoranda, and to amplify in fuller detail some of the conclusions then drawn.

History and Definition of the Term

History of the concept
Since the term has been used in so many different senses, no statistical investigation of the subject can have much value unless the investigators

first explain how the word is being used. We must therefore begin by formulating a definition of the term, sufficiently precise for practical purposes, and by setting forth, as succinctly as we can, the justification for the interpretation proposed.

Although new in ministerial publications, the notion of maladjustment is by no means new in psychology. The idea of adaptation or adjustment has formed a leading concept with nearly all the representatives of the British evolutionary school. 'Mental life,' so Spencer repeatedly declares, 'consists in a continual *adjustment* of inner processes to outer processes'. And Sully (1890) adopts much the same language: 'Mental development may be viewed as a progressive adjustment of the individual organism to its environment. . . . It is only as such adjustment is effected that the conditions of stable life are realized.' He goes on to apply the notion more particularly to define the distinction between the *normal* and the *abnormal*. 'There is no wide gap,' he says, 'between the two, such as the popular contrast suggests. The sound shade off into the unsound by a continuous succession of fine gradations. The normal is adjustment of the organism to its environment; the abnormal, simply maladjustment.' Moreover, he insists that 'the psychologist's reference to external conditions must above all include that social environment in interaction with which the individual thinks and acts. We cannot understand an individual mind in abstract separation: each thinks, feels, and acts as he does under the constant influence of social relations.'

In his *Teachers' Handbook of Psychology* (1886) Sully makes this doctrine the basis of his account of the mental development of the individual child. In its essential nature, we are told, it consists of 'successive adaptive modifications, issuing in a growing adjustment of the individual to the circumstances of his environment, and in a wider range of adaptations'. In a modern civilized society, he explains, we may discern three successive stages of increasing range: the adjustment of the child (i) to life in his family, (ii) to life at school, and (iii) to life in the community at large; while all the time there is an increasing need for (iv) self-adjustment.

Sully's view of mental abnormality was adopted by Mercier, and was even made the basis for his definition of insanity, a term which he used in a broad etymological sense to cover any form of mental ill-health. Such a conception, however, was too far removed from the current medical view of mental illnesses, which considered them to be classifiable into distinctive types according to the causes and the symptoms found *within the patient*; and Mercier was in consequence vigorously criticized by his colleagues for 'substituting vague speculation for clinical observation'. Quite recently, however, a number of psychiatric writers in this country have tentatively revived the term. Thus the various medical authorities who have contributed to the *Survey of Child Psychiatry* (1939) have used it sometimes to describe the causes of delinquent and psychoneurotic behaviour, occasionally to describe the effects of physiological and biochemical disturbances, and (most frequently of all) as a generic term to cover psychoneurosis, delinquency, and even educational backwardness.

Owing to the fact that they seemed to necessitate a teleological interpretation, the concepts of adjustment and maladjustment at first found little favour with American psychologists. But, since the decline of the more extreme behaviourist doctrines, several writers have sought to reintroduce a biological standpoint, and have thus made increasing use of these terms. Allport (1938), for example, in setting forth what he terms 'the biological theory of personality' makes 'adjustment' a key word. And a similar change in standpoint has appeared in American psychiatry.

Not only British writers, but also American, have frequently complained that, until quite recently, psychiatry in that country so insistently ignored the influence of social and psychological factors in the causation of mental disorders; and, 'largely because child guidance in America was, during its earlier stages, developed by psychiatrists rather than by psychologists or educationists, the importance of the sociological aspects remained' (so we are told) 'for long unrealized.' Reymert, for instance, points out that, at the time of Healy's early studies, 'the clinic staff did not include a social worker': 'the work [on mental subnormality] had expanded gradually from a consideration of the mentally retarded to that of the educationally retarded'; and only in the later development of the clinical study of children was it recognized that 'the feeble-minded and the maladjusted are separate problems', and that 'educational maladjustment is often only a part of a picture of general maladjustment.' In child psychiatry, as in other branches, this change of view-point is due in great measure to the teaching of Adolf Meyer and the 'school of psychobiology, which insisted that the psychiatrist is concerned "with the total individual in relation to the total situation" ' (Harms, 1947).

External and internal maladjustment

Unfortunately, both in America and in this country, those psychologists who use words like 'adaptation', 'adjustment', and 'maladjustment' seldom offer any explicit definitions of the meanings they attach to them; and psychiatric writers usually appear to employ them in a popular rather than a technical sense. Often, indeed, they evidently assume that the terms refer to what may be called 'internal' as distinguished from 'external maladjustment'.

Thus teachers are not infrequently told that 'the maladjusted child is the child whose personality is ill-organized or badly integrated: he is a machine whose parts do not fit; and, as with other machines in that condition, he must be sent to a repair-shop in order that the appropriate expert may effect the necessary readjustments.' From the very nature of their subjects, it is said, 'psychologists and physiologists are primarily occupied with the study of distinct functions in isolation, whereas psychiatrists are concerned with the study of the internal organization or "integration" of the personality as a whole.' Such criticisms are quite justifiable if (as seems to be the case) the critics are referring chiefly to the attitude of Titchener and his American followers, who persistently deprecated all attempts to apply psychology to social or practical problems. But they are scarcely true of British psychology. Ward, Sully, Stout, McDougall, and their followers have never tired of emphasizing 'the unity of the personality'. And they go further still. Again and again they remind us that the personality itself is an abstraction, and can never be adequately studied apart from the psychological environment. Indeed, it was to emphasize this latter point that terms like 'adaptation' and 'adjustment' were employed.

The concept of maladjustment in child psychology

Here we shall be concerned almost exclusively with 'maladjustment' as a term of child psychology. In this country the foundations of child study and child guidance were laid by Sully; and consequently his conception of adjustment and maladjustment has figured prominently in British writings on the subject from the very start.

As Sully himself repeatedly affirmed, the term was meant to stress the fact that the maladjusted child is not to be considered as a patient seen in isolation at the clinic consulting room: he is to be regarded as an individual personality interacting with the immediate bio-sociological environment. To borrow the language of 'dynamic psychology' which

McDougall made popular, the 'mental forces in the field' must be taken into consideration quite as much as the 'mental forces within the individual'. It follows that, in any statistical investigation on the problem of the so-called maladjusted child, it will be essential to secure data, not only in regard to the child's personal characteristics— his general and special abilities, his health and physique, and his temperamental, emotional, and moral characteristics, but also in regard to his past and present environment, at home, at school, at work (if he is already employed), and during his hours of play or recreation.

Definition

As we have seen, the appearance of this new category in official regulations has led to an increased number of speculative statements regarding the nature and causes of the conditions falling within its scope. Very little, however, seems so far available in the shape of empirically verified facts. Probably an acceptable definition of what the term implies can only be reached at the end of a systematic enquiry into the whole problem. But some preliminary formulation is necessary at the outset. For educational purposes, therefore, we provisionally suggest that a maladjusted child may be defined as one *whose adjustments to the recurrent situations of his everyday life are less adequate than might reasonably be expected from a child of his mental age, and whose condition or circumstances therefore require special study and treatment.*

The use of the term 'recurrent' is intended to imply that the maladjustment is not a temporary consequence of some passing crisis, but prolonged and relatively permanent. The recurrent situations will involve, on the other hand, (1a) the physical and perceptible needs of the child's material environment and (1b) the social and moral needs of his human environment, and, on the other, (2a) the conscious or non-conscious needs of the child himself and (2b) his capacity for fulfilling those needs. His adjustment may be described as 'inadequate' when these needs, as a whole, are not effectively fulfilled.

At its simplest the postulates required by such a definition are those suggested by early experiments on 'adaptive behaviour', like those of Lloyd Morgan and Hobhouse. We assume (i) that the individual possesses certain conative tendencies, inborn or acquired, which (under certain internal conditions) are aroused by some specific change in the external environment, and cease when some specific end-result is reached, i.e. when some need is satisfied; (ii) that the external situation not only arouses the conative impulse, but also impedes its immediate fulfilment by any automatic reaction, such as might result from pre-existing instinctive or habitual patterns of behaviour; (iii) that the immediate result of the external stimulation and obstruction is a state of disequilibrium or tension: (in metaphorical language we may say that the flow of energy is at once increased and temporarily blocked); (iv) that, in such a situation, the internal structure of the individual organism enables it to develop *alternative* patterns of activity (based on 'trial-and-error' or 'discriminative insight'); and (v) that, after a period of varied activity, and as a result of repetitive trial, discriminative insight, and eventual success (or some equivalent process), a *new* mode of reaction is eventually acquired, which in some degree provides a more or less adequate solution to the problem. It follows that, if the psychologist is seeking to aid a child in a condition of 'maladjustment', the assistance should take the form rather of 'training' the child to meet the situation (e.g. by assisting discrimination, encouraging alternative reactions, or simplifying the situation itself) than of medical 'treatment'. Adequacy is plainly a matter of degree; hence the need for the second clause in the definition above. Two main grades may conveniently be distinguished: (i) if the child merely requires individual assistance from the teacher, social worker, family doctor, or other adviser, we suggest that the condition may be described as one of *mild* maladjustment; (ii) if he requires the attention of a specially qualified expert (e.g. a psychologist at a child guidance centre), it may be described as *severe*. In a large mixed urban area, like London, surveys suggest that roughly 10 per cent of the school population fall into the first grade, and 2 per cent into the latter.[1]

The Need for Statistical Verification

Alternative methods of proof
Most of the descriptions given of the various conditions which are assumed to lead to maladjustment appear to be based on more or less plausible deductions from the writers' psychological preconceptions. It is our view that such assumptions are of little scientific value until they have been critically checked and verified by some sort of objective test. However, most writers on child psychiatry apparently hold that any attempt at statistical confirmation is not merely invalid but actually

impossible; in their opinion the only satisfactory mode of verification is the first-hand intuitive insight of the experienced practitioner actually handling such cases.

This point of view has been forcibly argued by a former Medical Director of the Child Guidance Council, and is frequently expressed by other writers on the subject (Maberley, 1946). They quote with approval the conclusion of one of the contributors to the *Survey of Child Psychiatry*. 'Any attempt to deal with the matter statistically is entirely unconvincing, so that in these matters the guesses of a clinician must be allowed more value than the statistician's argument.'

We fully agree that 'statistics alone can prove nothing', and that in the past statistical investigators have furnished some justification for such criticisms by confining themselves to 'tables of figures and brief supplementary comments'. Indeed, it is for that reason that we have prefaced our statistical analysis by a discussion of current views. But before we turn to the results of our own enquiries, our critics may feel that we should offer some brief defence of the procedure we propose. Perhaps the best way of meeting such objections is to examine the alternative method of proof, which is customarily followed. It relies rather on plausible generalization than on systematic verification.

In the opening chapter of the *Survey* just quoted, an attempt is made to demonstrate the importance of 'the physiological approach to psychiatric problems', which earlier 'child psychologists' were held to have neglected. To prove his case, the author cites the history of a girl of 10 referred for persistently stealing sweets or money for sweets. Being 'thin and lackadaisical', her blood-sugar was examined. Found to suffer from hypoglycæmia, she was put on a diet including regular supplies of glucose, and 'from that moment never stole anything again'. Now, when the blood-sugar level sinks, profound changes in cortical function may ensue, amounting to coma and death'. Accordingly (we are told) '*it is clear* that the low blood-sugar created a tension in the mesencephalic and diencephalic centres, *which was transmitted to the effector areas* in the frontal lobes.' Hence the thefts. At this point, however, a statistical argument (a little disguised) persisted in breaking in. Numerous patients have been found suffering from hypoglycæmia: do all of them (the reader naturally enquires) relieve this 'mesencephalic tension' by stealing, or, if not, how many do? The writer recognizes this gap in the proof; and adds 'we must postulate *some specially directed* spread of excitation here, for every case of hypoglycæmia does not steal sweets. Nevertheless, the *chief* stimulus was apparently the hypoglycæmia' (our italics).

But, of course, there are a good many alternative hypotheses, far more simple and far less speculative, which would equally well explain the 'cure', and which could perhaps have been partly confirmed, had some information been included about the general background of the case. Moreover, since the writer's object was to demonstrate the importance of 'biochemical needs' (as distinct from 'biological needs') in precipitating disorders of conduct, it would surely be helpful to learn in how many other cases, where habitual pilfering has been prompted by a childish desire for sweets, a similar hypoglycæmic condition has been discovered.

We do not for one moment wish to deny the possibility that bio-chemical conditions may profoundly influence the child's mental state. We merely contend that, before a single case of this kind can be regarded as typical and the proposed explanation accepted as proved, a statistical investigation is essential: we have first to show that the causes found are accompanied by the effects alleged with a frequency which cannot be explained by coincidence, and secondly to determine how important or how common such a factor may be.

Sources of data

In London it was part of the duties of the Council's psychologist to examine pupils whose mental development appeared to be hampered in any way, whether by personal or by environmental difficulties. To determine the number and types of children needing special investigation or treatment, surveys were carried out from time to time in different areas; and instructions were issued to teachers, care committee workers, and school medical officers, explaining what kinds of pupils should be referred. In addition to other types of case, it was suggested that they might submit for special examination 'children whose school progress, behaviour, or emotional condition appeared to indicate that they might be handicapped by some form of maladjustment'. The term was briefly explained along the lines indicated above; and special emphasis was laid on the fact that the maladjustment might be due, not only to conditions in the child himself, but also to those in his home, school, or everyday life.

There were practical reasons for the inclusion of some such category.

The earlier surveys had dealt chiefly with those who were actually backward, delinquent, defective, or otherwise subnormal. But terms like 'defective' or 'subnormal' had come to imply some pathological characteristic in the child—some intrinsic weakness or infirmity of the mind, rather than the effects of the constant interaction between the child on the one hand and his present or past circumstances on the other. In the absence of any such mental defect or illness, teachers were apt to assume that every pupil ought to adjust himself to the work of his class; and many failed to realize that often the only effective procedure was to adjust the choice of class or teaching methods to the needs of the child. Further, it became clear that the work of the psychologist should be preventive as well as curative. It therefore seemed urgently desirable to investigate, at the earliest possible stage, cases of *potential* backwardness, delinquency, or neurosis. However, to ask teachers and others to notify not only actual but also potential delinquents and neurotics would have been useless. The teacher regarded the discovery of neurotic conditions a matter for the doctor; the doctor considered his task to be the diagnosis of actual cases; and to pick out certain children as 'potential delinquents' seemed to be condemning them before they had committed any offence. Above all, it was desired to avoid the common misunderstanding that a child referred to the Council's psychologist (or 'mental expert', as he was sometimes described) must necessarily be either 'mentally defective' (in the technical sense of defective) or 'mentally ill' (in the strict sense of illness). 'Maladjustment'—the term so often used by Sully and other British educationists, and already part of every teacher's vocabulary—appeared to cover most of these points.

In addition to investigating cases referred by teachers and others, a careful watch was kept for similar cases during periodical surveys of the school population; and the data that we propose to analyse here are drawn mainly from these two sources. Since it appeared conceivable that the term 'maladjustment' might be interpreted differently by other investigators, we have also endeavoured to secure similar information about children who have been more recently referred to child guidance centres, and have then come under our own notice or that of other co-workers later on, usually in the course of researches upon some other topic. No significant differences seem discernible between the data reported for these various groups of cases. On the whole, therefore, we are inclined to conclude that, nowithstanding differences in

E

theoretical standpoint, in actual practice the term is now used, at any rate in London, in much the same way.

It should be added that children referred solely or primarily on the ground of actual educational backwardness or actual delinquency will not be included in the present series. A number of the cases still retained may no doubt have been sent forward partly because of undisciplined behaviour either at home or at school; others proved on investigation to have committed offences already, generally of a minor type; and a small proportion turned out to be educationally subnormal as well as maladjusted. But in every case considered in the following analysis, the ostensible ground of reference was some form of maladjustment as interpreted above.

From what we have said, it will be obvious that the group with which we are concerned is somewhat vaguely defined. It will be our task to analyse its nature more precisely, to discover what causes are mainly responsible for its existence, and if necessary to suggest some more exact method of classification.

A Factorial Study of Maladjustment
The chief characteristics of the maladjusted child
The first problem that calls for investigation is the validity of classifying certain children in this way. To what extent do those reported as suffering from maladjustment constitute a homogeneous class, or form a distinct psychological category of their own? Is there any definite attribute or component, no matter how complex, which underlies all these cases, and is characteristic of no other group? To answer such questions the most obvious procedure is to undertake a factor analysis for the main conditions reported. Since, as we have seen, the term necessarily refers to the relations or interactions between two sets of conditions—environmental on the one hand and personal on the other—it is necessary to collect detailed information as regards (I) the material and psychological conditions in the child's home, school, and places of business or recreation, and (II) the child's own health, intellectual, emotional, and moral characteristics, especially in so far as they affect his reactions to his environmental conditions.

Data
Fairly complete information was available for 273 cases. These were mainly children between the ages of 9:0 and 13:0. No significant

differences were found between boys and girls; and the groups were too small to permit of subdivision according to age. The conditions ascertained were classified under 24 sub-headings, as shown in table 9.1. For most of the personal characteristics (intellectual abilities and attainments measured by tests and emotional characteristics by a rating scale on the basis of direct observations), and for several of the environmental characteristics, the data obtained consisted of graded assessments; but for the majority of the latter the information related merely to the presence or absence of some specified condition.

On referring to our record cards we found that about 60 per cent of the cases could be sorted out into classes and sub-classes based on this classificatory system of table 9.1. The remainder show a good deal of overlapping. But, of course, it is precisely when the lines of classification are blurred and obscure that a factorial analysis is needed to establish the most appropriate scheme.

The conclusions to be drawn from the analyses seem clear. The cases put forward as cases of maladjustment form a decidedly heterogeneous collection. Children who are maladjusted in one respect are not necessarily maladjusted in others; and, no matter what the primary cause may be, the fact of maladjustment, so far as it is revealed by the child's behaviour, may manifest itself by a number of alternative reactions, differing from case to case. The requisite treatment must take this into account. Those who are 'maladjusted' because the work

TABLE 9.1

24 CONDITIONS ASSOCIATED WITH MALADJUSTMENT

I A.	*School*	II A.	*Physical*
	Absence		Developmental
	Inappropriate School		Pathological
	Inappropriate Class		
	Uncongenial Teacher	II B.	*Intellectual*
			General Intelligence
I B.	*Home*		Special Disabilities
	Economic Condition		Inferior Attainments
	Overcrowding		
	Parent-Child Relation	II C.	*Emotional*
	Parental Relations		General Emotionality
	Defective Relations		Extraversion
	Defective Discipline		Introversion
			Adolescent Instability
I C.	*Out of School and Home*		Alleged Neurosis
	Conditions at Work		Alleged Delinquency
	Conditions during Leisure		Conflict, etc.

TABLE 9.2

FREQUENCY OF CAUSES

Condition	Maladjusted Group Per cent	Control Group Per cent	Correlation
I. ENVIRONMENTAL			
A. IN THE SCHOOL			
Repeated Absence from School	7·3	0·2	0·19
Changes of School	6·8	2·4	0·11
Inappropriate School	5·7	1·9	0·10
Inappropriate Class:			
Work too Hard	16·4	6·0	0·17
Work too Easy	5·7	1·5	0·12
Uncongenial Teacher	12·7	1·2	0·23
Uncongenial Pupils	8·1	0·0	0·21
B. IN THE HOME			
1. Poverty and its Concomitants			
Very Poor	13·3	8·2	0·08
Poor	32·7	22·3	0·12
Comfortable	46·5	52·3	−0·06
Well-to-do	9·3	18·2	−0·14
Overcrowding	26·7	15·7	0·13
Lack of Facilities for Recreation	19·5	6·3	0·20
2. Defective Family Relations			
Father Dead or Absent	12·8	4·4	0·15
Father Deserted, Separated, or			
Divorced	7·3	0·5	0·17
Mother dead	15·3	3·1	0·23
Mother Deserted, Separated, or			
Divorced	7·5	0·2	0·19
Mother out at Work	12·7	4·1	0·16
Prolonged Absence from Parents	8·3	2·2	0·13
Step- or Foster-father	9·3	4·1	0·11
Step- or Foster-mother	15·1	1·9	0·24
Illegitimate	8·6	0·2	0·21
Only Child	10·9	3·6	0·14
Defective Pre-school Conditions	24·2	16·7	0·09
3. Defective Discipline, etc.			
Over-strict	17·7	2·2	0·26
Weak or Vacillating	14·3	4·1	0·18
Lack of Affection	23·9	1·5	0·34
Disagreement about Control	4·2	0·0	0·14
Parental Disagreement	5·1	1·2	0·12
Disagreement with Sibs; Jealousy	7·9	3·9	0·08
Neurotic Parents	3·6	1·5	0·07
4. Vicious Home			
Sexual Immorality	3·6	0·2	0·13
Drunkenness	9·6	0·5	0·22
Quarrelling	3·1	0·0	0·12
C. OUT OF SCHOOL AND HOME			
Excessive Facilities for Amusement	8·8	7·3	0·04
Defective Facilities for Amusement	9·6	5·1	0·07
Undesirable Companions	5·3	1·2	0·11
Lack of Companionship	5·3	2·4	0·08
II. PHYSICAL			
A. DEVELOPMENTAL			
Under-developed	5·5	1·7	0·11
Over-developed	7·8	1·5	0·16
Noticeable Peculiarities	8·3	2·2	0·14

TABLE 9.2—continued

FREQUENCY OF CAUSES

Condition	Maladjusted Group Per cent	Control Group Per cent	Correlation
B. PATHOLOGICAL			
General Ill-health	13·8	10·9	0·04
Specific Ailments (current)	7·3	6·8	0·01
Specific Ailments (past: excessive number of)	8·1	3·6	0·09
Neurological Disorders	3·4	0·5	0·12
Biochemical Disorders	5·6	2·4	0·08
III. INTELLECTUAL			
A. Apparently INNATE			
1. General Intelligence			
(a) Mental Deficiency	2·4	1·2	0·04
(b) Dullness	9·3	3·4	0·13
(c) Superior	6·2	0·0	0·17
2. Special Disabilities	5·3	0·5	0·14
B. Predominantly ACQUIRED			
1. General Educational Backwardness	37·1	3·4	0·42
2. Special Educational Backwardness			
(a) Reading	9·1	2·4	0·13
(b) Spelling	2·1	0·0	0·09
(c) Arithmetic	7·8	4·1	0·07
IV. EMOTIONAL			
A. Apparently INNATE			
1. General Emotionality			
(a) Unstable	48·3	6·5	0·47
(b) Temperamentally Defective	2·1	0·0	0·09
2. Temperamental Tendency			
(a) Excessive Extraversion	23·6	2·2	0·33
(b) Excessive Introversion	21·3	3·4	0·27
3. Specific Emotions			
(a) Timidity	3·1	0·0	0·12
(b) Anger	2·1	1·0	0·04
(c) Sex	4·8	1·9	0·07
(d) Wandering	2·9	0·0	0·12
B. Predominantly ACQUIRED			
1. Developmental or Normal			
Adolescent Instability*	8·3	0·0	0·21
Personal Sentiments	2·6	1·0	0·08
Impersonal Sentiments	2·3	0·0	0·10
2. Psychoneuroses			
Hysteria (chiefly Conversion)	1·8	0·0	0·07
Obsessions and Compulsions	0·5	0·0	0·03
Anxiety States	10·3	2·2	0·16
Neurasthenic States	4·8	1·2	0·11
Psychopathic or Pre-psychotic	2·9	0·0	0·12
C. Habitual Emotional REACTIONS†			
Conflict (including Ambivalence)	7·1	0·0	0·18
Regression	4·6	1·5	0·09
Perseveration	2·3	0·0	0·12
Feelings of Inferiority	9·3	1·2	0·17
Feelings of Superiority	2·1	0·0	0·10
Feelings of Insecurity	10·1	2·7	0·15
Irritability	2·6	2·2	0·03
Jealousy	4·4	3·6	0·02
Miscellaneous Grievances	6·5	2·4	0·11
Incontinence	4·1	1·2	0·09
V. MORAL‡			
1. Moral Conflicts	3·4	0·0	0·12
2. Religious Conflicts	1·5	0·0	0·08

* Mostly pupils over 14.
† These conditions are entered here only when they appear to be contributory causes to the maladjustment, not merely its effects.
‡ Cases referred for known delinquency have been excluded from this series.

at school is too hard require entirely different measures from those
who are unhappy at home or those whose difficulties are emotional
rather than intellectual; those who respond actively by inferior or
undesirable adjustments require a different type of training or treatment
from those who react by withdrawal or passive regression.

The Causes of Maladjustment

Data

As in investigating the causes of juvenile delinquency or educational
backwardness, our main procedure has been to compare the conditions
observed in cases of maladjustment with those observed in a parallel
control group of well-adjusted pupils. To a large extent the control
groups used in the earlier investigations were employed for the present
study. The figures in the preceding tables are based on data obtained
from 394 maladjusted boys and girls, aged 6 to 14, and an equal
number of normal children, of corresponding age and sex, and drawn
for the most part from the same schools.

For these cases information has been systematically collected
according to the schedules described in the reports on juvenile
delinquents and backward pupils. Accordingly, there will be no need
to repeat the accounts there given of the methods used or to explain
in further detail the meanings attached to the various headings. These
will be found fully discussed in the publications on these subjects
(Burt, 1925, 1933).

Results

In table 9.2 we have brought together figures showing the frequency of
the more relevant conditions in both the maladjusted and the normal
groups. However, the reader may not find it easy to judge the relative
importance of each causal condition when the results are expressed in
the form of two proportions. Hence, to obtain a single index-figure,
we have calculated a point-distribution correlation based on the
assumption that the samples to be compared are equal in number. Any
coefficient numerically exceeding 0·10 may be taken as statistically
significant. The more conspicuous items under each of the various
headings call for a word or two of comment.

One point should be emphasized at the outset. Merely to establish
a significant correlation between maladjustment and some particular

condition does not of itself prove that this condition has operated as a cause of maladjustment. On the other hand, the fact that the correlation falls so near to zero as to be non-significant, even with large samples like the present, would yield strong presumptive evidence that the condition is not an important cause. As we have already seen, in discussions on maladjustment the favourite method of demonstrating causation is to deduce or at least to illustrate, from a few first-hand case-studies, some intelligible process by which the alleged cause is likely to have resulted in maladjustment. It will now, we think, be clear that such arguments can seldom be convincing, particularly when (as is so often asserted) the process postulated is assumed to be unconscious. What is needed is a combination of the case-study method with the statistical method, such as one of us has already attempted in the case of mental deficiency, educational disabilities, and juvenile delinquency (Burt 1925, 1933). But perhaps the most conclusive proof is that afforded by the eventual failure or success of specific methods of treatment, directed to remove or counteract this or that presumable cause. However, a completely cogent demonstration can rarely be secured except in a carefully planned investigation, where the conditions can be varied separately, or where their variations can be statistically distinguished.

I. Environmental conditions

A. In the School. In dealing with school conditions it is comparatively easy for a psychologist holding an official position in the school inspectorate to check his inferences by watching the effects of different methods of treatment. The evidence gathered in this way leaves little doubt that in many cases the main, if not the sole, cause of maladjustment arises out of current conditions at the child's school. This is confirmed by the figures in the table.

In many of the cases there noted the pupil's own mental characteristics proved to be perfectly normal. Thus a child of average ability working in a class or school attended by pupils whose general ability is much higher than his, or again a bright child attending a school in a poor neighbourhood where the intellectual level is decidedly low, may easily become maladjusted. Judged by the percentages, the condition most frequently reported was the assignment of the child to a class where the work is too hard; yet the size of the correlation coefficient suggests that its influence may not be so important as might be inferred. More often it is the personal relations between the child, his teacher, or his school fellows that provide the chief aggravating factors. Among these cases the commonest are those in which the child's class teacher is in some way uncongenial, unsympathetic, or lacking in understanding. The heading 'uncongenial pupils' refers mainly to cases of teasing, bullying, or snobbishness, usually on the ground of social or physical peculiarities. Absence from school, whether as a cause or as an effect of maladjustment, is the third most commonly reported condition. Change of school or department plays a significant part both with older and younger children: with older children the commonest type of case is that of the scholarship winner from a relatively un-cultured home, who was the star pupil in the primary school, but turns out to be a backward pupil in the secondary or grammar school to which he has been sent; with younger children maladjustment not infrequently follows promotion from the infants' school to the junior: such a change is very liable to produce maladjustment when the methods of teaching are abruptly altered, particularly in the case of those who are dull or suffer from special disabilities. It should be observed that a significant correlation also arises in the case of bright pupils who have been left in classes or schools where the work is too easy and so affords insufficient outlet for their abilities or ambitions.

The importance we are led to attach to school conditions in so many cases of maladjustment runs counter to the view that has recently been put forward in several quarters. 'The *primary* causes of maladjustment,' it is said, 'are to be found within the individual and in the structure of his relations with the rest of his family, especially as they operate during the first five years': when conditions in the school *appear* to produce maladjustment, what has really happened is that 'a hidden disturbance has become manifest in response to school stresses'. Now, in following up the after-histories of the earlier cases, we have found that, in quite a high proportion, remedies directed solely to an alteration of the school conditions have been followed by a complete and apparently permanent disappearance of every overt sign of maladjustment. On this point the records kept by one of us over a period of nearly 20 years furnish ample evidence: thus, in 124 instances where a change of school was arranged, reports were available regarding the child's subsequent progress, and in 73 per cent a complete improvement seems to have occurred; in 186 cases a change of class was carried out, and a similar improvement occurred in 68 per cent; in many of these the main factor appears to have been a change to a more congenial teacher. Often, where special disabilities are concerned, simply altering the teaching methods has proved almost equally effective. This was conspicuously the case with young children suffering from a disability in reading that appeared to have provoked a widespread emotional reaction: here, out of 54 cases studied at different times, a satisfactory result was obtained in 35, i.e. in nearly two-thirds.

B. *In the Home.* In the reports on home circumstances a large number of different conditions were noted, and were frequently put forward as the main or sole cause. But once again the mere frequency with which such conditions are found is by no means a safe guide to their actual influence.

Poverty is a common characteristic among maladjusted children of the elementary school type; but the correlation is not high. A study of the individual cases falling under this head suggests that poverty only becomes a contributing factor when it tends to limit the natural development of the child's intellectual capacities or emotional interests. Thus an exceptionally bright child coming from a very poor home where there are few opportunities for indulging its intellectual interests, a lively and adventurous type of child brought up in a restricted slum environment, the child from a poor but highly respectable home sent by its parents to a school attended by wealthier children—all are apt to develop symptoms of maladjustment.

In the main the psychological conditions of the home are much more important than the economic or material. Our data fully bear out Sully's contention: the mental and moral influence of the home on the adjustments made by the child is 'far greater than that of any other single factor', for four main reasons: (i) 'first, its influence is far more comprehensive than that of school or other external circumstances'; (ii) 'it acts much earlier, at a time when first impressions are formed'; (iii) its effects are far more sustained; (iv) finally, 'family relations, involving warmer relations and more intimate intercourse, give a peculiar intensity to the influence of the home' (Sully, 1886).

Defective family relations play much the same part in maladjustment as they do in the causation of delinquency.[2] The absence of one or both parents, or the removal of a child from its parents for an appreciable period, is often followed by maladjustment, though, as a rule, such causes appear to be contributory rather than primary. The condition that has the most direct and the most powerful influence upon the child's

E*

adjustments to its daily life at home is the attitude of its parents or of those who act *in loco parentis*. From our experience it would be easy to classify the parents of such children into the four suggestive groups, somewhat picturesquely described by Lafore (1945), namely, (i) 'dictators', (ii) 'appeasers', (iii) 'temporizers', and (iv) 'cooperators'. Contrary to what is found in the investigation of delinquency, it is the 'dictators', with their excessively strict disciplinary treatment, who seem to be responsible for the most serious cases of maladjustment: but the weak or vacillating discipline of the 'appeasers' and the 'temporizers' may also have effects that the casual visitor may scarcely suspect. The largest coefficient of all is associated with what can only be described as a general lack of affection. This includes a few instances of grave neglect (2·7 per cent) or even downright cruelty (0·5 per cent); but the majority are cases of mere indifference or selfishness.

Out of the long list of conditions reported as characterizing the child's home circumstances, seven stand out as yielding high correlations (coefficients over 0·20), namely, lack of affection, over-strict discipline, the presence of a step- or foster-mother, the death of the child's own mother, drunkenness, illegitimacy, and lack of adequate facilities for recreation. Several characteristics frequently stressed in the literature appear to have less importance than is commonly supposed; for instance, prolonged absence from parents during earlier childhood, disagreement between the parents in regard to the child's own management or other affairs, and the fact that one or other parent (usually the mother) is highly neurotic. So far as possible, we obtained detailed information regarding the child's early history before reaching school age. For this we relied, not only on the mother's recollection, but on reports from teachers, social workers, and others, who had often been acquainted with the household for over a long period of time. Among the maladjusted group there were a large number of cases in which material and emotional deprivations were reported, together with stories of early difficulties and injudicious handling in regard to such problems as weaning, feeding, cleanliness and the like. But in the control group (where our information is probably less complete) a high proportion of such cases was also reported. Hence, as will be seen from table 9.2, the coefficient of correlation is barely significant.[3]

The environment outside the home and the school plays a smaller part here than it does in cases of juvenile delinquency or among those who have already left school.

II. *Personal characteristics*

A. *Physical Conditions.* Unless they affect the nervous system, physical weakness and disease appear to have comparatively little direct influence. Where change of school involves a change in social or cultural environment (e.g. the weakly scholarship winner sent to a secondary or residential public school), physical ill health and lack of bodily strength may prove important; but our list contains only a few instances of this type, and most of them should perhaps be primarily regarded as cases of an unsuitable school. Irregular development in physical characteristics, particularly among girls, may occasionally prove a temporary factor; and the presence of some conspicuous physical peculiarity—a squint, a stammer, a cleft palate, left-handedness, or even red hair—may indirectly lead to maladjustment, though as a rule such cases are referred on other grounds. If our data can be trusted, therefore, the importance of physical conditions and pathological defects has been greatly exaggerated.

The only significant correlation is that for neurological disorders, which are however decidedly rare. Under this heading the conditions noted were similar to those reported in the investigation on delinquency (Burt, 1925); by far the commonest were post-encephalitic conditions, migrainous headaches, and chorea (usually associated with rheumatism): we have also included three cases in which the maladjustment appeared to be due almost exclusively to partial deafness. Under biochemical disorders the majority of cases consisted of disturbances of endocrine functions and of carbohydrate metabolism, together with a few alleged cases of vitamin deficiency and intolerance of fat: so far as our evidence goes, it seems clear that the importance of such conditions cannot be very great.[4]

B. *Intellectual Characteristics.* Our case-histories leave little doubt that innate disabilities, both general and special, may form a predominant factor in the production of maladjustment. But from the table it appears that the correlation of maladjustment with acquired educational backwardness is far higher than its correlation with disabilities that are presumably innate: the figure, indeed, is one of the highest in our list. However, judged by the after-histories, the condition would seem to be quite as often an effect of the maladjustment as its cause.

As we have seen, in the present series most of the cases falling under this head were not, in point of fact, referred primarily on the ground that the child was dull or backward. Often this was discovered only incidentally. Indeed, in many cases the amount of retardation was too slight for the child to be regarded as dull or backward in the technical sense, or (as it would now be called) 'educationally subnormal'. It may be noted that an innate degree of general intelligence *above* the general average is apparently a more effective (though not a more frequent) cause than an innate degree *below* the general average. Often the difficulty can be remedied by a change of school or class. But quite as frequently it arises out of school and in the home: the boy who is much brighter than his parents, or than his brothers and sisters, sometimes presents an exceptionally puzzling problem; and it is one which seems rarely to be noted in the literature.

C. *Emotional Characteristics.* If we may judge by the total percentages, emotional conditions appear to be far more important than any that we have considered hitherto. Their numerical predominance in the present series, however, is due partly to the fact that cases referred specifically on the grounds of intellectual subnormality or delinquency were not included. In the cases falling under this general heading, the most conspicuous feature is the presence of a high general emotionality, producing what is sometimes termed an unstable temperament. This furnishes the largest correlation in the whole list.

Among a few of the older children the instability proved to be a temporary condition, incidental to puberty or adolescence; but in the vast majority it appeared to be innate.[5] Often other members of the household, particularly the parents, were equally unstable, so that environmental causes were operative as well.

Among the cases referred by teachers, the extraverted, aggressive, self-assertive type was the commonest; among those referred by school medical officers or discovered in the course of school surveys, it was rather the introverted child, suffering his deprivations and discomforts in silence, and appearing worried or unhappy for no obvious cause, that was most frequently noted. Both these more extreme types seem to find it difficult to make spontaneous readjustments to the shortcomings and frustrations which at one time or another confront so many children in homes of limited means.

In an appreciable proportion of the cases, the maladjustment proved to be the cumulative outcome of unfavourable or uncongenial conditions that had lasted for a period of years, and had thus gradually built up undesirable but habitual emotional reactions—continual mental conflicts or a deep sense of inferiority or insecurity. The highest correlation in this sub-group is found in the case of mental conflict. A study of the individual cases, however, suggests that, even when conflict appears as a cause rather than as an effect, it nevertheless remains a contributory factor only: it is chiefly when repeated or prolonged conflict is associated with material or psychological restrictions imposed by the environment that symptoms of maladjustment are likely to ensue.

The high percentage given for 'feelings of insecurity' is perhaps due to the fact that we have here grouped together rather a wide variety of different reactions, based chiefly on statements or impressions obtained during interviews with the children: they have not been counted as potential causes of maladjustment unless they amounted to fairly persistent states of anxiety (as a rule by no means baseless). The percentage for the normal children is probably too low, since they were not studied so intensively. In 14 per cent of the maladjusted cases these emotional reactions took the form of symptoms that would be generally regarded as definitely pathological or abnormal, so that the child has been diagnosed as psychoneurotic or (in 3 per cent) as psychotic.

We should add that it is clear from our data that the incidence and relative importance of the various conditions differ appreciably in different districts, among different social classes, and, in a lesser degree, among different age-groups. But our total groups are too small for these variations to be studied in detail. We venture to suggest that the next most fruitful topic for research might well be the differences between the causes chiefly operative (a) at different ages and (b) in different social groups.

Summary and Conclusions

1. The correlations between 24 conditions reported among 273 maladjusted children have been factorized. Only a small general factor was found. The first bipolar factor indicates a broad classification into environmental conditions and personal conditions respectively; the second, a cross-classification into intellectual conditions and emotional. The group factor analysis suggests a corresponding subdivision into four distinguishable types; these, however, show considerable overlapping. It is concluded that cases of maladjustment can hardly be regarded as forming a single relatively homogeneous group.

2. The frequencies of the various conditions have been examined in

fuller detail among a series of 394 cases of maladjusted children, and have been compared with those obtaining among a control group consisting of the same number of normal children. Point-distribution correlations have been calculated from the percentages found. Judged by these coefficients, a wide variety of conditions shows significant correlations with maladjustment. The most important appear to be the following: (i) in the school, the presence of an uncongenial teacher, and assignment to a class where the work is too difficult; (ii) in the home, lack of affection, over-strict discipline, presence of a step- or foster-mother, death of the child's own mother, drunken parents, illegitimacy, and lack of adequate facilities for recreation; (iii) as regards intellectual characteristics, general educational backwardness, often (though not always) the result of innate intellectual disability, either general or specific; (iv) as regards emotional characteristics, general emotional instability, excessive extraversion, excessive introversion (often accompanied by anxiety states, conflicts, or feelings of inferiority), and (among the older children) adolescent instability. There are appreciable variations according to age, locality, and social class.

Notes

1 This figure is based on the assumption that not only 'educationally subnormal children' (the dull, backward, or mentally defective), but also the delinquent, will be enumerated in separate categories of their own. If, however (as the Ministry's regulations would seem to imply), the delinquent are to be included among the maladjusted, then the proportion must be increased to at least 3 per cent. The difference between 'mild' and 'severe' degrees of maladjustment correspond to the differences between 'mild' and 'severe' retardation in intelligence, as connoted by the phrases 'dull' and 'mentally defective' respectively, and could indeed be defined in terms of a mental age for adjustment. The two groups together would seem to be roughly covered by Carl Rogers' category of 'seriously maladjusted', in which the maladjustment, though 'serious', is not necessarily 'severe'. Rogers' criterion, however, was somewhat different, namely, maladjustment in at least four different directions as specified by his various criteria, which to some extent depended on general and special intellectual disabilities.

2 It has of late been the fashion to lay special stress on 'broken homes' and similar conditions as regular causes of maladjustment and delinquency. The low figures in our table do not support this view.

3 We cannot help thinking that the emphasis placed on early conditions in psychiatric writings is due partly to unverified theories based on psychoanalytic studies of adults, partly on the fact that the psychiatric specialist is far more

familiar with early conditions in middle-class and well-to-do homes than he is with conditions among the general elementary school population. Methods of parental treatment, such as are quite common in large families in poorer neighbourhoods, would seem positively shocking if found, say, in a family of the professional classes. At the same time we have no wish to deny the importance of home treatment during the first few years of life, particularly in its effects on the formation of acquired emotional and social characteristics: in the case of delinquents, for instance, the correlation, though not high, is unquestionably significant.

4 In three cases where 'acidosis' or 'glysopenia' was reported, the alleged maladjustment cleared up after appropriate treatment. But, in the interests of the children, the treatment always included a number of different measures, and the inferences to be drawn were never very clear. As regards endocrine disturbances our results are fully in keeping with the views expressed by Professor Moncrieff: 'sweeping and unscientific claims for endocrinal disorders as factors in mental disturbances are not supported by satisfactory proof: clear-cut examples occur in the literature; but in general, therapy based on speculative relations of this type is futile' (Gordon, 1939).

5 Those who have criticized the hypothesis of innate differences in general emotionality generally do so on the ground that such differences, though appearing early, are attributable to the treatment of the child during the first year or two of life: in particular, it is alleged, 'an emotional mother is apt to produce an emotional child by her postnatal treatment of the infant rather than by her transmission of an hereditary trait'. But this view does not explain the existence of wide differences among siblings treated in the same fashion, nor the high and significant correlations that can be demonstrated between children and remoter relatives. The fact that, by selective breeding, it is possible within eight generations to produce distinct groups of rats—one highly emotional and the other markedly unemotional, as shown in situations causing conflict or other forms of maladjustment—appears to confirm our hypothesis: (cf. for example, Hall, C., *Sigma Xi Quarterly*, XXVI, 1938, pp. 17f.).

PRINGLE, M. L. K. and BOSSIO, V.

10. Early Prolonged Separation and Emotional Maladjustment

Introduction

In the current literature, the term 'deprived' is used to describe a child who, for one reason or another, is unable to live with his own family but is being brought up in an institution (Home Office, 1946; United Nations, 1952; Ford, 1955). The term is also used for children who, although now living in their own homes, have early in life been separated from their parents, particularly the mother, or who are unloved and rejected by her. Like institutionalization, early separation and 'maternal deprivation' are considered to be detrimental to children's development (Bowlby, 1946; Fitzgerald, 1948; Bowlby, 1951). In recent years considerable research has been devoted to these topics, yet there have been comparatively few systematic investigations of unselected groups of deprived children. There has been a tendency for special categories such as pre-school, hospitalized or delinquent children, or for certain aspects, such as emotional adjustment or social maturity to be studied (Goldfarb, 1943; Rheingold, 1943; Spitz, 1945; Bowlby, 1946; Bodman et al., 1950). Our investigation aimed at a comprehensive enquiry into the development and achievement of some unselected samples of deprived children, to examine the interrelationship between their abilities and attainments and to make comparisons with ordinary children wherever possible. In addition, three hypotheses were tested regarding the results of deprivation: that its ill-effects are more marked (a) where the first separation from the mother occurred at an early age; (b) where deprivation has been severe; and (c) where there has been a prolonged period of institutionalization.

Pringle, M. L. Kellmer, and Bossio, V. (1960) 'Early prolonged separation and emotional maladjustment.' *Journal of Child Psychology and Psychiatry,* 1, 37–48. Reprinted as Chapter 4 in Pringle, M. L. Kellmer (1965) *Deprivation and Education.* London: Longmans (second edition, 1971).

When studied, all the children (N = 188) were in care and living in large children's homes. The main results of this study have been reported elsewhere (Pringle and Bossio, 1958). Though a considerable proportion of children showed symptoms of maladjustment, some 30 per cent were considered to be stable by their teachers and the house staff, when rated on the *Bristol Social Adjustment Guides*. Thus our findings suggested that previous views had been incorrect, or at least overstated, and that separation and institutionalization do not necessarily result in children becoming affectionless or psychopathic personalities. In a subsequent study, Bowlby and Ainsworth (1956) came to the same conclusion. To gain further insight into the dynamics of deprivation and personality reactions, it was decided to make an intensive, clinical study of two groups of children selected from our main sample of 142 cases according to the following criteria:

(a) That the first removal from home had occurred before the age of 5 years.

(b) That the child had continued to live apart from his parents for more than half of his life.

(c) That he had been rated either 'notably stable' or 'severely maladjusted' on all the following measures:

(i) The *Bristol Social Adjustment Guides* completed by the house staff.

(ii) The same Guides completed by the class teachers.

(iii) The results from a personality test (*Raven's Controlled Projection Test*).

(iv) The clinical observations made by the investigators throughout the individual testing and interviewing of each child.

(d) That he should be of average ability (i.e. I.Q. range on the full WISC between 85 and 114).

In that way the most severely deprived children were chosen and the possibly complicating factor of low or high intelligence was excluded. Applying these criteria, we found eleven 'severely maladjusted' and five 'notably stable' children, some from each of the age groups of the main sample, namely 8-, 11- and 14-year-olds. A detailed case study was made of each of the sixteen children, eleven boys and five girls, and this is the subject of the present paper.

Summary of the Case Studies

The results of the individual tests and assessments used with the main sample and two intensively studied groups are shown on table 10.1. The main sample and the maladjusted group are markedly backward in language development which was assessed by the *Mill Hill Vocabulary Scale*, and in comprehension reading, tested on Schonell's *Silent Reading Test B*. The stable group achieved average mean scores on both these measures.

Similarly, the mean coefficient of conformity on *Raven's Controlled Projection Test* is considerably below the expected mean of 100 both for the main sample and the maladjusted group. A qualitative analysis of the responses given by the latter shows many answers indicative of aggression, a feeling of hopelessness or anxiety about parents and general insecurity, as well as ambivalent and guilt feelings. The drawings made while answering the test questions are rather poor in content, detail, colour and movement, suggesting a paucity of ideas, general immaturity and restricted powers of self-expression. On the other hand, the answers given by the stable group to the personality test contain fewer 'unique responses' and the mean 'coefficient of conformity' is consequently higher. The drawings made while answering the test items are quite pleasing and lively, showing a free use of colour, variety in content and an eye for detail.

Though both groups receive an average score for social competence on the Vineland Scale, the children in the maladjusted group were reported to show from time to time regressive tendencies in social behaviour, both in the home and at school.

The main test results for each child in the two groups are shown on tables 10.2 and 10.3. The close correspondence of all the results obtained by the identical twins, Roger and Allan, are noteworthy. The descriptions of the children's outstanding personality traits are a summary arrived at by combining the assessments made both by the school and home staffs on the *Bristol Social Adjustment Guides*. Perhaps the most outstanding feature is the inability of the maladjusted children to make relationships with adults or children or both, while being overanxious for adult approval and over-attentive to any newcomers. This attachment is, however, only temporary and soon gives way to indifference or uncertainty. In contrast, the stable group are all reported

TABLE 10.1

TEST RESULTS OBTAINED FOR THE MAIN EXPERIMENTAL SAMPLE AND FOR THE INTENSIVELY STUDIED GROUPS

Tests	Main experimental sample N = 142		Severely maladjusted group N = 11		Notably stable group N = 5	
	Mean quotient	Range	Mean quotient	Range	Mean quotient	Range
WISC Full Scale	89·84	62–128	91·72	86–100	99·00	90–107
WISC Verbal Scale	86·47	58–130	84·72	77– 96	89·80	77– 99
WISC Performance Scale	95·60	55–136	100·36	86–100	108·80	100–114
Mill Hill Vocabulary Scale (Oral Definitions)	74·88	45–120	72·90	59– 97	93·60	85–109
Schonell Silent Reading Test B	80·13	51–124	75·18	63– 92	98·20	90–112
Vineland Social Maturity Scale	104·67	70–138	102·63	80–116	112·00	106–117
Raven's Controlled Projection Test (Coefficient of Conformity)	51·36	17– 85	42·36	30– 50	78·00	70– 85

TABLE 10.2

TEST RESULTS AND PERSONALITY ASSESSMENTS FOR THE SEVERELY MALADJUSTED GROUP

Name	WISC V.Q.	WISC P.Q.	WISC F.Q.	L.Q.	R.Q.	S.Q.	C. of C.	P.Q. V.Q. discrep.	S.Q. I.Q. discrep.	Outstanding personality traits
1. John	81	103	91	63	71	108	41	22	+1·29 D.S.	Craves affection and attention, moody, resents correction; lacks interests and persistence; severe nail-biting and body scratching
*2. Roger	80	104	91	65	67	108	30	24	+1·36 D.S.	Apathetic but shows aggressive resentment if corrected; careless and destructive with property and toys; solitary and unpopular among children, detached, secretive and has formed no close relations with anyone but his twin brother
*3. Allan	77	106	90	66	81	109	42	29	+1·46 D.S.	Is described in almost identical terms to those used for his twin brother Roger
4. Charlotte	81	110	94	69	80	102	45	29	+0·59 D.S.	Craves adult attention to the point of making herself a constant nuisance to teachers and house staff; aggressive to other children; moody, destructive; severe bedwetting, nail-biting and thumb sucking
5. Paul	90	86	88	71	83	116	41	—	+2·32 D.S.	Timid and cries easily; has no friends at school; neat worker but often day dreams; in the home he is often depressed, 'wrapped up in himself'; a deeply unhappy, lonely boy who has never apparently accepted separation from mother and sister
6. Sandra	96	100	98	97	86	103	46	4	+0·41 D.S.	Moody, restless, temper outbursts; over-anxious for adult approval and jealous of other children; lies and steals food and money; distrusts adults

TABLE 10.2 (continued)

Name	WISC V.Q.	WISC P.Q.	WISC F.Q.	L.Q.	R.Q.	S.Q.	C. of C.	P.Q. V.Q. discrep.	S.Q. I.Q. discrep.	Outstanding personality traits
7. Kathleen	96	104	100	76	92	107	45	8	+0·67 D.S.	Stammers, bites nails and has temper tantrums; gets fond of children and adults but attachments do not last; many fears and very restless
8. Colin	85	93	88	59	63	84	40	8	−0·72 D.S.	Very backward at school, moody, violent if corrected; nail-biting, body scratching and enuresis are among his many symptoms; craves adult approval yet hostile to them
9. Leonard	79	94	86	88	64	80	41	15	−0·90 D.S.	Moody, temper outbursts and full of infantile fears; steals from and spiteful to other children; extremely attached to his mother, lives for her infrequent letters and visits; has made no lasting relationship to any other adult
10. Nicholas	85	107	95	74	77	112	45	22	+1·47 D.S.	Stammers, moody; defiant to adults and distrustful; boasts, craves attention and is restlessly and aimlessly 'on the go'
11. Terry	82	97	88	74	63	100	50	15	+0·80 D.S.	'Wrapped up in himself', hostile to women and rather solitary; lies, boasts and rebuffs kindness from adults as if mistrusting them

* Identical twins.

WISC V.Q. = WISC Verbal Quotient
WISC P.Q. = WISC Performance Quotient
WISC F.Q. = WISC Full Scale Quotient
L.Q. = Language Quotient

R.Q. = Reading Quotient
S.Q. = Social Quotient
C. of C. = Coefficient of Conformity
D.S. = Difference between standard score in terms of I.Q. mean and standard deviation

to have established good relationships, both with adults and contemporaries.

The life history and family background of each child are.summarized on tables 10.4 and 10.5. The severely deprived group came into care rather younger than the stable children, all but two having been separated from their mothers for the first time by 1 year of age or before. Most of the maladjusted children had been deserted by their mothers or abandoned near children's homes, police stations or in churches. Both groups have experienced a number of placements. Fostering had been tried for five children in the maladjusted group, but their difficult behaviour led to a breakdown in the arrangements and a return to a children's home. This was not done for the stable children, as they had dependable ties with a parent or other adult even though they could not live with them. Most of the children had been in hospital but only one boy had been seriously ill (No. 9 Leonard with rheumatic fever). John had numerous periods in hospital for observation of an eye defect which was soon to be operated upon; otherwise his health was good, except that he had gastro-enteritis at the age of 10 months. It is worth noting that in the case of eight of the maladjusted children their first stay in hospital occurred near the time of the first separation from their mothers.

The records relating to the children's parentage were found to be rather scanty. This may well have been because there had been several placements and because the children have been in care for a long time. A little more is known about the parents of the stable group, but there is insufficient information for a comparison between the two groups. It is evident, however, that the rate of illegitimacy is much higher among the maladjusted children.

The most marked difference between the two groups is in the amount of contact maintained with parents or parent substitutes. 'Regular' means that contact has consistently been maintained by the same people, in the form of letters, parcels, visits, outings and holidays for the children; 'occasional' means that for some years there has not been continuous and regular contact and even that has only been forthcoming at the repeated requests of the Children's Officer; 'none at all' means that the child has never known a continuing relationship with any adult outside the children's home, whether relative or friend. All the stable children have experienced a dependable, lasting relationship

TABLE 10.3

TEST RESULTS AND PERSONALITY ASSESSMENT FOR THE NOTABLY STABLE CHILDREN

Name	WISC V.Q.	WISC P.Q.	WISC F.Q.	L.Q.	R.Q.	S.Q.	C. of C.	P.Q. V.Q. discrep.	S.Q. I.Q. discrep.	Outstanding personality traits
1. Elizabeth	81	111	95	85	98	110	75	30	+1·28 D.S.	Friendly, responsive and well-behaved; popular with contemporaries; works well at school and takes care of her belongings; very attached to younger brother, house mother, 'official aunt' and her teachers
2. Jacqueline	77	106	90	86	90	113	70	29	+1·90 D.S.	Affectionate, responsive and liked by children and adults; very attached to her mother and siblings but has warm relationships with house staff
3. Peter	99	114	107	109	92	117	80	15	+1·08 D.S.	Helpful, friendly and well-behaved; does well in school; gets on well with contemporaries; very good relationships with his mother, 'aunt', teachers and house parents
4. Dennis	95	113	104	89	112	106	85	18	+0·31 D.S.	Well-behaved, responsive and hard working in school where he is doing very well; mixes well; fond of his father and sisters and good relations with most adults
5. Roy	97	100	99	99	99	114	80	3	+1·39 D.S.	Cheerful, good natured and well liked by children and adults; very fond of his foster-mother

WISC V.Q. = WISC Verbal Quotient
WISC P.Q. = WISC Performance Quotient
WISC F.Q. = WISC Full Scale Quotient
L.Q. = Language Quotient

R.Q. = Reading Quotient
S.Q. = Social Quotient
C. of C. = Coefficient of Conformity
D.S. Difference between standard score in terms of I.Q. mean and standard deviation

with a parent or parent substitute, whereas only one child in the maladjusted group has had such a contact.

Discussion and Conclusion

Although the number of cases upon which this study is based is small, they were chosen from a fairly large and unselected sample of deprived children in institutional care. The criteria governing their selection ensured that they had been separated from their mothers at an early age and had continued to live apart from them for considerable periods. In fact most of the sixteen children had spent virtually all their lives in children's homes only interrupted by unsuccessful periods in foster homes. How then can we account for the difference in emotional adjustment found between them? Constitutional inferiority and thus greater susceptibility to emotional instability in the face of environmental stresses might be one hypothesis. Though only meagre evidence was available on the children's parentage, the very high incidence of illegitimacy among the maladjusted group together with subsequent parental rejection could be interpreted as indicating greater parental instability than was operative in the stable group. Alternatively, however, one could argue that parents whose children come into care almost permanently are likely to be themselves unstable and too disorganized to provide, and cope successfully with, normal family life. The loss of contact and rejection among the many illegitimate children in the maladjusted group could be due largely to the social stigma and other practical difficulties encountered in our society by the unmarried mother. The very young age at which the illegitimate children first came into care also supports this view. Moreover, some of these women were known to have married subsequently and to be providing a home for their legitimate offspring. Thus we must conclude that we have insufficient evidence regarding the influence of hereditary or constitutional factors.

More factual information is available on environmental influences. The first mother–child separation occurred before the first year for nine of the maladjusted children. In Bowlby's terminology (Ainsworth and Bowlby, 1954) they suffered from complete 'privation of a mother–child relationship, implying that one has never existed'. Complete privation is defined as separation in very early infancy before a stable and secure dependency relationship has been established, and subsequent rearing

TABLE 10.4

SUMMARY OF THE LIFE HISTORY AND FAMILY BACKGROUND OF THE SEVERELY MALADJUSTED GROUP

Name	C.A. at time of study Yrs Mths	Age at first separa- tion Months	Reasons for coming into care	No. of place- ments	No. of hospital- izations	Legit./ illegit.	Family background		
							Father's occupat. status	Mother's reported status or mentality	Contact with parent or parent- substitutes
1. John	7 6	8	Unsuitable living conditions	4	5	Illegit.	Unknown	Illiterate	Occasional
2. Roger	7 7	7	Mother deserted	3	None	Illegit.	Taxi driver	Mental Hosp.	Occasional
3. Allan	7 7	7	Mother deserted	3	None	Illegit.	Taxi driver	Mental Hosp.	Occasional
4. Charlotte	8 4	1	Abandoned by mother	5	1	Illegit.	Unknown (Negro)	Unstable	Not at all
5. Paul	8 8	11	No home	3	1	Illegit.	Unknown	Dom. servant	Occasional
6. Sandra	10 0	11	Parents divorced; children to father	3+	1	Legit.	No job for 6 yr.; died 1 yr ago	In prison	Not at all
7. Kathleen	10 3	5	Mother deserted	6	2	Illegit.	Labourer (Maltese)	Dom. servant	Not at all
8. Colin	11 1	19	Abandoned by mother	4	2	Illegit.	Unknown	Very dull	Occasional
9. Leonard	11 6	2	Unsettled home	5	3	Illegit.	Labourer	Unknown	Regular
10. Nicholas	14 6	18	Ill-treated and abandoned	5	2	Illegit.	Unknown (Cypriot)	Illiterate	Not at all
11. Terry	14 8	12	Mother dead; father no home	3	1	Legit. mother dead	Labourer	Dead	Not at all

TABLE 10.5

SUMMARY OF THE LIFE HISTORY AND FAMILY BACKGROUND OF THE NOTABLY STABLE GROUP

Name	C.A. at time of study Yrs Mths	Age at first separation Months	Reasons for coming into care	No. of placements	No. of hospitalizations	Legit./illegit.	Family background		Contact with parent or parent-substitutes
							Father's occupat. status	Mother's reported status or mentality	
1. Elizabeth	8 6	36	Evicted, no home since	2	3	Legit.	Labourer	Unknown	Regularly till recently (both parents)
2. Jacqueline	8 7	46	Mother deserted; father abroad	3	1	Legit.	Regular army	Unstable	Regular (with mother)
3. Peter	10 1	25	Mother chronic T.B.; father neglectful	5	1	Legit.	Coal-loader	Chronic T.B. in sanatorium	Regular (with 'nurse')
4. Dennis	10 8	36	Mother's death leaving four children	2	None	Legit.	Gas-meter reader	Dead	Regular (with father)
5. Roy	13 11	12	Evacuation, then beyond control	3	2	Illegit.	Unknown	Responsible	Regular (with 'aunt')

of the child in an institution where he is cared for in a more or less impersonal way by a variety of adult figures. Secondly, for the maladjusted children separation was accompanied by lasting parental rejection. Lastly—and this may be equally if not more important— none of the maladjusted group had had the opportunity or the ability to build up and consolidate stable relationships with parent figures.

In contrast, all but one child in the stable group remained with its mother until well after the first year of life, by which time a stable relationship is likely to have been established. Separation appears to have been caused by unfortunate circumstances rather than by the rejection of the child. Even the mother who deserted her family (table 10.5, case No. 2) continued to keep in touch with the child. Three children never experienced a complete severance of family relations but a prolonged physical separation; the other two children in this group (table 10.5, Nos. 3 and 5) formed a stable and lasting relationship with a mother-substitute. It is worth noting that they never lived permanently in the homes of their mother-substitutes but visited regularly and spent holidays there. Our maladjusted group may be described as being psychologically deprived, while the stable group was deprived of family life and physically separated but nevertheless loved and cherished by adults who were important to them.

The fact that the maladjusted group was found to be markedly backward in language development and reading attainment, supports the view that emotion and learning are inseparably linked (Pringle, 1957, 1958). Similarly, people working with young deprived children have noted that separation from the mother is often followed by indifferent physical health, in some cases necessitating entry into hospital. This was found to be so for the majority of children in our maladjusted group.

Thus our evidence supports the hypothesis that the child who is rejected very early in life and remains unwanted is likely to become insecure, maladjusted and educationally backward. Never having experienced lasting love and loyalty from any adult, the child becomes unable to develop these qualities in his human relationships. Some of the children in our maladjusted group were beginning to show the characteristics of the so-called 'affectionless character', although many seemed still to be searching for and attempting to form affective ties.

It almost seems as if children in our society need to feel they matter and are valued as individuals by someone outside the children's home where the adults are paid for the job of looking after them. Physical separation and prolonged institutionalization by themselves do not necessarily lead to emotional difficulties or character defects. Susceptibility to maladjustment and resilience to the shock of separation and deprivation appear to be determined by the quality of human relationships available to the child during critical periods of growth. Further research is needed to verify this hypothesis and to investigate whether and when this process becomes irreversible.

The main practical implication of our evidence lies in the need to ensure that every child in institutional care has the opportunity to make a stable relationship with an adult in the outside world. At present the emphasis in Child Care is firstly on the prevention of the break-up of the family and secondly on its reunification at the earliest possible moment. There is perhaps some doubt about the wisdom of this policy in every case of separation. If it is accepted that a child can suffer deprivation of emotional needs without physical separation from his mother and family, a return to a home where he is rejected is not necessarily a desirable solution. Rather there should be increased practical recognition of a child's need to feel valued by a dependable adult and increased emphasis to such adults (whether parents, relatives or friends) on the fact that it is essential to maintain their contacts with the child regularly and reliably over a period of years.

GOLDENBERG, H. and GOLDENBERG, I.

11. School Phobia: Childhood Neurosis or Learned Maladaptive Behaviour?

If, as many authorities claim, phobias in general are the neuroses of childhood, then school phobias in particular represent a most virulent form. Typically, the child dreads some aspect of the school situation—the teacher, other children, the journey, other aspects of school life—as well as dreading physical separation from home and mother. Somatic complaints appear, only to disappear when the child is assured he does not have to go to school.

Lippman (1956) describes as fairly typical the following parental reaction to the school phobic child:

> Driven by their anxiety, parents first urge their child to go back to school, beg him, and then try to bribe him with gifts. When these methods fail they often resort to punishment, in the belief that the child is being wilful and stubborn. When parents become panicky about the child's not going to school, their anxiety intensifies the child's suffering. . . . The child feels ashamed of his helplessness and guilty. . . .

From the above, the parent-child interaction is clear in the maintenance, if not the production, of the child's phobic reaction.

The school phobic child must be differentiated from the truant, whose motives in not attending school may be many and complex, but rarely resemble the intense and irrational fear of the phobic child pressed to attend school (Johnson, Falstein, Szurek, and Svendsen, 1941). Kessler (1966) points out that the child in real danger of failing in school rarely becomes phobic. She notes the curious paradox that youngsters with clear cut learning difficulties 'do not express a reluctance to go to school, they want to go even though they may have little success'.

While school phobia may occur at any age, Goldberg (1953) reports

Goldenberg, H. and Goldenberg, I. (1970) 'School phobia: childhood neurosis or learned maladaptive behavior?' *Exceptional Children*, 37, 3, 220–6.

the majority of youngsters show their first signs of such reactions early, usually between 5 and 10 years of age. The educational as well as the psychological implication of the child's conflicts are serious and may result in long term damage and deficit. Serious learning gaps may occur from frequent absence from school. Ability to establish adequate peer relationships may be damaged. Negative attitudes toward school or later learning in general, may result. School phobias, while unique to childhood, may be prodromal of adult phobic states (Warren, 1960).

The phobic child feels great distress when confronted with the necessity to separate himself from familiar people, notably his mother, and familiar surroundings. Yet the development of a unique, autonomous, independent self demands of every person that he successfully make such a separation. The process of separation is as vital for growth as it is filled with dangers. It therefore can rarely be navigated without risk.

Separation—An Essential Process in Normal Growth

In defining separation Allen (1955) makes the differentiation between separation as a *process* and as an *event*. The normal child, whose physical and emotional needs are satisfied particularly through his relation to his mother, gradually moves out of his dependent state and develops a growing sense of individuality and self-awareness.

Allen points out that the term separation is used in two different ways. One concerns the premature removal of the child from his biological mother. Separation in this sense is a tearing apart, or *event*. We have a great deal of information about what occurs at these times from studies on hospitalization, death of a parent, and institutionalization.

The second aspect of separation deals with the differentiating *process* between parent and child. While the first aspect deals with actual physical separation and the deprivation effects on the child, the second aspect concerns separation as a dynamic psychological process between parent and child. It is here that studies on the transactions between the parent and the school phobic child have focused. Separation, in this sense, is a process of differentiating oneself from the mother, and is an essential phenomenon of normal growth.

The relationship between mother and child is in constant change, beginning slowly but becoming more discernible in later stages, such as weaning and learning to walk. The child is using what he is getting from the mother to nourish his growing sense of himself as a separate 'I' (Bettleheim, 1967).

Animal studies such as those by Harlow and his students with monkeys underscore these findings. Saiy and Harlow (1965) found that when normal jungle-raised monkeys reach a certain age, the mothers push the children away from them physically, literally propelling them into the social world. If as is the case of the neurotic laboratory-raised mothers, this separation does not occur, the infant monkeys do not develop normally, showing many behaviors that resemble symbiotic or autistic behavior patterns in humans.

Disturbed Separations

If we accept the premise that healthy personality development is dependent on an early close and satisfying relationship with the mother, succeeded by a gradual process of separation and self-development in the growing child, then it follows that the loss or interruption of such loving maternal care may have deleterious consequences.

Yarrow (1964) insists on the distinction between *maternal separation* and *maternal deprivation*, pointing out that published studies that purport to show the effects of separation may actually be measuring the results of other conditions, such as maternal deprivation. (Deprivation here refers to a reduction or lack of tactile, kinesthetic, auditory, or other kinds of stimulation normally provided by the mother.) It may represent, typically, how children may be cared for outside their homes—in inadequate institutions, foster homes, day nurseries, and hospitals. Maternal separation, on the other hand, involves a break in the continuity of the mother-child relationship, after a meaningful focused relationship has been established. Before such a relationship has been established, the results of physical separation are unpredictable, and depend on the physical environment, stimulation, mother substitutes, etc. After the meaningful focused relationship is established, separation from the mother is a serious loss of a significant loved one. Perhaps even more significant may be the circumstances of separation: death, chronic illness, economic disaster, or war, for example. Moreover, the trauma of separation from the child's natural parents may simply be the prelude to a long, unpredictable and often disturbing and inconsistent series of changes in foster homes or institutions.

Yarrow (1964) reviews the literature of at least six major varieties of separation which might be assumed to represent psychologically different experiences to the young child.

1. Single brief separation followed by reunion with parents (e.g. vacations, short term hospitalization of child or parent, nursery school).

2. Repeated brief separations with reunions (same example as above, but with increased frequency).

3. Single long term separation with reunion (e.g. hospitalization for chronic illness, severe family crisis, wartime separation).

4. Repeated long term separation with reunion (e.g. periodic placement in foster home or institutions of children from families in constant crisis).

5. Single permanent separation (e.g. death or permanent physical or mental disability of parents, resulting in foster home placement or adoption).

6. Repeated permanent separations (e.g. permanent separation from parents, followed a series of foster homes or institutions and frequent changes of mother substitutes).

Yarrow reminds us that certain variables must be accounted for in evaluating studies of separation. He includes (a) the developmental stage of the child at the time of separation, (b) the character of the relationship with the mother prior to separation, (c) the character of maternal care during separation, and (d) individual experiences as well as individual vulnerability to separation.

All separation experiences cannot be equated. They vary from minor events which are part of, and indeed may facilitate, normal development, to traumatic interruptions which may be permanently damaging. In addition, the effects of the separation experience *per se* sometimes cannot be differentiated from the reinforcing conditions following separation, particularly traumatic separation.

With these cautions in mind, the next section reviews the literature concerned with one common and frequently traumatic example of a disturbed separation—school phobia.

Etiology of School Phobia

Theories of the etiology of any emotional or behavioral disorder are best understood by examining the general personality theory from which they emerge. In the case of school phobia, it is the psychoanalytic school that has paid the greatest attention and offers the most comprehensive explanations, although recently other schools, namely behavior modification, have become interested in understanding and treating the child with this problem.

This section will describe and elaborate the various explanations offered for the development of school phobia, bearing in mind that no single explanation of the mechanics of the onset of school phobia will explain all cases, and recognizing that a combination of several of the following are involved in every case—with different combinations for different children.

Separation anxiety

This is perhaps the most common view shared by many psychoanalysts. Eisenberg (1958) states categorically that 'school phobia has been shown to be a variant of separation anxiety'. Separation anxiety, in turn, is defined by Estes, Haylett, and Johnson (1956) as 'a pathologic emotional state in which the child and parent, usually the mother, are involved in a mutually hostile dependent relationship characterized primarily by an intense need on the part of both to be in close physical proximity to each other'. The point to be underscored here is that the anxiety is experienced and shared by both mother and child.

The psychoanalysts go further, insisting that school phobia is a childhood neurosis. Moreover, as Estes, Haylett, and Johnson (1956) put it, the child's neurosis never exists in isolation, but is 'always intimately associated with a complementary neurosis in the mother'. Fear of school is fear of separation or fear of abandonment, and may be experienced by both mother and child. Johnson (1941) who did some of the pioneering work on school phobic children, points out that mothers of such children have poorly resolved dependency relationships with their own mothers. The immature mother will have difficulty in trying to cope with fear and anxiety in her child, and her discomfort may reinforce, rather than alleviate, the problem.

Mother-child symbiosis

This view is an elaboration of the previous one, again put forth primarily by psychoanalysts. Eisenberg (1958) describes the cues within the mother-child transaction where each unconsciously communicates his anxiety about separation to the other. The mother who herself

F

thinks of school as a cold, impersonal place, is overly sympathetic with the child's reluctance to attend school. The child senses that the mother wishes, at least unconsciously, that the child remain at home. Each communicates his discomfort and each looks to the other to be reassured and comforted.

Aggression, regression, dependency

Coolidge, Tessman, Waldfogel, and Willer (1962) emphasize the mother's neurotic conflict about the aggression involved in disciplining her child: 'The mother's guilt about her own hostile impulses underlies a similar concern in the child and is a source of his prodigious anxiety.' The mother may resent giving emotionally when she herself wishes to be dependent and feels she herself has not received enough from her own mother. She exaggerates the child's needs because there is a reawakening in her of her own infantile feelings of unfulfillment, which she projects onto the child. The child is afraid of his aggression and defends himself by regressing to increased dependence on the mother and displacing the anger to the outside world, notably school.

Unrealistic self-image

Turning from the mother-child interaction, some authors have looked elsewhere in attempting to understand the etiology and dynamics of school phobia. These authors (Kessler, 1966; Leventhal and Sills, 1964), argue that the same mother-child transactions in other families have been observed without producing school phobic problems. Secondly, within the same family, why is only one child affected? Thirdly, why do these children not have difficulties separating from their mother in other areas of their lives? In this vein, Leventhal and Sills question the psychoanalytic model of phobic development. Instead, they stress the child's self-image, narcissism, and omnipotent fantasies. They believe such children 'commonly overvalue themselves and their achievements and then try to hold onto their unrealistic self-image'. When this is threatened in the school situation, they 'suffer anxiety and retreat to another situation where they can maintain their narcissistic self-image'. Usually this means wanting to re-establish close contact with the mother.

Leventhal and Sills believe these children overestimate their own power and ability to master persons and events, and avoid situations which threaten this overcontrolling self-image. Their need for school success is great and when this is threatened, whether in reality or fantasy, they retreat back to the indulgent mother who gratifies their infantile demands and thereby restores within the family their disproportionate sense of power, at the same time helping to avoid the external reality of school.

School avoidance and positive home reinforcement
Leventhal and Sills' position cited above is a transitional one between the views of those with a psychoanalytic orientation and those favoring behavior modification. Among the latter, Garvey and Hegrenes (1966), as typical behavior modifiers, are less concerned with etiology than treatment, although in general they believe that school phobia is a learned maladaptive pattern of behavior. In the case of Jimmy, aged 10, described in their paper, they speculate in learning theory terms how he acquired a fear of school. They reason that Jimmy had an intense fear of losing his mother, as indicated by his fantasies about harm coming to her or her leaving the family. His mother reinforced the fears by telling him that some day she would be dead, that he would want help and she would no longer be there. This danger signal—losing mother—was repeatedly paired with the neutral stimulus of school; she told him that one day, upon his returning from school, she would be gone. School eventually became a conditioned stimulus capable of eliciting the conditioned response of fear. When the fear finally became too intense, Jimmy refused to go to school.

By refusing school and staying home, his fear was reduced, and thereby the avoidance response was strengthened. Secondly, the many positive reinforcements at home (greater freedom, less pressure, etc.) strengthened the school avoidance response. School phobia, according to this line of reasoning, is a learned maladaptive response which calls for counter-conditioning procedures to eliminate the phobic symptom.

Therapeutic Strategies

The nature of any therapeutic intervention is dependent on the specific and unique aspects of the presenting problem, as well as the techniques and theoretical framework available to the therapist attempting to treat the problem. In the case of school phobia, the usual considerations are complicated because treatment involves the collaboration of many people; the child, the therapist, the mother (or perhaps the entire family), the school, and the teacher. Davidson (1961), in reviewing 30 cases of school phobia, points out the need for the school to make concessions for irregular attendance, provide individual tutoring, and help the child maintain academic progress. Kessler (1966) notes that the teacher may need to 'seat the phobic child close to herself, meet him at the door, modify toilet or lunch rules for him, and above all, accept him on whatever terms are necessary'.

All writers, from whatever theoretical persuasion, agree to the necessity of returning the child to the classroom, or at least to the school building, as soon as possible. Waldfogel, Tessman, and Hahn (1959) urge early intervention when the teacher suspects an incipient school phobia. Their results indicate that in 25 of 26 cases where treatment was begun promptly, school attendance resumed in a few weeks. However, in the cases where it was delayed beyond a semester, it persisted for months or even years.

Various therapeutic innovations, in addition to the traditional individual psychotherapy or psychoanalysis, have been reported in the literature. Messer (1964) believes that school phobia expresses publicly a disruption of the family equilibrium, and urges treatment of the entire family unit. Leventhal, Weinberger, Stander, and Stearns (1967), following up on the paper reported in the previous section on the phobic child's unrealistic self-image and unrealistic power beliefs, attempt to assess the complicity of all the family members, and perhaps even school personnel, in this power struggle.

Traditional psychoanalytic approaches have been used, sometimes in the orthodox way, and sometimes, interestingly enough, in combination with desensitization procedures aimed at returning the child to school as quickly as possible. Thus, the advantages of psychoanalysis (e.g. providing an understanding of the effects of early trauma) and behavior modification (e.g. providing a simple, easily understood, systematic effort at symptom removal) are combined. Sutterfield (1954) reports on five cases where the treatment was psychoanalytic and the psychodynamics pointed to maternal rejection, preference for siblings on the part of the mother, and excessive dependency on an overprotective mother.

Lazarus, Davison, and Polefka (1965), behavior modifiers, describe the application of classical and operant conditioning procedures in treating school phobic children. They attempted to deal with the intense fear of school by systematic desensitization, such as taking the child back to school for short visits accompanied by the therapist. In addition, operant conditioning techniques were used such as rewarding the child with tokens for remaining in school.

Returning to the case of Jimmy described in the previous section, Garvey and Hegrenes (1966) describe the step-by-step desensitization procedures carried out in the school environment with the cooperation of the school officials. Jimmy and his therapist began by sitting in a car together in front of the school, and then they systematically proceeded over the next 20 days to approach the school steps, go to the door, enter the school building, approach the classroom a certain distance each day down the hall, enter the empty classroom, be present with the teacher in the classroom, be present with the teacher and two class-mates in the room, and finally be present with the entire class. The return to the full class proceeded at the pace Jimmy could tolerate. By the twentieth day, according to the authors, Jimmy voluntarily returned to class, saw another youngster occupying his desk and told him politely to leave. A 2-year follow-up has indicated no subsequent manifestation of the phobia.

Conclusions and Implications for Future Research

If, as this paper presumes, separation from the mother is essential to normal growth and if disturbances in the interaction between mother, child, and school may cause separation difficulties which lead to school phobia, then we must answer numerous questions about the nature and quality of this disturbed interaction.

Although many of the theoretical models and techniques discussed are fruitful, it appears that a number of variables have been omitted. With the trend toward earlier school attendance and the growth of preschool programs, it becomes incumbent on us to examine more closely the effects of social class and ethnic or racial variables on this phenomena.

If, as Eisenberg (1958) believes, an important aspect of this problem is the mother's perception of the school as a cold, rejecting place, how does the lower-class mother view the middle-class-oriented school? If programs such as the one described by Caldwell and Richmond (1964) (educationally-oriented day care for culturally deprived children between 6 months and 3 years of age) are to be instituted to provide for inadequacies in the home environment, then the importance of brief separation and its relation to chronological age and developmental level becomes paramount. In addition to programs for the culturally deprived, the emergence of the modern woman as a continued part of the work force and the insistence by many of these women that child care should start earlier and be more inclusive, raises other problems.

The practical solutions to many of these problems will reside not only in the therapeutic strategies for dealing with school phobia but in the preventive measures that can be developed. These may involve such things as home visits for the teacher prior to the child's arrival at school for the first time, or repeated observations in the school for both the child and the mother prior to school entrance. Information for teachers to help them understand the special vulnerability of the poor, the minority, or the first-time mother in their initial contacts with and perceptions of the school, must be provided.

It is very possible that time spent by the school psychologist in the preschool or kindergarten at the beginning of a school year identifying and working with children who appear to have separation difficulties might save more intensive work later on.

Separation from the mother at the nursery school door the first day at school holds enormous significance for both mother and child. To the child this is the first contact he makes with the institution where he will be spending a major portion of his social existence. The mother often feels that this is a test of her adequacy as a parent. The teacher too needs to feel competent in her first contacts with the child. If the adults both feel comfortable in their roles the child can venture forth into the new environment, but if there are hesitations, self-doubts, and conflicts on the part of parent or teacher, the groundwork for future maladaptive learning such as that demonstrated in school phobia is laid.

Methods of Treatment

Introduction

This section consists of four articles, the first two of which examine the traditional approach to treatment which has often been used in the last thirty or forty years: referral to a clinic for psychotherapy. Levitt, in the first article, reports a survey of investigations into psychotherapy with children which has become a classic illustration of some of the difficulties inherent in claiming success for this type of treatment. It would be wrong for Levitt to claim with certainty that there is no difference between the results obtained with psychotherapy and those obtained without, since as he himself admits, there is no guarantee that the groups which he compares were matched, that is, that they consisted of children with equivalent difficulties and other characteristics.

The second paper makes a more exact attempt to match two sets of children in this way. One set was being treated at child guidance clinics for behaviour disorders, whereas the other set was not. It is interesting to note how Shepherd and his co-authors, although they do not quote the Levitt work, do in fact find improvement rates which are very similar to those which Levitt himself found. Again it would be quite wrong to equate the findings of this article with a condemnation of the value of child guidance clinics. It is just as wrong to conclude this as it is to assume that child guidance clinics are solely psycho-therapeutic in their orientation and do not include other types of treatment.

The last two articles illustrate the behaviour modification approach which is currently gaining some favour among educational psychologists. They show the way in which children's behaviour in classroom situations can be altered in different directions by using the techniques of conditioning and behaviour modification. Again it would be wrong to conclude from the successes which are reported in these articles that the effects of behaviour modification are markedly superior to those of psychotherapy. The type of comparison which Levitt and Shepherd advocated in the first two articles is not illustrated in the last two articles. The important point, however, is to note the way in which, when faced with a child with a specific behaviour problem in the classroom, it is sometimes possible through careful observation and objective use of planned techniques to change that behaviour in the direction which the teacher wishes.

12. Psychotherapy with Children: A Further Evaluation

Preliminary considerations

In 1957, the author reviewed articles involving the evaluation of the results of psychotherapy with children for the period 1929–55 (Levitt, 1957a). A total of 18 reports of evaluations at close and 17 at follow-up were found. Of the total of nearly 8,000 child patients, two-thirds were rated as improved at close and three-quarters at follow-up. Using 'defectors' from treatment (i.e. children who had been accepted for treatment but who never began treatment) as a control baseline, approximately the same percentages were found for respective control groups. It was concluded that the results failed to support the contention that psychotherapy with children is effective.

This conclusion was supported by the results of a long-range, follow-up study at the Institute for Juvenile Research in Chicago (Levitt, 1959), one of the largest community child guidance clinics in the United States. Treated groups were compared with defector controls from the same clinic population on 26 variables, and no differences were found.

The review has been criticized by Eisenberg and Gruenberg (1961), Heinicke (1960) and Hood-Williams (1960).[1] The major point is that defectors (alternatively 'terminators' or 'discontinuers') constitute an inappropriate control group because they may be less disturbed individuals who are able to respond favourably to the diagnostic procedure alone. The hypothesis certainly appears reasonable, though none of the critiques actually cite experimental findings which bear directly on it. There are, however, a number of investigations which do have direct bearing.

One study (Levitt, 1957b) shows that defector cases and those who

---

Levitt, E. E. (1963) 'Psychotherapy with children: a further evaluation.' *Behaviour Research and Therapy*, 1, 45–51.

have had some treatment do not differ on 61 factors, including two clinical estimates of severity of symptoms, and eight other factors relating to symptoms. Another study (Levitt, 1958a) found that experienced mental health professionals were unable to detect a difference in severity of symptoms between treated and defector child cases, based on case records. On a 5-point scale, the mean severity ratings were 3·02 for the defector children and 2·98 for the treated cases. Judgments of motivation for treatment also did not distinguish the two groups.

Ross and Lacey (1961) found that the defector cases had fewer histories of developmental difficulties, fewer 'unusual behaviours' (confusion, disorientation, panic reactions, unpredictable, meaningless and self-destructive acts), a lower incidence of specific somatic complaints, and less parental 'marital disharmony' (not including divorce and separation). The defectors also tended to have had shorter waiting periods between application and intake interview. There was no relationship to socio-economic status. Lake and Levinger (1960) did find a relationship with socio-economic status, with the defectors tending to come from lower strata, but they found no relationship between continuing into therapy and the length of the waiting period. They report positive correlations between continuing into treatment and motivation of the parent for treatment.

A follow-up study of 142 defectors (Levitt, 1958b) disclosed that a family member was clearly resistant to treatment in 24 per cent of the cases, but 52 per cent attributed defection to deficiencies of the clinic, or to environmental circumstances.

Overall, the findings seem to be in conflict. Some of the studies appear to indicate that the defectors are less disturbed, but some appear to show no differences. One study shows a relationship to the socio-economic status, while another does not. The waiting period and parental motivation were found to be associated with termination in one study, but not in another.

The problem in attempting to reconcile these conflicting findings is that the definitions of 'treated' and 'defector' vary among studies. In the Levitt (1957b, 1958a) studies, a treated case was one which had at least five treatment interviews; in the Ross and Lacey study (1961) a minimum of 16 interviews. The term is not defined specifically in the Lake and Levinger investigation (1960). A defector in the Levitt studies is a case which had had a complete diagnostic work-up, had been accepted for therapy, and had failed the appropriate appointment when it was offered. For Ross and Lacey, a defector is one who had less than 5 treatment interviews, and terminated against clinic advice. In the Lake and Levinger study, a defector is a case which broke contact with the clinic after a complete application procedure, including an interview, but no diagnostic work-up. It is entirely possible that these differences in definition lie at the root of the discrepancies in findings.

Ideally, the defector should be an individual who has been procedurally identical with the treated case except for the factor of formal treatment itself. In the Ross-Lacey investigation, the defectors could have had as many as four treatment interviews. In the Lake-Levinger study, the defectors had not been subjected to diagnostic evaluation, and had evidently, therefore, not actually been accepted for treatment. Only in the Levitt investigations does the handling of the defector case appear to satisfy the criterion. If we accept the results of these studies (Levitt, 1957b; Levitt, 1958a) then the conclusion is that there does not seem to be any basis for the view that the defector cases were more or less seriously disturbed than treated cases, at the time of diagnostic evaluation.

It is probably true that a defector group contains a percentage of cases which have noticeably improved in the interim between the diagnostic evaluation and the offer of therapy.[2] The critics of the 1957 review speculate that the defector group may be a poor control because it is likely to contain substantially more of such cases than will the group which eventually goes on to formal treatment.

There are several arguments against this contention. It has been pointed out (Levitt, 1960) that follow-up interviews with parents of defector cases suggest that about 18 per cent terminated contact with the clinic because of the interim symptomatic improvement. Only about 12 per cent offered this as the sole explanation for termination. This percentage could, of course, affect an inter-group comparison, but it hardly seems sufficient to account for an overall improvement rate of some 65 per cent.

The second point is simply that the treated group might also have an interim improvement rate, which would balance, or partly offset, this phenomenon in the defector group.

Interim improvement is usually a corollary of the hypothesis that the defectors are less seriously disturbed initially, since such a child is more apt to be improved by a brief contact. Another argument against the idea of interim improvement as a bias follows from the evidence which appears to suggest that the defectors are not, in fact, less seriously disturbed.

Summing up, we can say that the defectors may be a biased control group, though the available evidence appears to indicate otherwise. The need for such a control is undeniable and no one has yet suggested a superior method of establishing the baseline of spontaneous remission.

Eisenberg and Gruenberg (1961) and Eisenberg, Gilbert *et al.* (1961) believe that failure to distinguish among diagnostic categories tends to obfuscate an evaluation of outcome. They argue that it would be more revealing to match treated and defector control groups by diagnosis. The contention appears reasonable; spontaneous remission is usually variable among illnesses. Unfortunately, data on defector groups by diagnostic categories are not available. It is possible, however, to determine whether outcome varies by diagnosis among treated cases, which is the logical first step. The present review of evaluation studies will attempt to accomplish this.

The present review

The present review is based on twenty-two publications in which evaluative data are presented.[3] More than half of these are evaluations at follow-up rather than at close, but no distinction is made in this review. Some of the follow-up intervals are very short, and the interval is not stated in some studies. Furthermore, the combined breakdowns into diagnostic categories and into follow-up and close studies would fractionate the data to the point where comparisons would be unfeasible.

Data from the investigations are divided into five groups according to diagnostic criteria. Two groups are reasonably clear cut; psychotic children (Annesley, 1961; Bender and Gurevitz, 1955; Hamilton *et al.*, 1961; Kane and Chambers, 1961; Kaufman *et al.*, 1962), and those with special symptoms such as enuresis, tics, and school phobia (Hersov, 1960; Lazarus and Abramovitz, 1962; Phillips, 1961; Rodriguez *et al.*, 1959; Zausmer, 1954). A third group deals with cases of delinquency, aggressive behaviours, antisocial acting-out, etc. (Annesley, 1961; Cytryn *et al.*, 1960; Eisenberg *et al.*, 1958a; Morris *et al.*, 1956; Rexford *et al.*, 1956). The fourth group is roughly analogous to the adult neurotic (Annesley, 1961; Dorfman, 1958; Eisenberg, Gilbert *et al.*, 1961). The fifth group, which is by far the largest, is a mixed one in which a number of different diagnostic categories are represented, and includes accounts of general or unclassified child guidance clinic samples (Chess, 1957; La Vietes *et al.*, 1960; Miller, 1957: O'Neal and Robins, 1958a; Phillips, 1960; Seidman, 1957). The groupings are not entirely pure, but there is little overlap. By and large, cases of organicity have been excluded.

The establishment of a separate category for children with special symptoms does not imply that such a symptom may not be pathognomic of a more extensive psychological disorder. The distinction is required by the fact that the evaluation of therapy in these cases is based solely on outcome of treatment of the special symptom.

The therapy procedures which are represented in the studies cover a fairly broad range, including counselling with parents, environmental manipulation, techniques based on learning theory, nondirective counselling of children, and the use of adjunctive drugs. Shock therapies, chemotherapy as the exclusive approach, and other somatic treatments have been excluded. Several recent innovations in therapeutic methods are also excluded, largely because the numbers of cases are small, or because a system evaluation procedure does not appear in the study. Included in this category are Charny's 'isolation treatment' (Charny, 1961), and the operant conditioning techniques of Ferster and DeMyer (1961).

Results

The data from the twenty-two evaluation studies are summarized in table 12.1. The customary trichotomous breakdown is employed: Much

TABLE 12.1
SUMMARY OF EVALUATION DATA FROM TWENTY-TWO STUDIES

Type of disorder	Number of studies	Much improved (N)	Much improved (%)	Partly improved (N)	Partly improved (%)	Unimproved (N)	Unimproved (%)	Total (N)	Overall (%) improved
Neurosis	3	34	15	107	46	89	39	230	61
Acting-out	5	108	31	84	24	157	45	349	55
Special symptoms	5	114	54	49	23	50	23	213	77
Psychosis	5	62	25	102	40	88	35	252	65
Mixed	6	138	20	337	48	222	32	697	68
Total	24*	456	26·2	679	39·0	606	34·8	1741	65·2

* The study of Annesley (1961) contributed data to three classifications

Improved includes any classification indicating great improvement, or 'cured'; any classification indicating lesser degree of improvement, such as 'partly', 'moderately', or 'slightly', is subsumed under Partly Improved; the Unimproved class also takes in 'worse'.

The overall improvement rate for the 1,741 cases in the present review is 65·2 per cent. Since evaluations at close and follow-up are not separated, the pooled defector rate of 72·5 per cent must be used as the baseline (Levitt, 1957a). This rate is significantly greater than the 65·2 per cent rate found in the present study. However, if we eliminate the psychotic and acting-out children (an attempt was made to do this in the earlier review) the adjusted figure becomes 68·3 per cent which does not differ significantly from the defector rate of 72·5 per cent.

If we pool all evaluation studies in the 1957 review, we find that 73·3 per cent of the cases show improvement. This is significantly higher than the improvement rate for studies in the present review. Again, an elimination of the psychotic and acting-out children from the present group makes the comparability more exact. We find, nonetheless, that the adjusted improvement rate of 68·3 per cent in the present study is still significantly lower than the rate for studies in the 1957 review. However, a difference of 5 per cent could easily be due to differences in sampling, treatment procedures, evaluation methods, and other sources of variation. Its clinical significance is certainly negligible.

Discussion

The results of this second review of evaluations of outcome of therapy with children are similar to those of the earlier review, and like those earlier findings, do not differ markedly from results obtained with defector cases. And again, the inescapable conclusion is that available evaluation studies do not furnish a reasonable basis for the hypothesis that psychotherapy facilitates recovery from emotional illness in children.

Apart from this global inference, the data suggest that there is merit in Eisenberg's contention that comparisons of treated and defector cases ought to be made within diagnostic categories. It appears that the improvement rate with therapy is lowest for cases of delinquency and antisocial acting-out, and highest for identifiable behavioural symptoms, like enuresis and school phobia. However, until the required comparisons are actually made, it would be incautious to conclude that therapy is more or less successful with any diagnostic group. It is perfectly possible that the spontaneous remission rate, as indicated by appropriate defector control groups, is also lower for the delinquents and higher for the special symptoms, and that the differences which are found in table 12.1 simply reflect these facts.

Strupp's statement (1962) that we have not yet arrived at the appropriate time for a definitive outcome study is probably quite true. It also appears true that in recent years, research attention has turned away from the evaluation of outcome *per se* and has taken up the therapist and the therapy process as phenomena for investigation. However, the study of therapeutic dyad or of the personality of the therapist as a variable, or other process phenomena, does not obviate the need for precise measurement of outcome. To find the personality or the process which makes for successful treatment, we must still have an appropriate evaluation of that treatment. As Strupp (1962) says, 'Concerted effort is needed to develop meaningful and measurable criteria of therapeutic outcome.' It is hard to see how this can be done without continuing to evaluate the outcome of therapy itself.

Notes

1 By restricting his analysis of data to only two studies, Heinicke was able to arrive at the conclusion that treated children at least showed a greater degree of 'successful adjustment', while the control cases showed a greater percentage of 'partial improvements'. In addition to the obvious potential effect of selecting two investigations from many, those who are experienced psychotherapists cannot help but be struck by the greater difficulty in distinguishing among degrees of improvement, as opposed to distinguishing between any improvement and no improvement whatsoever. This suggests that the distinction between 'successful' and 'partial' will usually be relatively unreliable. Eisenberg classified neurosis in children as a 'disorder for which there is reasonable likelihood of response to treatment', but admits that no definite conclusion concerning the efficacy of psychotherapy can be ventured at present. Despite his criticisms, Hood-Williams accepts the defectors as a control group, 'albeit with reservations, whose very nature demands that conclusions drawn from them should be highly tentative'. A detailed rebuttal of his critique has already appeared (Levitt, 1960).

2 It is a common belief among clinic workers that this improvement is a function of therapeutic properties of the diagnostic procedure. If this is indeed true, then

the amount of such improvement is likely to vary considerably from clinic to clinic, as the evidence (Filmer-Bennett and Hillson, 1959; Phillips, 1957) indicates that the diagnostic procedure varies. However, the etiology of the improvement is not relevant to the argument.

3 As in the earlier review, several studies have been excluded because of overlapping, and other reasons. Eisenberg's data (1958b) are included in the later study of Rodriguez et al. (1959). A second publication by O'Neal and Robins (1958b) includes data of an original publication (1958a). The latter is used because of its more complete presentation. The general improvement–non-improvement findings are similar. Most of the results of the study by Cytryn et al. (1960) are included in the subsequent paper by Eisenberg et al. (1961). The article by Cunningham et al. (1956) appeared in the earlier review as an unpublished paper. The study of Michael et al. (1957) is inappropriate since only 25 of 606 treated cases were located at follow-up.

SHEPHERD, M., OPPENHEIM, A. N. and
MITCHELL, S.

13. Childhood Behaviour Disorders and the Child Guidance Clinic: An Epidemiological Study

Introduction

The Buckinghamshire Child Survey

The disturbances of behaviour exhibited by children who are referred to child guidance clinics raise two fundamental questions. The first turns on the distribution in the general population of behavioural characteristics which child psychiatrists have traditionally taken to signify morbidity. Here Kanner (1957) has commented with justice on the tendency by clinicians to disregard the selective nature of their case-material: 'This selectiveness, in the absence of "normal controls", has often resulted in a tendency to attribute to single behaviour items an exaggerated "seriousness" with regard to their intrinsic psychopathologic significance . . . in clinical statistics, those same symptoms, figuring among the traits found in the histories of "problem children", are apt to be given too prominent a place, far out of proportion to their role as everyday problems or near-problems of the everyday child.'

The second question arises from the fact that most clinical observation of children's behaviour is initiated by intermediate lay observers who bring the child to medical attention. For this reason much of our knowledge of behaviour disorders in childhood depends on the reports of adults, especially parents and teachers. Again, Kanner (1960) elucidates the situation: '. . . There is no absolute criterion for the normalcy of any of the common forms of behaviour problems of

Shepherd, M., Oppenheim, A. N. and Mitchell, S. (1966) 'Childhood behaviour disorders and the child guidance clinic: an epidemiological study.' *Journal of Child Psychology and Psychiatry, 7*, 39–52.

children. Their evaluation is bound up tightly with the general outlook of the evaluating agent. . . . A mother who is preoccupied with calories, vitamins and the weight chart will have a different notion about her child's food intake from one who is wholesomely casual about the whole matter of eating. . . . In fact, the very term "feeding problem" implies that a child's ingestion of food is at least as much an issue of the feeder as of the eater.'

In the light of these considerations it is surprising to find how few studies have been concerned with the patterns of juvenile behaviour in the general population and the part played by key adults in the interpretation of that behaviour (Macfarlane et al., 1954; Ministry of Education, 1955; Glidewell et al., 1963; Lapouse et al., 1964).

Such work clearly demands a broad epidemiological framework. This has been provided by the present authors in a large-scale survey carried out in the county of Buckinghamshire where, in 1961, questionnaires were sent out to the parents and teachers of a one in ten sample of children attending local authority schools in the county. The sample children were identified from every tenth card in the records of the school medical services for the county. The relevant class teacher was then asked to complete a questionnaire about each survey child and also to act as an agent for transmitting and returning the questionnaires to the children's parents. Of 6,920 forms sent out to parents, 6,287 (91 per cent) were received back completed. Teachers filled in questionnaires for 6,632 (96 per cent) of the children.

The questionnaire which went out to parents was based on that used by Cattell and Coan (1957), modified to record behaviour problems rather than personality variables as in the original version (see p. 185). From the material collected in this way quantitative information was obtained about the reported behaviour of a large, representative sample of children between the ages of 5 and 15. It was also possible to compare the socio-medical differences between sub-groups defined in behavioural terms (Mitchell, 1965). In addition, however, the data suggested the need to investigate another problem, for many of these supposedly normal children displayed not only individual items of behaviour which in intensity or frequency lay towards the apparently pathological extreme of each behavioural continuum; a proportion of them were also reported to exhibit combinations of 'problems' which appeared to be virtually identical with those encountered commonly among patients at child guidance clinics. Accordingly, it was clearly of practical as well as of theoretical interest to compare such children with those who are referred to medical care for ostensibly similar complaints. This study was designed to make such a comparison.

Method

The core of the investigation consisted in a comparison between a group of 50 children attending child guidance clinics for the first time in 1962, and a group of matched children from the main sample who had never attended such a clinic. The clinic group was obtained so far as possible by taking each consecutive new case attending for diagnostic interview. Since one of the purposes of the study was to investigate voluntary attendance at child guidance clinics by children and their parents, it was decided to exclude from the survey all children who were attending a clinic for a court report or as a condition of probation (5 cases), and those who were in residential schools or children's homes (6 cases); 3 families in which another child was already attending the clinic were also excluded. Further, since the intention was to match the children attending clinics with those with similar behaviour from the main school sample, children were also excluded if they were younger than 5 years of age (12 cases) or older than 15 years (4 cases); if they were suffering from psychosis, epilepsy, or brain damage (4 cases); or if their problems were of a type not covered by the questionnaire used in the main survey, e.g. sexual delinquency, attempted suicide (15 cases). To these exceptions were added two refusals, one removal, and three children seen by clinic staff at domiciliary visits. The excluded categories involved most of the more 'severe' cases seen at the clinics. In all they amounted to 27 per cent of the children aged 5 to 15 years attending clinics. It therefore appears that the group of 50 children included in the study may be taken as reasonably representative of three out of four children of school age attending child guidance clinics.

The parent of each clinic child was interviewed by the research worker either at the first visit to the clinic or as soon as possible thereafter. At this semi-structured interview the parent described the 'problems' that had led to the child's referral, the attitudes and reactions of family members and other persons to the child's behaviour, any action taken to deal with it, the route to the child guidance clinic, and parental feelings about referral. Information was also obtained about the parents' social educational and occupational background, and their physical and mental health. In addition, each parent was asked to complete one of the questionnaires used in the main sample survey and a report was obtained from the child's school.

From the questionnaire completed by the parent of the clinic child a Hollerith card was punched to show the child's age, sex and behaviour. A special note was also made on each card of the presenting symptoms at the clinic. The cards of all children in the main sample of the same age and sex as the clinic children were sorted, and those which recorded behaviour similar to the presenting problems of the clinic children were extracted. The sample cards were then compared by eye with those for the clinic attender, and the child who showed the most similar behavioural profile was selected to make a matched pair for the corresponding clinic child. To avoid having to repeat this procedure if the matched child were, for some reason, unobtainable other suitable children were also listed at the same time.

The mothers of the matched children were then interviewed by the research worker in their own homes and invited to give an account of the behaviour specified on the questionnaire. The following pairs of case-histories illustrate the nature of the information and the quality of matching:

1 (a) *Clinic child*

M.X., a girl aged 12 yr, was referred to a child guidance clinic because of difficult behaviour at home. She had violent tantrums every two or three days in which she stamped, cried, shouted that no one loved her and rushed up to her bedroom where she stood in front of the mirror with tears pouring down her face. If asked to help her mother she would either 'gaze in front of her and pretend she doesn't hear' or do it very slowly 'one fork at a time' while complaining about how ill-used she was. She had several times said that she was leaving home but had never been farther than the bottom of the road. She told numerous lies. For instance, she had told her mother that school did not start until 9.10 a.m. when, in fact, she should have been there at 9 o'clock; she then told her teacher that she was late because her mother would not make her breakfast in time. For about twelve months she had been enuretic during the day at home but not at school. She would then change and leave the wet pants all round the house. The enuresis had, however, stopped about one month before the interview after a visit to the family doctor.

The only person with whom she had a good personal relationship was said to be her maternal grandmother, with whom the family had lived for the first three years of her life. With her own parents she made little response to affection or attempts to reason with her. She was very jealous of her younger brother and would provoke him. She did not mix much with the other children in the area and was becoming so rude and unpleasant to adult visitors that her parents had become reluctant to invite visitors to the home.

(b) Matched child

S.Y., a girl aged 13 yr, had been a difficult child since an admission to hospital with scarlet fever when she was 2½ yr old. As a baby had cried so much that the mother stated: 'When I got pregnant again I said I hope I don't have another grizzly little bitch like that one.' She had always been quick-tempered and would lie on the floor and scream if crossed in any way. When chastised she became distraught. These outbursts occurred almost daily. She was underweight (70 lb on her thirteenth birthday) with a very small appetite and, when upset, she refused all food. The mother complained that she would not do anything to help in the house and that she would not obey either of her parents. She got on better with her father and with the older brothers but 'hated' her mother and her younger sister. She had no sympathy with her mother's disability arising from an arthritic shoulder which she regarded as 'just laziness'. She had one friend at school but otherwise no social contacts. Her only interest was the school drama club; otherwise she just stayed at home watching television most of the time.

2 (a) Clinic child

M.P., a boy aged 10 yr, was referred to a child guidance clinic because of refusal to leave his home for the past three months. Previously he had been an energetic boy, good at sport, popular with his school-mates and sufficiently independent to undertake an unescorted coach journey to visit his grandparents. He had begun to complain of feeling 'weak and dizzy', stating that his 'stomach turned over' if he took food or drink and that his 'head wanted to burst out of his skin'. He had become very faddy about food. On some days he would eat nothing, though on others he was still capable of taking a good meal. The only liquid he would take was about half a pint of lemon squash daily. He said that he felt too 'dizzy' to go to school and, if delivered there forcibly by his father in the car, would cry violently, threaten to jump out of the moving car and, on arrival, either run away or stand sobbing in the cloakroom. He had become very tearful and irritable; he cried and threw things if he were crossed in any way. He took no interest in his friends but would spend his time in the house using his Meccano set or making model aeroplanes.

(b) Matched child

B.G., a boy aged 10 yr, had suffered from a stream of minor ailments for the previous two years. He had constant sore throats and colds; he had headaches several times a week; and he developed 'water blisters' of unknown causation. He had become very anxious about his health. He washed his hands frequently because of 'germs'; he gargled; he brushed his teeth frequently; and he made his mother examine his ears and throat every day. He was afraid of dogs; he was afraid to go upstairs by himself, particularly in the dark. He was faddy about food and would not eat fish, eggs or milk. He worried a lot, had bad dreams and occasionally walked in his sleep. He disliked school intensely and would go off in the morning looking very tearful and sometimes 'downright ill', so that neighbours had asked if he ought not to be kept at home. Sometimes he vomited in the morning and often refused to eat his breakfast, but unless he had a temperature he was sent to school where he ceased to complain. It was the process of leaving home that he could not bear. He was regarded as backward at school and had been unable to read when he entered junior school at the age of eight though he had since made progress. He had friends at school but once he had returned home he was unwilling to go out again to play with them. His brothers teased him a lot and he reacted with tears and tantrums; his relationship with his father was poor.

In 1964 the parents of both the clinic and the non-clinic children were again approached and re-interviewed by the research worker whenever possible. Psychiatrists treating the clinic children were given advance notice that the parents were to be approached. In two instances the doctor asked that the interview should be omitted on the grounds that such enquiries would interfere with the relationship between psychotherapist and child. In all other cases there were no obstacles imposed by the medical authorities. Four sets of clinic parents refused to be re-interviewed and only an incomplete interview was possible with another three. Among the non-clinic children, seven sets of parents could not be contacted. The remaining 87 parents were seen in their own homes and asked about any changes in behaviour which had taken place since the last interview. The original problems were discussed in detail and, in most cases, a standard (follow-up) parents' questionnaire was also completed at the interview.[1] This procedure made it possible to detect and investigate any new problems which had appeared during the interim period.

Results

The results of this investigation fall logically into two categories: (A) the initial differences between the child guidance cases and their 'matched' controls; and (B) the outcome of both groups.

A. Comparisons between children referred to child guidance clinics and matched children
1. *Factors associated with the process of referral*
   (a) *Severity of disturbances.* It was manifestly imperative at the outset to eliminate the possibility that referral to a child guidance clinic depended only on the degree of behavioural disturbance. To obtain a clinical assessment of severity, ratings of behaviour were made for each child by five raters, four psychiatrists and one clinical psychologist,

TABLE 13.1

AVERAGE 'DISTURBANCE RATING' SCORE OF 50 CLINIC CHILDREN AND 50 MATCHED CHILDREN

Average rating score	No. of children	
	Clinic children	Matched children
1 ⎫	1	1
⎬ (mild)		
2 ⎭	12	23
3 (moderate)	29	22
4 (severe)	8	4
Total	50	50

$$\chi^2 = 5\cdot 5;\ 2\ df.;\ p < 0\cdot 10 > 0\cdot 05$$

all of whom assessed the records of each child independently. Each rater was given a typewritten profile from which details bearing on contacts with child guidance clinics and related agencies were omitted; the 100 case-histories were presented in random order so that no indication of matching was given. A five-point rating scale was employed, ranging from 'very severe' to 'very mild'. As we were chiefly concerned with inter-rater comparisons each rater was permitted to employ an individual frame of reference in defining these categories. A 'disturbance rating' was obtained by scoring, adding and averaging the original ratings.

Table 13.1 shows there to have been a non-significant trend towards more severe ratings for the clinic children; the ratings for matched pairs were identical in 27 instances and for a further 11 pairs the difference in average rating score was less than one point. In three-quarters of the pairs there was the same rating for both children of a matched pair by at least one rater. The degree of disturbance could not, therefore, be taken as the sole determinant of referral.

(b) *Other factors.* A close examination was made of (i) *geographical distance from the clinic,* (ii) *the presence of young children in the household,* (iii) *gainful employment of the mother,* and (iv) *parental reactions* to the children's behaviour. Of these factors only parental reactions distinguished between the two groups.

Parental reactions to children's behaviour. These reactions were assessed by the research worker at the interview. The assessment was based partly on the parent's own description of her feelings and those of her husband, in response to direct questioning, and partly on the terms in which the child and his problems were described spontaneously, and the actions already taken to deal with them. Table 13.2 shows that the most obvious difference lay in the number of non-clinic mothers who accepted their children's behaviour as a temporary difficulty and saw no reason to seek medical advice for it. This general trend towards increased tolerance was particularly obvious among the mothers of the matched girls; by contrast, only one clinic mother expressed herself in this way and her child had arrived at the clinic after admission to hospital as the result of an accident.

Clinic-attending mothers worried significantly more about their children and were correspondingly more puzzled and helpless about coping with them. Compared with non-clinic parents they discussed their children's problems significantly more with the school authorities (62 : 26 per cent) and, probably as a result, with the school doctor (26 : 4 per cent) though there was little difference in the proportions consulting their family doctor (70 : 60 per cent). Mothers of girls who came to clinics expressed themselves as being more irritated and

TABLE 13.2

MOTHER'S REACTION TO CHILD BEHAVIOUR

Mother's reaction	Number of boys		Number of girls	
	Clinic children (N = 29)	Matched children (N = 29)	Clinic children (N = 21)	Matched children (N = 21)
Problems not seen to exist	2*	2	1*	2
Problem seen to exist but regarded as inevitable because due to developmental phase or environmental pressure‡	—	5	—	10
Primarily worry about the child's future welfare or present unhappiness‡	10	5	10	3
Primarily bewilderment, inability to cope†	5	2	7	1
Exasperation and irritation	13	14	10	4
Fear of delinquency or Court proceedings for absence from school	3	1	2	1
Problem regarded as educational only	—	1	—	—
Problems regarded as purely physical	—	3	—	4

N.B. It is possible for one child to appear in more than one category: the column total is not therefore the same as the number of children in the group.

    * Attended clinics under pressure from the child's school

    † For both sexes combined, χ^2-test (with Yates' correction: $p < 0.05$

    ‡ For both sexes combined, χ^2-test (with Yates' correction): $p < 0.001$

exasperated by their children's behaviour than did their matched counterparts; this difference was not so apparent among the boys' parents.

2. Background factors

(a) *Occupational class of father.* The occupational class of father was measured by the Hall-Jones scale (Hall and Jones, 1950). There proved to be a significant difference between the two groups, the proportion of fathers in non-manual jobs being twice as great among the clinic children (40 per cent) as among the others (20 per cent) (x^2 test: $p < 0.05$). This difference was particularly marked in the upper strata of each occupational group, but it may, to some extent, reflect the methods by which the control group was selected: all matched children were taken from the main sample of children attending local authority schools and the exclusion of private school pupils must have eliminated a number of children in the upper social classes.

(b) *Age of parents.* This factor proved to be very similar in both groups, whether recorded as the parental age at the child's birth or age at the time of survey.

(c) *Family disruption, death or separation experiences.* Among the clinic children, ten had lost at least one parent permanently, compared with three in the non-clinic group. The loss of a father, by desertion or divorce, was significantly more marked among the clinic boys (6 cases) than among the others (no cases) (Fisher's exact (2-tailed) test, $p = 0.0186$). There was also a tendency for the clinic children to have suffered the loss of an older sib more often than the non-clinic group (7 cases to 3) but this difference is not statistically significant.

(d) *Mental health of parent.* More clinic-attending mothers (34) saw themselves as 'suffering from nerves' than those in the non-clinic group (27 cases). In particular the clinic mothers were more apt to describe themselves as anxious and easily upset by stress which caused them to faint, vomit, and develop diarrhoea or pains; as feeling mildly depressed, tired and unappreciated, and as finding it difficult to cope with their house, husband and children. Fourteen clinic-attending mothers fell into this category compared with 6 non-clinic mothers. Though the difference is not significant these findings support Winnicott's (1965) thesis that there is a tendency for some mothers to bring their children to clinics in an attempt to obtain relief for their own mild depression.

Furthermore, there appeared to be some evidence to suggest a possible relationship between the presence in a parent of a degree of mental illness sufficient to require treatment either by a psychiatrist or by the family doctor, or which had been severe enough to limit the person's activities (fear of leaving the house, fear of crowds in shops, for instance), and the severity of the child's disturbance. Thus of the 31 children, one of whose parents suffered from such a disability, 7 (23 per cent) were assessed as severely disturbed and 9 (29 per cent) as mildly so compared with 5 (7 per cent) and 28 (41 per cent) respectively of the 68 other children who were resident with parents or step-parents.[2]

B. Comparison of outcome of the two groups

Status at follow-up interview. The information provided by the parents about the child's state in 1964 was written-up as before, and the degree of improvement or deterioration shown by the children's status at follow-up was assessed by three of the observers who had made the original ratings. In each case the assessor was provided with both the old and the new profiles and the original rating. Again, all references to any treatment received by the child were omitted and the raters had no means of knowing which children had attended psychiatric clinics. The assessment was rated on a five-point scale.

According to these ratings 55 children (63 per cent) had improved over the interim period; 21 children (24 per cent) had remained in the same state as before, though not necessarily with the same behavioural disturbance; and only 11 children (13 per cent) had deteriorated. Most strikingly, table 13.3 shows that there was no significant difference between the two groups in respect of improvement or deterioration.

TABLE 13.3

STATE AT FOLLOW-UP OF 50 CHILDREN WHO HAD ATTENDED
CHILD GUIDANCE CLINICS AND 50 MATCHED CHILDREN

Average improvement/ deterioration rating at follow-up	Clinic-attending children		Matched children	
	No.	%	No.	%
Improved	29	65	26*	61
Unchanged	8	18	13*	30
Worse	7	16	4	9
Total Number of Children	44	100	43	100

$\chi^2 = 2\cdot81$; 2 *df.*; not significant

* Including one child in each category who had been referred to a child guidance clinic during the follow-up interval and had received treatment

An analysis was then made of the amount of treatment received. A comparison of the mean number of visits paid to a psychiatrist, with the change in rated status, revealed there to have been virtually no difference in the average number of clinic attendances between those who improved and those who deteriorated. The children whose state was assessed as unchanged were those with the largest average number of attendances, averaging 15 psychiatric sessions each compared with approximately nine sessions for the other two groups. Further, in the group of children who did improve, were 83 per cent of those who attended clinics for from one to five sessions, 33 per cent of those with 6–15 sessions and 63 per cent of those who had received more intensive treatment or who had received special schooling.

It can, of course, be argued that the children showing most improvement on minimal treatment were those who were least disturbed initially, and those failing to improve after more lengthy treatment were those who were most disturbed originally. This did not prove to be the case (table 13.4). Of the 9 clinic children who were originally rated as 'severely disturbed' 8 were improved at follow-up but only 2 had received more than 5 sessions with a psychiatrist, and none had received special education. Again, among the 5 originally 'mild' cases who had failed to improve 4 had received more than 5 sessions of psychiatric help.

TABLE 13.4

OUTCOME OF CHILDREN BY INITIAL RATING OF DISTURBANCE AND FREQUENCY OF ATTENDANCE AT A CHILD GUIDANCE CLINIC OR CLINIC-INITIATED CLASS OR SCHOOL

| Original level of disturbance | No. of attendances made at clinic or class | Outcome | | | |
| | | Improved | | Not improved | |
		No.	%	No.	%
'Mild'	None (controls)	14	67	7	33
	5 or fewer	3	75	1	25
	6 or more*	4	50	4	50
'Moderate'	None (controls)	9	53	8	47
	5 or fewer	6	75	2	25
	6 or more*	9	53	8	47
'Severe'	None (controls)	2	67	1	33
	5 or fewer	6	100	—	—
	6 or more*	2	67	1	33

For all grades of severity combined overall χ^2 shows no significant association between number of attendances and outcome ($\chi^2 = 5\cdot25$; $df. = 2$; $0\cdot10 > p > 0\cdot05$).

* This category includes all those attending classes and schools

Discussion

A psychiatrically sophisticated general practitioner has commented of his own practice that '. . . for each child referred to child guidance clinics there are five, equally disturbed, not referred' (Ryle, 1963). The findings of this study demonstrate that a supposedly normal population can include children with behaviour disturbances comparable to those of patients at a child guidance clinic. For these children referral to a child guidance clinic is related chiefly to parental reactions. The mothers of clinic children were more apt to be anxious, depressed and easily upset by stress; they were less able to cope with their children, more apt to discuss their problems and to seek advice. Even though our clinic population was deliberately selected to exclude the most severe cases, the case material was otherwise unselected and represented the majority of children seen by child psychiatrists in the county.

The most obvious inference to be drawn from these data is the existence of a large pool of morbidity in the community which, it might be maintained, should be countered by expanded public health measures, in particular by an increase in the number of child guidance clinics. Caution, however, is enjoined by the results at follow-up: while 63 per cent of the clinic cases had improved after 2 years, so had 61 per cent of matched children who had not attended the clinics, and whose parents had at interview confirmed the existence of disturbed behaviour.

On the basis of this study, then, we would suggest that many so-called disturbances of behaviour are no more than temporary exaggerations of widely distributed reaction-patterns. The transient nature of these reactions is demonstrated by the tendency to spontaneous improvement in the untreated children and also by a follow-up study of a larger group of 400 children (Mitchell, 1965). Clearly childhood behaviour cannot be deemed morbid without some knowledge about its frequency, intensity, duration, and association with other forms of behaviour, and the setting in which it occurs. The limits of deviance have to be closely defined in this field.

The implications of this viewpoint for medical services are equally important. They have been adumbrated by Buckle and Lebovici (1960) as follows: 'all children show signs of disturbed behaviour at some time or another, and professional intervention is justified only if the disorder persists long enough to authorize a prognosis of lifelong disorder, or when the disturbance is serious . . .'. At the present time, the prognosis of most behaviour disorders is difficult to make because of the small number of longitudinal studies. If, however, it can be shown that certain types of children are more likely to improve spontaneously and that certain problems are likely to disappear with increasing age, then such children and their parents could be provided with support or advice. The greater portion of limited resources could be devoted to those children with behaviour patterns or family circumstances which indicate that spontaneous remission is unlikely to occur.

Notes

1 The behavioural items on this questionnaire were identical with those of the original (see appendix); only subsequent changes in social and personal circumstances were recorded.

2 The numbers involved are too small to use a χ^2-test to assess the significance of this association. Using Fisher's exact (2-tailed) measurement of probability, however, the probability level is $p = 0.054$. This just fails to attain significance.

Appendix

QUESTIONNAIRE ADMINISTERED TO PARENTS

CHILD HEALTH SURVEY

A

Below are some descriptions of illnesses and health problems which can affect children. If any item is true of.................will you please put a line under *Yes*. If the item does not apply to this child then please put the line under *No*.

This child

1. Wears glasses always ...... Yes No
2. Wears glasses sometimes ... Yes No
3. Is having treatment for eyes at clinic or hospital .... Yes No
4. Has had persistent ear-ache or running ear during the last twelve months .... Yes No
5. Seems to have difficulty in hearing sometimes .... Yes No
6. Has a hearing aid .... Yes No
7. Suffers from sick headaches Yes No
8. Gets travel-sick in car, bus or train .... Yes No
9. Has frequent colds or sore throats .... Yes No
10. Has a persistent and trouble-some cough .... Yes No
11. Is overweight .... Yes No
12. Is underweight .... Yes No
13. Has fainted more than twice in life .... Yes No
14. Is highly strung .... Yes No
15. Has suffered from a rash or other skin trouble which lasted for two weeks or longer .... Yes No
16. Has to wear special support for bone or muscle disorder (for instance, iron on leg, built-up shoe, etc.) .... Yes No
17. Has to wear brace on teeth Yes No
18. Has a stammer .... Yes No

Has a *doctor* ever said that this child suffered from
19. Any disease or disorder of the bones (*Not* a broken bone) .... Yes No
20. Any disease or disorder affecting muscles .... Yes No
21. Heart trouble .... Yes No
22. Eczema .... Yes No
23. Asthma .... Yes No
24. Tuberculosis .... Yes No
25. Any chronic lung trouble (such as chronic Bronchitis) Yes No
26. St. Vitus Dance .... Yes No
27. Meningitis (Brain Fever) ... Yes No
28. Migraine .... Yes No
29. Cerebral Palsy ('Spastic') ... Yes No
30. Fits or Convulsions .... Yes No
31. Diabetes .... Yes No
32. Rheumatic Fever .... Yes No
33. Hare-lip or Cleft palate ... Yes No
34. Any disorder of the glands (*Not* just swollen neck glands) .... Yes No
35. Any other physical handicap or *chronic* illness. If so, what is it? Please write it below .... Yes No

....

....

For *Girls* only:
36. Have periods started yet? .... Yes No
37. At what age was first period (write in number) ....
38. If periods have started, does she
   (a) Worry about it.
   (b) Feel sick.
   (c) Complain of pains.
   (d) Have to stay away from school or go to bed.
   (e) Usually have no trouble or worry at all.

Please underline any of these items which you think apply to this girl.

For *Boys* only:
39. Has his voice broken yet? .... Yes No
40. If so, at what age did this happen? ....

B

Below are some statements which describe the way that children behave. In each group of three, please underline the description that best suits at the present time.

45. Seldom or never purposely destroy things.
About as destructive as most children of the same age.
Very destructive.
46. Very much afraid of one or more animals (that is ordinary British animals, not lions, tigers, etc.).
A little afraid of some animals.
Not at all afraid of animals.
47. Has no fear of meeting new people.
A little afraid or shy of new people.
Generally fearful of unfamiliar people.
48. Afraid of the dark when in bed at night.
Seems a little uneasy unless a dim light is left on.
Has no fear of the dark.
49. Always tells the truth.
Tells an occasional fib.
Tells deliberate untruths quite often.
50. Likes school very much.
Likes school about as much as most children.
Dislikes going to school.
51. Never takes anything that belongs to someone else.
Has helped himself to someone else's things at least once or twice (including taking things belonging to other members of the family).
Has stolen things on several occasions.
52. Very irritable, easily becomes cross or annoyed.
Occasionally becomes cross (for instance, if tired or provoked by other children).
Very placid nature, practically never gets cross or annoyed.
53. Rather fussy about food, will eat certain things.
Has fairly definite food preferences but will eat most foods if hungry.
Will eat nearly anything.
54. Not at all shy, mixes freely with other children.
A little shy with strange children.
Very shy, bashful, fearful of other children.
55. Always hungry, eats a great deal both at meals and as snacks between meals. Can't stop him eating.
Eats about as much as others of the same age.
Small appetite, inclined to pick at food.
56. Very carefree, doesn't worry about anything.
Occasionally worries (for instance, about tests at school or illness in the family).
Often seems worried, worries about many things.
57. Complains and whines a lot, hard to satisfy.
Complains about as much as most children of the same age.
Seldom or never complains or whines.
58. Very restless and fidgety, cannot sit still for a minute.
About as active as most children of the same age.
Less active than average, likes sitting still as much as possible.
59. Tends to be very jealous.
Occasionally shows jealousy.
Seldom or never jealous.
60. Never wanders off from home without saying where going.
Loiters on way home from school or may go to play with friends without telling parents.
Wanders off for long distances or long periods without parents knowing where.
61. Almost daily has times of being drawn into self and out of touch with other people.
Occasionally seems lost in a dream world.
Seldom or never day dreams.
62. Always does things when told.
About as obedient as most children.
Usually resists when asked or told to do things.
63. Plays truant from school more than once or twice a month.

Plays truant more than three to four times a year.

Never plays truant.

64. Has a very noticeable twitch of face or body, or mannerism, which takes place most of the time.

Has occasional twitches or mannerisms which occur when tired, bored, etc.

Has no twitches or mannerisms.

65. Moods very changeable, on top of the world one minute, down the next for no particular reason.

Occasional changes of mood in response to things that happen.

Runs on very even keel, always the same except under very unusual circumstances.

66. Seemed to have difficulty in learning to read.

Learned to read as quickly as most children.

Good reader, learned to read more quickly than other children.

67. Is there anything about your child's behaviour or habits which worries you but which we have not mentioned? If so, please tell us about it here ....

....

Questionnaire continues overleaf

G

Below is a list of minor health problems which most children have at some time. Please tell us how often each of these happens to this child by putting a tick (√) in the appropiate column.

Example. If this child complains of headaches about once a month you would put the tick (√) in column (e) where it says 'About once a month'. If this child has only had a headache once or twice in his or her whole life, then you would put the tick (√) in column (h) where it says 'Never or less than once a year'.

	(a) Every day or almost every day	(b) Two or three times a week	(c) About once a week	(d) About once every two weeks	(e) About once a month	(f) About once in two or three months	(g) Two or three times a year	(h) Never, or less than once a year
68. Has constipation								
69. Has headaches								
70. Has nightmares or unpleasant or frightening dreams								
71. Is restless in sleep, tosses and turns, kicks off bedclothes, or walks in sleep, etc.								
72. Wets the bed								
73. Has pains in stomach								
74. Vomits								
75. Has diarrhoea								
76. Poor control of bowels, soils self								
77. Cries								
78. Sulks for hours on end								
79. Has real temper tantrums (that is complete loss of temper with shouting, angry movements, etc.)								
80. Bites nails								
81. Sucks thumb or finger								
82. Has bitter quarrels with other children								

ALLEN, K. E., TURNER, K. D. and EVERETT, P. M.

14. A Behaviour Modification Classroom for Head Start Children with Problem Behaviours

Head start programs across the country represent a diversity of educational models. Klein (1969) described a number of these: the traditional nursery school approach exemplified by the Bank Street program, the Deutsch-type programs based on sequential programing with heavy emphasis on listening, the autotelic-discovery approach espoused by Nimnicht and the Far West Laboratory, the cognitively oriented programs modelled after Weickart's work at Ypsilanti, and the 'pressure-cooker' approach of Engelmann and Becker, to name a few. These programs have demonstrated, in varying degrees, their effectiveness in ameliorating the accumulated deficits of young poverty children.

But what about the children with severe behavior disorders who seem to profit little or not at all from a head start program? Although they are relatively few in number, perhaps only one or two in a head start class (about the same ratio as in middle-class nursery schools), they do exist, regardless of the educational model upon which the class is based. These children exact a heavy toll of teachers' time and energy, often to the detriment of the other children.

The Demonstration Project

It is imperative that effective programs be created for these children. One possible approach is described in this paper. The project, entitled the Demonstration Head Start Classroom (Haring, Hayden, and Nolen, 1969), has three major goals: (a) to furnish remedial services for

Allen, K. E., Turner, K. D. and Everett, P. M. (1970) 'A behavior modification classroom for Head Start children with problem behaviors.' *Exceptional Children,* 37, 2, 119–27.

children with marked behavioral excesses or deficits; (*b*) to provide a training program for the teachers of these children; and (*c*) to conduct research in behavior modification procedures through analyses of teacher-child interactions.

Twelve to fifteen children are enrolled in the class at one time with individual enrollment periods varying from 3 weeks to 6 months. The children are referred by head start teachers in consultation with a head start interdisciplinary team. Some of the reasons given for referral include severely disruptive, excessively withdrawn, lacking in communication skills, hyperactive, incontinent, schizoid, echolalic, and brain damaged.

The ideal program for each child study contains four phases:

1. Observation of the child and his teachers and the accumulation of baseline data in the home classroom prior to the child's entry in the demonstration class.

2. Enrollment in the demonstration class for a period of time adequate to ameliorate the child's problems.

3. Involvement of home classroom teachers in an in-service training program.

4. Return of the child to his home classroom with collection of follow-up data and guidance for the teacher.

Behavior Modification Procedures

The overall philosophy of the demonstration class is based on the application of behavior modification techniques derived from principles of reinforcement. An abundant literature attests to the effectiveness of such procedures in dealing with the aberrant behaviors of preschool children. A few examples include: regressive crawling (Harris, Johnston, Kelley, and Wolf, 1964), hyperactivity (Allen, Henke, Harris, Baer, and Reynolds, 1967), operant crying (Hart, Allen, Buell, Harris, and Wolf, 1964), and mutilative self-scratching (Allen and Harris, 1966).

A single unifying theme is apparent in each of these experimental analyses: The common, everyday social behaviors or responses of preschool teachers are powerful determinants of child behavior. Therefore, the child behaviors that teachers respond to will increase while the child behaviors that teachers fail to respond to will decrease. If a teacher wishes to eliminate the isolate tendencies of an excessively shy child (Allen, Hart, Buell, Harris, and Wolf, 1964), she withholds her smiles, nods, conversation, suggestions, and presentation of materials as long as the child isolates himself from the group. But the moment the isolate child moves toward a peer or a peer-group activity, the teacher immediately directs attention to him, reinforcing (providing consequences for) his first approximations to social behavior. By controlling the timing of responses, that is, holding responses contingent on the child's emission of appropriate rather than maladaptive behaviors, preschool teachers have demonstrated that beneficial behavior changes can be effected (Harris, Wolf, and Baer, 1964).

Individualized Programing

In accordance with the principles of systematic application of behavior modification procedures, the demonstration class emphasizes an individualized program for each child within the context of a typical preschool program. The daily schedule, though flexible, has a basic structure which enables children to acquire skills in self-management. Such skills are, or should be, one of the major educational goals of a well-designed preschool program. However, the program is also organized to promote each child's acquisition of social, verbal, pre-academic, and motor skills. To this end, a variety of quiet, sedentary activities are balanced by vigorous play activities; child-initiated activities are balanced by teacher-structured and teacher-directed activities. Regardless of the activity in progress, the teachers are continually on the alert to reinforce target behaviors peculiar to each child's individual needs.

During outdoor play, for example, when the overall emphasis is on free play and vigorous large motor activities, a dozen different programs may be in effect: for one child, the teachers may be reinforcing appropriate peer contacts; for another, constructive use of materials; for a third child, more creative use of the equipment. Several different verbal development programs may be in progress: reinforcement of one child for more audible verbal output, of another for simply joining two words, of a third for asking for instead of grabbing. Span of attention, sharing, concept development, visual and auditory discriminations—all of these skills and many more, a teacher can teach (reinforce) in the context of a free-play situation if she has carefully specified in advance the target learning or behaviors for each child.

Part of the daily program is devoted to a more formal, pre-academic work time when the children sit at tables in small groups. The tasks consist of activities designed to extend attention span, increase perceptual-motor skills, refine visual and auditory discrimination skills, and develop basic concepts of size, shape, color, equivalence, seriation, and spatial relationships. Again, the program is individualized and is based on the skill levels of each child at the time of his entry into the class. Materials used are those found in every preschool classroom: puzzles, pegboards, matching cards, color cubes, formboards, and a variety of teacher-made materials. The materials are carefully sequenced, however, so that each child acquires specific learning in gradual increments. Correct responses and error-rates over time are recorded by the teacher on each task for each child (Nolen, Hulten, and Kunzelmann, 1968). These data provide the teachers with a basis for preparing individual lesson kits so that maximum success comes to each child as he acquires the basic school performance skills.

Natural Contingencies

The natural reinforcers in the environment are also carefully monitored by the teachers. For example, receiving a snack is contingent on completion by each child of his pre-academic tasks. However, for a new child or an excessively active child, material may be so programed that he is required to attend to academic tasks for as little as 3 minutes at first (30 seconds has been a beginning requirement in some cases). The time depends entirely on the individual child's behavior. The crucial factor is that the teacher set the first approximation in accordance with the target behavior.

Another example of the monitoring of the natural reinforcers in the preschool environment is the opportunity to go out of doors. Going outside to play is always contingent on the child's putting away blocks, housekeeping materials, or whatever else the child was playing with at the time. Thus, in the demonstration class, all activities and teacher attention are devoted to molding appropriate behaviors, and nothing is expended on attending to maladaptive responses. Three adults can effectively manage and provide a sound educational program for 12 to 15 children who only a short time before were causes for grave concern in their home classrooms. To illustrate individual modification programs, two case studies are presented.

Case Study 1

Townsend was 4½ years old when he was transferred to the demonstration class. Collection of data (according to the system described by Bijou, Peterson, Harris, Allen, and Johnston, 1969) continued after his transfer to the demonstration class, where the teachers were instructed during the baseline period to replicate as nearly as possible the home-room teachers' methods of handling Townsend: rechanneling his disruptive activities, comforting him during outbursts, and physically restraining him when he attacked other children. Maladaptive behaviors continued at a high rate during baseline conditions.

Tantrum behavior

On Townsend's eleventh day in the demonstration classroom a first step in behavior modification was initiated. All tantrums, regardless of duration or intensity, were to be ignored, that is, put on extinction. Absolute disregard of the tantrum, no matter how severe it might become, had to be thoroughly understood by the teachers inasmuch as there are data (Hawkins, Peterson, Schweid, and Bijou, 1966) which indicate that when tantrums are put on extinction, extremes of tantrumming may temporarily ensue. Townsend's data were no exception to the classic extinction curve. His first tantrum under the non-attending contingency lasted 27 minutes (average duration of previous tantrums had been 5 minutes), becoming progressively more severe up to the 20-minute point. When it became obvious that the tantrum was going to be lengthy, the other children were taken to the playground by a teacher and a volunteer while the second teacher stationed herself immediately outside the classroom door. When Townsend quieted down, the teacher opened the door to ask in a matter-of-fact voice if he was ready to go to the playground. Before the teacher had a chance to speak, Townsend recommenced his tantrum. The teacher stepped back outside to wait for another period of calm. Twice more Townsend quieted down, only to begin anew at the sight of the teacher. Each time, however, the episodes were shorter (6, 3, and 1 minutes, respectively).

On the second day of tantrum intervention there was one tantrum of 15 minutes with two 2-minute follow-up tantrums when the teacher attempted to re-enter the room. On the third day there was one mild 4-minute tantrum. No further tantrums occurred in the demonstration class nor was there a recurrence when Townsend returned to his regular head start class.

Disruptive behaviors

Modification of generally aggressive and disruptive behaviors such as hitting and kicking children, spitting, and running off with other children's toys was instituted on the sixteenth session. On the first day of modification the teachers were instructed to give their undivided attention to the child who had been assaulted, while keeping their backs to Townsend. Nine episodes of aggressive behavior were tallied on this day. During the next eleven sessions, there was a marked decrease (an average of three per session). During the twelfth session, there was an upswing to seven episodes, then a gradual decrease until finally, no more grossly aggressive and disruptive acts occurred. A zero rate was recorded for the remainder of the sessions.

Bus program

Another behavior modification project with Townsend involved the use of consumable reinforcers. Townsend had been banned from the head start bus for failing to sit in a seat with the seat belt fastened, attempting to open the doors while the bus was in motion, playing with the instrument panel, and throwing himself upon the bus driver while the latter was driving. Staying buckled in the seat was the target behavior.

On the first day of the program Townsend's seat belt was fastened, and the teacher immediately put a peanut in Townsend's mouth commenting, 'Good, you are sitting quietly, all buckled up snug in your seat belt.' She then quickly dispensed peanuts to every child on the bus with approving comments about their good bus-riding habits. Rounds of peanut dispensing and approving comments were continued at 30- to 90-second intervals throughout the 15-minute bus ride. The peanuts were dispensed at longer intervals for the next 4 days. On the following 3 days the peanuts were saved until the children got off the bus.

On the ninth day, Townsend rode the bus without a rewarding adult other than the bus driver who had been instructed to praise the children for their good bus-riding behavior as he let them off the bus and to ignore Townsend if he had not stayed buckled. When the teacher and social worker, waiting at the bus stop, heard the bus driver praise Townsend, they voiced approval and gave him a small sucker as they accompanied him to his house. Gradually all consumable reinforcement was eliminated and only occasional social reinforcement, in the form of praise for Townsend's independent bus-riding, was used.

Shaping play skills

Establishing appropriate behaviors incompatible with his maladaptive behaviors was the area on which his teachers concentrated the greatest time, energy, and planning in Townsend's program. Data from the home classroom indicated that he had few play skills and also, that he had a low rate of interaction with other children. It seemed futile to attempt to build cooperative play with children until Townsend had acquired some play skills. Therefore, the teachers began a step-by-step program of teaching play with each of the materials considered important in a preschool program. For example, a teacher helped Townsend to duplicate what at first were simple block models. If he refused to participate in a play lesson he forfeited the attention of all adults in the classroom. The moment he returned to the play materials, the attention of the teacher was again forthcoming. He was also reinforced for all divergent or unique uses of materials and equipment as long as the divergence was within the broad limits acceptable to preschool teachers.

Between sessions 6 and 26 Townsend acquired a functional repertoire of play skills with a variety of materials and equipment. It was decided, therefore, to change reinforcement contingencies: Adult social reinforcement would be available only when Townsend engaged in constructive use of play materials and interacted appropriately with another child. The change in contingencies appeared to have a positive effect. Between sessions 26 and 32 (figure 14.1) there was a steady increase in the rate of cooperative play.

Return to home classroom

Analysis of the data at this point indicated that it was an appropriate time to return Townsend to his home classroom. Townsend's original teachers had had 3 days of in-service training in the demonstration classroom and had worked with the staff person who had been assigned to Townsend's home classroom. The staff person provided coaching on sessions 33 to 36 (figure 14.1), at which point the data indicated that Townsend's teachers were able to continue the contingency management procedures on their own. Not only were there no incidents of

G*

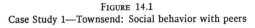

FIGURE 14.1
Case Study 1—Townsend: Social behavior with peers

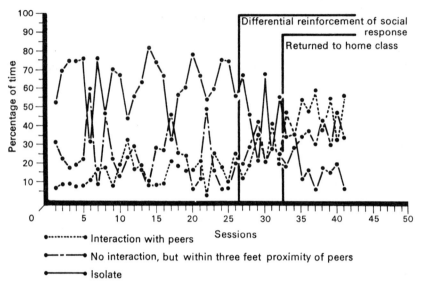

FIGURE 14.1
Case Study 1—Townsend: Social behavior with peers

disruptive behaviors, but Townsend's social skills continued to hold at a high stable rate as measured by the amount of cooperative play (figure 14.1, sessions 37–41). Several post-checks were made throughout the remainder of the school year. These indicated that Townsend continued to function in an acceptable manner.

Case Study 2

Doreen was $4\frac{3}{4}$ years old when she entered the demonstration class. The reasons for referral were many: immaturity, incessant crying, frequent physical attacks on other children, excessive dependency on adults, severe deficits in large motor skills, little interaction with peers, and speech that was either echolalic or unintelligible mumbling. Data taken for six sessions in the home classroom prior to her transfer to the demonstration class confirmed referral reports.

Shaping motor skills

Where does one begin with a child displaying so maladaptive and deficient a repertoire? As with Townsend it was reasoned that a child needs play skills to participate even minimally in the preschool program.

However, in Doreen's case, basic motor skills had to be developed first. Therefore, a program was planned beginning with very simple skills such as walking a low, wide board and progressing to more complex activities like climbing on the outdoor equipment, riding the wheel toys, and pumping on the swings. A teacher's hand and other forms of physical contact were forthcoming only when Doreen was making an effort to engage in a motor task. At all other times the teachers disengaged her hands and turned away when she clung to them or to their clothing. Within 5 weeks Doreen was using all the outdoor equipment competently and independently. One data photography sequence shows her going up and over a 6-foot climber without assistance. Concurrently, the teachers ignored totally her repeated attacks on children. They gave their attention to the child who had been attacked, inserting themselves between Doreen and the other child, with their backs to Doreen. Attacks on children became infrequent, occurring only once or twice a week.

Differential reinforcement of verbal behavior
Doreen's verbal behavior continued to be of a low order. The verbal data were broken down into two categories: (*a*) appropriate verbalizations as specifically defined, e.g. intelligible words relevant to the situation, and (*b*) inappropriate verbalizations or vocalizations as specifically defined. The latter included her whimpering cries, echolalic or parroted responses, and unintelligible monologues. The baseline data taken in the classroom indicated that the teachers tended to respond more to her inappropriate verbalizations than they did to her appropriate ones (figure 14.2, sessions 1–6). When Doreen entered the demonstration class, the teachers were instructed to attend as frequently as possible to her appropriate verbalizations and to attend as infrequently as possible to her inappropriate ones. As can be seen in figure 14.2, the teachers rarely succeeded in totally ignoring the inappropriate verbalizations. Nevertheless they did, for the most part, give a proportionately greater share of their attention to the appropriate responses. Under this regimen, appropriate verbalizations began an irregular increase with inappropriate verbalizations slowly declining at an irregular rate; the latter eventually constituted a relatively small percentage of the child's total verbal output (figure 14.2, sessions 34–39). Six days of data taken after Doreen's return to the home classroom indicated that appropriate verbalizations continued to dominate her verbal output and, further,

that her teachers were responding in an appropriately differential fashion.

No specific program to increase Doreen's social interaction with peers was instituted though the question was posed: Will amelioration of the major behavior disorders be accompanied by improved social interaction with peers? The data indicate that cooperative interaction with peers did increase from an average of 10 per cent of each session during baseline in the home classroom to an average of 26 per cent (figure 14.3) in the demonstration class. It seems probable that as assault behaviors decreased, verbalizations became less bizarre and improved motor skills enabled her to use the play equipment, Doreen became a more desirable play companion, thus making peer as well as adult social reinforcement available to her.

Conclusions

These behavior modification projects have been described in detail in order to illustrate the application of reinforcement principles by pre-school teachers in a field setting. The principles and techniques as they relate to these specific case studies follow:

1. Preschool teachers can readily employ reinforcement procedures to produce desired changes in children's behavior. To do so effectively, a teacher must assess children objectively, select specific target behaviors, keep continuous records, and use these records as a basis for program planning and continuous assessment.

2. Modification of only one or two of a child's behaviors at a time is essential to a successful program. A teacher's responses may become scattered and unsystematic if too many contingencies must be kept in mind for each child.

3. Every adult involved in a child's environment is potentially a powerful social reinforcer. Thus, every adult who interacts with children in the preschool situation must carefully monitor his responses to each child. When strict monitoring is not exercised, progress will be slower and more irregular.

4. The preschool environment abounds in natural reinforcers—play materials, snack time, outdoor play, special games and activities. Preschool teachers must make these reinforcers work for the child by making them available contingent on responses which will enhance the child's progress.

FIGURE 14.2

Case Study 2—Doreen: Proportion of appropriate to inappropriate verbal behavior;
ratio of adult social reinforcement for each category

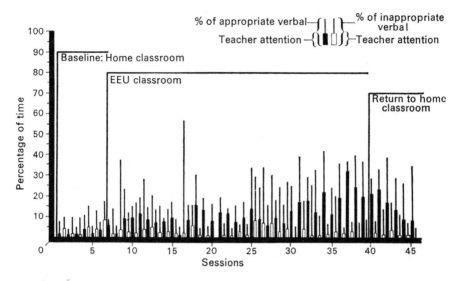

FIGURE 14.3

Case Study 2—Doreen: Social behavior with peers

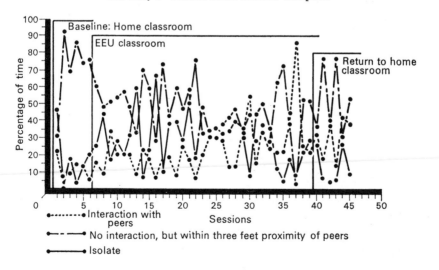

5. Though the extinction process (withholding reinforcement) is a highly effective means of freeing a child of his maladaptive response, it does not automatically provide an alternate set of appropriate behaviors. Therefore, it is critical that teachers give their attention to desired behaviors so that the child may acquire a functional response repertoire.

6. Reinforcement of successive approximations to the target behaviors (shaping) is essential to achieve successful behavior modification. Reinstatement of Townsend as a bus-rider is one example of shaping procedures.

7. A careful step-by-step reduction in the amount of reinforcement (leaning the schedule) is necessary if a response is to be self-maintained. The bus-riding sequence is again cited as an example.

8. Elimination of maladaptive behaviors simultaneous with shaping of appropriate behaviors often correlates with other favorable changes in the child's behavioral repertoire. The concurrent changes in improved cooperative play patterns in the second case study demonstrate this effect, an effect which has been noted previously (Allen, Henke, Harris, Baer, and Reynolds, 1967).

It would appear from this demonstration project, as well as from many other experimental analyses of behavior, that the teacher's differentiated responsiveness is the crucial variable in determining what and how the young child learns. No educational model, no preschool curriculum alone can insure optimum progress for a child. The deciding factor is the teacher's behavior and appropriate reinforcement techniques. Successful behavior modification depends on correct teacher-child interaction.

BECKER, W. C., MADSEN, C. H., jr.,
ARNOLD, C. R. and THOMAS, D. R.

15. The Contingent Use of Teacher Attention and Praise in Reducing Classroom Behaviour Problems

The influence of the teacher's attention, praise, nearness and other social stimuli in maintaining deviant as well as positive social behavior in children has been repeatedly demonstrated with pre-school children (e.g. Allen, Hart, Buell, Harris and Wolf, 1964; Harris, Johnston, Kelley and Wolf, 1964). The expectancy that attention in almost any form may maintain deviant behaviors lies in the high probability that attentional responses from adults will be repeatedly followed by relief from aversive stimulation or the presentation of positive reinforcers in the history of most children. With such a history, stimuli produced by attentional responses are likely to become positive conditioned reinforcers which function to strengthen responses that are followed by such attentional stimuli. An essentially similar process is involved in the establishment of the effectiveness of praise comments such as 'good boy', 'that's fine', 'you're doing great', which acquire conditioned reinforcement value through their repeated pairing with positively reinforcing stimuli.

Various forms of attention by nursery school teachers have been used to modify such behaviors as 'regressive' crawling, isolate behavior, excessive orientation to adults, 'aggressive' rather than cooperative peer interactions, and lethargy or passivity, among others. In addition, a similar procedure has been used to train mothers to modify the demanding-aggressive behavior of their children (Hawkins, Peterson, Schweid and Bijou, 1966). There is little question in the face of the

Becker, W. C., Madsen, C. H., Arnold, C. R. and Thomas, D. R. (1967) 'The contingent use of teacher attention and praise in reducing classroom behavior problems.' *Journal of Special Education*, 1, 287–307.

extensive research by Sidney Bijou, Donald Baer and their students that a powerful principle for influencing the development of social behaviors has been isolated.

The group of studies to be reported here demonstrate how the selective use of teacher attention and praise can be effectively applied in managing behavior problems in elementary classrooms; the studies also explore methods of training teachers to be more effective in this regard.

The Setting

The studies were carried out in Urbana, Illinois, in an elementary school whose population was 95 per cent Negro. Our research group was invited into the school because it was believed that we could provide a service and they would provide us with a research laboratory. Seven teachers (half of those invited) agreed to participate in a workshop and seminar on the application of behavioral principles in the classroom. This report covers studies involving five of these teachers, carried out between February and June, 1966.

The conduct of our research was guided to some extent by the necessity of establishing good relationships within the school system. Even though we had been invited by the school administration to see what we could do, there was still a need to convince teachers to participate, to keep them participating and to help them feel comfortable with observers in their classrooms. The comments of one of our teachers expresses better than we can the background into which the research had to be adapted:

At one time few teachers wanted to work at our school, and only those who could not find a better position would teach. Suddenly the school found itself qualified under Title I of the Elementary and Secondary School Act to receive Federal aid. A large percentage of its population was termed 'culturally deprived' or perhaps more aptly, 'deprived of middle-class culture.' The school was bombarded with specialists, aids, volunteers, and experimental groups from the University of Illinois, all wanting to borrow the children or to help the children. By planning carefully, class interruptions were held to a minimum, but even then planning was done around a music teacher, an art teacher, a language teacher, special small-group speech classes and language classes. With all of this going on, plus many other items I shall leave unmentioned, it became increasingly more difficult to develop a continuous daily program. A self-contained classroom was a thing of the past. My attitude began to become very negative. I am not capable of judging the merits or demerits of this program, only time will measure this,

I am merely attempting to describe briefly the setting, from my vantage point, into which a class in 'behavior modification' was introduced. The enthusiasm held by some for the possibilities of behavior modification did not particularly excite me. The observing would interrupt my class and make it very difficult for me to function comfortably. The plan of the experiment was a bit nebulous, since too much knowledge of what was to be done would affect the results. To add to all this, these people were *psychologists!* My reinforcement history of working with psychologists need not be discussed here. I will simply state my relationship with them was inconsequential and negative; their reports were read carefully for some new information, but, finding none usually, the reports were filed as useless.

I vacillated for days on whether to take part in the class or not, finally deciding, despite my anxiety about the observation, that the only way to make educational psychology practical was to allow psychologists into the classroom to observe for themselves the classroom situation and problems.

Because of the need to sell ourselves to the teachers and maintain close contact with them, the seminar workshop was initiated at the beginning of the second semester. At the same time we began to train observers, select target children and make baseline recordings of the children's behavior. This sequence of events is not ideal, since even though instructed otherwise the teachers were likely to try out the procedures they were learning in the workshop before we wished them to do so. The fact that they did this is suggested by an occasional decreasing baseline of problem behavior for a target child. Most changes, however, were dramatic enough that this potential loss in demonstrating an experimental effect did not grossly distort possible conclusions.

Most work in this area has used designs of the ABAB type. After baseline (A) an experimental effect is introduced (B), withdrawn (A), and reintroduced (B). We did not use this design (though we had an accidental counterpart to it in one room where the second (A) condition was provided by a student teacher) because: (*a*) we were afraid it might jeopardize the teacher's support; (*b*) the values of the experimental processes involved have been repeatedly confirmed; (*c*) 'accidental' influences which might have produced changes in behavior would be unlikely to happen to ten children at the same time in five different classrooms; (*d*) we are unimpressed by arguments that Hawthorne effects, time alone or other 'uncontrolled' variables such as the 'weather' are causative in view of (*b*) and (*c*) above. By electing not to use an ABAB design we were also able to show the persistence of effects maintained by conditioned reinforcers over a longer period of time (nine weeks) than is usually the case. As a result of our caution and our success, we are now in a position where teachers and administrators in other schools are permitting us to establish controlled designs in return for our helping them with their problem children.

Procedures

Selection of target children. The authors began by observing in the classrooms of the teachers who had volunteered for the project, and then discussing possible problem children with them. After tentative selection of two children in each class, explicit behavior coding categories were evolved and tested. The final selection was contingent upon demonstration that problem behavior did occur frequently enough to constitute a problem and could be reliably rated.

Rating categories. During the first four weeks the rating categories were repeatedly revised as reliability data demanded. Where it was not possible to get rater agreement for a category above 80 per cent, a new definition was sought or a category abandoned. For example, in three classes (A, B and C) inappropriate talking and vocal noise were rated as separate categories (see table 15.1). In two classes (D and E) the behavior patterns made it difficult to discriminate between these behaviors, so they were combined. The general rules followed in establishing categories were as follows:

1. They should reflect behaviors which interfered with classroom learning (time on task), and/or,
2. They should involve behaviors which violated the rules for permissible behavior established by the teacher and/or,
3. They should reflect particular behaviors a teacher wanted to change (e.g. thumbsucking).
4. The classes should be constituted by behaviors which were topographically similar in some important way.
5. The classes should be mutually exclusive.
6. The definitions must refer to observables and not involve inferences.
7. The number of classes should not exceed ten.

As table 15.1 indicates, some codes were usable with all ten target children; others were devised especially for a particular child. For convenience we will speak of the Categories A and B in table 15.1 as 'deviant behaviors'.

Observer training and reliabilities. Observers were obtained from under-graduate classes in psychology and education and were paid $1.50 an hour. Initially they worked in pairs, often in conjunction with one of the authors. After each rating session of 40 minutes, ratings were compared and discussed and reliability examined by category. Definitions were clarified and changes made when necessary. Reliabilities were above 80 per cent before the baseline period was begun. Several reliability checks were made each week throughout baseline and periodically thereafter. As indicated in figures 15.1 to 15.5, reliability only occasionally fell below 80 per cent when calculated by dividing the smaller estimate by the larger.

The observers were carefully trained not to respond to the children in the classes. They were to 'fade into the walls'. This procedure quickly extinguished the children's responses to the observers. Several incidents were reported where children were surprised to see the observers respond to a request from the teacher to move. After a while it was possible for other visitors to come into the class without distracting the children as they had in the past.

Rating procedure. Except for a few occasional absences, target children were observed for 20 minutes a day, four days a week. In the experimental phase of the study frequency of reliability checks were reduced so that ratings of teacher behavior could also be obtained. Each observer had a clipboard with a stop watch taped to it. Observers would start their watches together and check for synchronization every five minutes (end of a row). They would observe for 20 seconds and then take ten seconds to record the classes of behavior which occurred during the 20-second period. All data are reported in terms of the percentages of the time intervals during which deviant behavior was observed to occur. The activities in which the children were involved varied considerably from day to day and contributed to daily fluctuation. For this reason only weekly averages are reported.

Ratings of teacher behavior. At the beginning of the experimental phase for four teachers, and for a week prior to the experimental phase for teacher E, a 20-minute sample of the teacher's behavior was also obtained. The rating categories are given in table 15.2. The main

TABLE 15.1

CODING CATEGORIES FOR CHILDREN WITH TEACHERS A, B AND C

SYMBOLS	CLASS LABEL	CLASS DEFINITIONS

A. Behaviors Incompatible with Learning: General Categories

X	Gross Motor Behaviors	Getting out of seat; standing up; running; hopping; skipping; jumping; walking around; rocking in chair; disruptive movement without noise; moving chair to neighbor.
N	Disruptive Noise with Objects	Tapping pencil or other objects; clapping; tapping feet; rattling or tearing paper. *Be conservative, only rate if could hear noise with eyes closed. Do not include accidental dropping of objects or noise made while performing X above.*
A	Disturbing Others Directly and Aggression	Grabbing objects or work; knocking neighbor's book off desk; destroying another's property; hitting; kicking; shoving; pinching; slapping; striking with object; throwing object at another person; poking with object; attempting to strike; biting; pulling hair.
O	Orienting Responses	Turning head or head and body to look at another person; showing objects to another child; attending to another child. *Must be of seconds duration to be rated. Not rated unless seated.*
!	Blurting Out, Commenting and Vocal Noise	Answering teacher without raising hand or without being called on; making comments or calling out remarks when no question has been asked; calling teacher's name to get her attention; crying; screaming; singing; whistling; laughing loudly; coughing loudly. *Must be undirected to another particular child, but may be directed to teacher.*
T	Talking	Carrying on conversations with other children when it is not permitted. *Must be directed to a particular child or children.*
//	Other	Ignoring teacher's question or command; doing something different from that directed to do (includes minor motor behavior such as playing with pencil when supposed to be writing). *To be rated only when other ratings not appropriate.*

B. *Special categories for children with teachers A, B and C (to be rated only for children indicated)*

+	Improper Position Carole and Alice	Not sitting with body and head oriented toward the front with feet on the floor, e.g. sitting on feet; standing at desk rather than sitting; sitting with body sideways but head facing front. *Do not rate if chair sideways but head and body both oriented towards the front with feet on the floor.*

TABLE 15.1 (continued)

SYMBOLS	CLASS LABEL	CLASS DEFINITIONS
S	Sucking Alice and Betty	Sucking fingers or other objects.
B	Bossing Carole	Reading story out loud to self or other children (*do not rate! in this case*); acting as teacher to other children, as showing flash cards.
//	Ignoring Charley	This category expanded to include playing with scissors, pencils, or crayons instead of doing something more constructive during free time.
C. Relevant Behavior		
——	Relevant Behavior	Time on task, e.g. answers question, listening, raises hand, writing assignment. *Must include whole 20 seconds except for orienting responses of less than 4 seconds duration.*

purpose of the ratings was to ensure that the experimental program was being followed.

Experimental phase instructions. Following a five-week baseline period (for most children) teachers were given instructions to follow for the nine-week experimental period. In all classes the teachers were given general rules for classroom management as follows (typed on a 5″ × 8″ card to be kept on their desks):

General Rules for Teachers
1. Make explicit rules as to what is expected of children for each period. (Remind of rules when needed.)
2. *Ignore* (do not attend) behaviors which interfere with learning or teaching, unless a child is being hurt by another. Use punishment which seems appropriate, preferably withdrawal of some positive reinforcement.
3. Give *praise* and *attention* to behaviors which facilitate learning. Tell child what he is being praised for. Try to reinforce behaviors incompatible with those you wish to decrease.
   Examples of how to praise: 'I like the way you're working quietly.' 'That's the way I like to see you work.' 'Good job, you are doing fine.'
   Transition period. 'I see Johnny is ready to work.' 'I'm calling on you because you raised your hand.' 'I wish everyone were working as nicely as X,' etc. Use variety and expression.

In general, give praise for achievement, prosocial behavior and following the group rules.

In addition to these general rules, teachers in classes A to D were given specific instructions with respect to their target children. An example follows:

Special Rules for Alice

Attempt to follow the general rules above, but try to give extra attention to Alice for the behavior noted below, but try not to overdo it to the extent that she is singled out by other children. Spread your attention around.

1. Praise sitting straight in chair with both feet and chair legs on floor and concentrating on own work.
2. Praise using hands for things other than sucking.
3. Praise attention to directions given by teacher or talks made by students.
4. Specify behavior you expect from her at beginning of day and new activity, such as sitting in chair facing front with feet on floor, attention to teacher and class members where appropriate, what she may do after assigned work is finished, raising hand to answer questions or get your attention.

The fifth teacher was given the general rules only and instructed not to give the target children any more special attention than was given

TABLE 15.2

TEACHER CODING CATEGORIES

SYMBOLS	CLASS LABEL	CLASS DEFINITIONS
C	Positive Contact	Positive physical contact must be included—such behaviors as embracing, kissing, patting (on head), holding arm, taking hand, sitting on lap, etc.
P	Verbal Praise	This category includes paying attention to appropriate behavior with verbal comments indicating approval, commendation or achievement such as: 'That's good.' 'You're studying well.' 'Fine job.' 'I like you.'
R	Recognition in Academic Sense	Calling on child when hand is raised. (Do not rate if child calls teacher's name or makes noises to get her attention.)
F	Facial Attention	Looking at child when smiling. (Teacher might nod her head or give other indication of approval—while smiling.)
A	Attention to Undesirable Behavior	This category includes the teacher's verbally calling attention to undesirable behavior and may be of high intensity (yelling, screaming, scolding or raising the voice) or of low intensity ('Go to the office.' 'You know what you are supposed to be doing,' etc.) Calling the child to the desk to talk things over should also be included, as well as threats of consequences. Score the following responses to deviant behavior separately:
L	Lights	Turning off the lights to achieve control.
W	Withdrawal of Positive Reinforcement	Keeping in for recess, sending to office, depriving child in the classroom.
/	Physical Restraint	Includes holding the child, pulling out into hall, grabbing, hitting, pushing, shaking.

the rest of the class. This procedure was decided upon because our observers felt that general classroom management was a problem for Mrs E. She relied heavily on negative control procedures, and the general level of disruptive behaviors in the room was high. In view of this, we decided to see if the two target children in her class might not be used as barometers of a more general effect on the class of a change in control procedures.

When we first initiated the experimental phase of the study, we attempted to give the teachers hand-signals to help them learn when to ignore and when to praise. This procedure was abandoned after the first week in favor of explicit instructions, as given above, and daily feedback on their progress. While hand-signals and lights have been found to be effective in helping parents learn to discriminate when to respond or ignore (Hawkins, Peterson, Schweid and Bijou, 1966), the procedure is too disruptive when the teacher is in the middle of a lesson and is consequently placed in conflict about which response should come next.

At this point, the seminar was used to discuss and practice various ways of delivering positive comments. For some teachers, delivery of positive comments was difficult, and their initial attempts came out in stilted, stereotyped form. With time, even our most negative teacher was smiling and more spontaneous in her praise (and enjoying her class more). Shortly after the experimental phase began, one teacher commented, 'I have at least 15 minutes more every morning and afternoon in which to do other things.'

The experimental phase was initiated March 30th and ended May 27th. A breakdown in the heating plant in part of the building for the week of April 8th (Week 7) accounts for the loss of data for some children that week.

Results

The main results are presented in figures 15.1 to 15.5. The average 'deviant' behavior for ten children in five classes was 62·13 per cent during baseline and 29·19 per cent during the experimental period. The t-test for the differences between correlated means was significant well beyond the ·001 level. All children showed less deviant behavior during the experimental phase. However, differential teacher attention and praise were not very effective with Carole and did not produce much change in Dan until his reading skills were improved. Each child and class will be discussed in more detail and a breakdown of the behaviors which changed will be examined.

Teacher A

Mrs A is an anxious, sensitive person who expressed many doubts about her ability to learn to use 'the approach' and about whether it would work with her middle-primary adjustment class. Both of the children on whom data were collected (figure 15.1) changed remarkably, as did Mrs A and other members of her class. The teachers' views of what happened to themselves and to members of their classes are very instructive and will be presented elsewhere.

Albert (age 7:8) tested average on the Stanford-Binet, but was still on first-grade materials during his second year in school. He was selected because he showed many behaviors which made learning difficult. He talked, made other noises, did not attend to teacher and got in and out of his seat a lot. He loved to be 'cute' and arouse laughter. In Mrs A's words:

He was a very noisy, disruptive child. He fought with others, blurted out, could not stay in his seat, and did very little required work. I had to check constantly to see that the minimum work was finished. He sulked and responded negatively to everything suggested to him. In addition, he was certain that he could not read. If I had planned it, I could not have reinforced this negative behavior more, for I caught him in every deviant act possible and often before it occurred. I lectured him and, as might be expected, was making only backward motion. In November Albert came to me to tell me something and I was shocked by the intensity of his stuttering. He simply could not express his thought because his stuttering was so bad. I declared an 'I Like Albert Week'. I gave him a great deal of attention, bragged about his efforts and was beginning to make some progress. This turned out to be the basis upon which an 'ignore and praise' technique could be established. When the class began, I could see quickly what had happened to my relationship with Albert and had to fight to keep up my negative remarks until the baseline was established. Finally, I was free to use the technique. He quickly responded and his deviant behavior decreased to 10 per cent, the lowest recorded. Along with the praising and ignoring, I attempted to establish a calmer atmosphere in which to work, and carefully reviewed class behavior rules. A good technique with Albert was to have him repeat the rule because 'he was following it.'

During Weeks 8 and 9 Albert showed less than 12 per cent deviant behavior on the average. His worst performance out of seven observation days was 18·77 per cent and he was under 5 per cent deviant four out of seven days. Then an unplanned experimental reversal occurred.

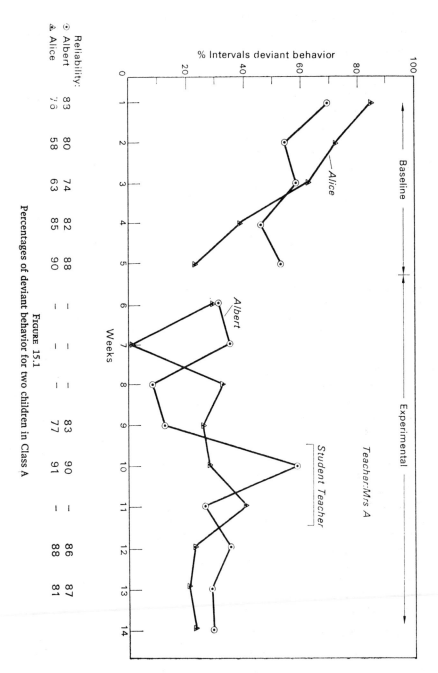

FIGURE 15.1

Percentages of deviant behavior for two children in Class A

Mrs A relates what happened:

As my student teacher gradually assumed more and more of the teaching load, the deviant behavior increased again. She made the same mistakes that I had. I deliberately planned her work so that I would be working with Albert most of the time. She felt the efficiency of the direct command, but she also realized that this was not modifying Albert's behavior in a lasting way. Gradually, she accepted the positive approach and in the last week or two of her work the deviant behavior began again to decrease. She had learned that with so negative a child as Albert, only building rapport by using positive reinforcement would succeed.

Albert has improved delightfully. He still blurts out, but makes an effort to stop this. He is often seen holding his hand in the air, biting his lips. He completes his work on time, and it is done well. Often, when he has to re-do a paper, he takes it cheerfully and says, 'I can do this myself.' No sulking. He still finds it difficult to sit for a long period of time, but time on task has increased. He works very hard on his reading and has stated that he can read. His stuttering has decreased almost to zero. When the observers were questioned concerning this, they had detected little, if any stuttering. Most important to me, Albert has become a delightful child and an enthusiastic member of our class who feels his ideas are accepted and have merit.

Examination of the separate categories of behavior for Albert only serves to confirm the teacher's reports about which behaviors were most frequent and which changed the most.

The record of Mrs A's behavior showed that she attended to and praised positive behaviors more than 90 per cent of the time during the experimental period. Similar effective following of procedures was demonstrated for all five teachers.

Alice (age 7:8) scored 90 on the Stanford-Binet and was doing low first-grade work. The data on Alice are less clear than those for Albert since her average deviant behavior showed a decline prior to the experimental phase. Mrs A considered Alice a 'sulking child'. She would withdraw at times and not talk. She would sit inappropriately in her chair, suck her thumb, and make frequent movements of her hands and legs. Mrs A said that Alice would report headaches after being scolded.

Mrs A also indicated that two weeks before the end of baseline she told Alice that she was 'disgusted with your sulking and would you please stop it'. Mrs A felt that this instruction in part accounted for the drop in deviant behavior prior to the experimental phase. Analysis of Alice's separate classes of behavior indicates, however, that the motor category declined from 45 per cent to 25 per cent to 8 per cent the first three weeks of baseline and remained under 12 per cent the rest of the experiment. Following this decline in 'getting out of seat', frequency of odd sitting positions went from 0 per cent to 25 per cent to 18 per cent over the first three weeks of baseline and declined to zero over the next two weeks. There was also a decline in talking during the first two weeks of baseline. In other words Mrs A got Alice to stay in her seat, sit properly and talk less prior to the experimental change. The behaviors which show a correlation with the experimental change are decreases in *orienting, sucking* and *other* (ignoring teacher) response categories.

It is probable that the maintenance of Alice's improvement, except for the short lapse when the student teacher took over the class, can be attributed to the experimental program. Mrs A reported at the end of the year as follows:

Alice is a responsible, hard-working student who now smiles, makes jokes, and plays with others. When a bad day comes, or when she doesn't get her way and chooses to sulk, I simply ignore her until she shows signs of pleasantness. Through Alice I have learned a far simpler method of working with sulking behaviour, the one most disagreeable kind of behavior to me. Alice is a child who responds well to physical contact. Often a squeeze, a pat, or an arm around her would keep her working for a long while. This is not enough, however. Alice is very anxious about problems at home. She must have opportunity to discuss these problems. Again through the class suggestions, I found it more profitable to discuss what she could do to improve her problems than to dwell on what went wrong. Alice's behavior is a good example of the effects of a calm, secure environment. Her time on task has lengthened and her academic work has improved.

Teacher B

Mrs B had a lower intermediate class of 26 children. Before the experimental phase of the study, she tended to control her class through sharp commands, physical punishment and withholding privileges. The two children on whom observations were made (figure 15.2) showed considerable change over the period of the experiment. Observers' comments indicate that Mrs B was very effective in following the instructions of the experimental program. Only occasionally did she revert to a sharp command or a hand slap.

Betty (age 9:7) scored average on various assessments of intelligence and was doing middle third-grade work. Her initial problem behaviors included 'pestering' other children, blurting out, sucking her thumb,

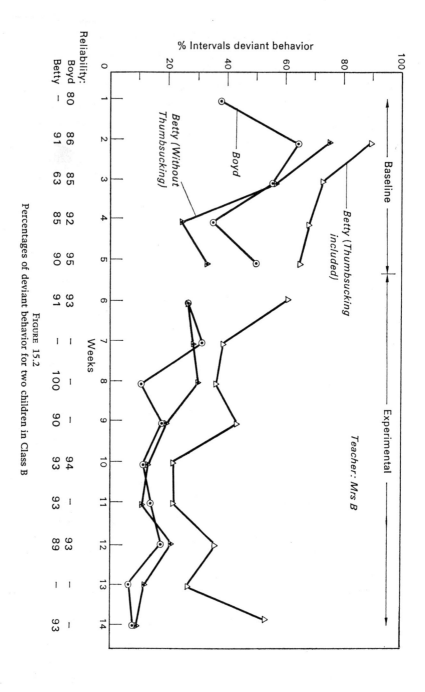

FIGURE 15.2
Percentages of deviant behavior for two children in Class B

making noises. She also occasionally hit other children. Often she said or did things that evoked laughter from others. As figure 15.2 shows, many of her problem behaviors showed a reduction during the baseline period (as happened with Alice), but thumbsucking did not. The experimental program brought thumbsucking under control for a while, but it increased markedly the last week of the experiment. Betty's other problem behaviors showed continued improvement over the experimental period and remained at a level far below baseline for the last five weeks of the experimental period.

Boyd (age 9:7) was of average I.Q. His achievement test placements varied between second- and third-grade levels. During baseline he scored high on getting out of his seat and making other gross movements, talking out of turn and making noises. Mrs B also reported that Boyd had difficulty 'saying words he knows', giggled a lot and would not try to do things alone. He very much liked to be praised and tried not to do things which led to scolding. During this period Boyd was getting a great deal of teacher attention, but much of the attention was for the very behaviors Mrs B wished to eliminate. Through a gradual shaping process Boyd learned to sit in his seat for longer periods of time working on task. He has learned to work longer by himself before asking for help. Mrs B reports that he is less anxious and emotional, although we have no measure of this. Blurting out was not stopped entirely, but now he usually raises his hand and waits to be called on in full class activities and waits for his turn in reading.

Teacher C
Our biggest failure occurred in Mrs C's middle primary class of about 20 children. Mrs C was one of our most positive teachers, and we underestimated the severity of the many problems she was facing. With our present knowledge, we would likely have gone directly to a more potent token economy system for the whole class (see O'Leary and Becker, 1967). The above misjudgment notwithstanding, the experiment reported below is still of considerable value in pointing to one of the limits of 'the approach', as our teachers came to call it. Besides focusing on Carole and Charley, as described below, we assisted Mrs C in extinguishing tantrums in Donna (beginning Week 8), and in reducing swearing and hitting by Hope. The work with Donna was very successful.

Carole (age 7:5) scored from 78 to 106 on various intelligence tests.

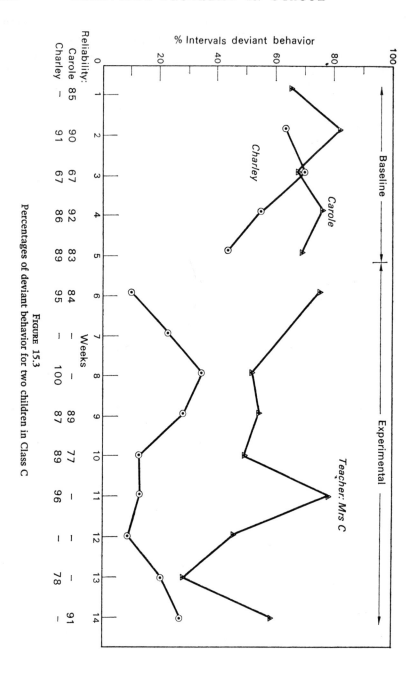

FIGURE 15.3
Percentages of deviant behavior for two children in Class C

She was working at the mid first-grade level. Carole is an incessant beehive of activity. She scored high on response categories which indicate that she spent much time talking out of turn, turning in her seat, getting out of her seat, bossing other children and hitting others. Her most frequent behavior was talking when she should have been quiet. She was very responsive to peer attention. At times she would stand at the back of the room and read out loud to everyone. She liked to play teacher. She was also described as good at lying, cheating, stealing and smoking. Like most of the children in the study, Carole came from a deprived, unstable home. Descriptions of home backgrounds for most of the children in this study consist of sequences of tragic events (see Mrs D).

The experimental phase of the program reduced Carole's average deviant behavior from about 75 per cent during baseline to 55 per cent for Weeks 7 to 9. A detailed analysis of Carole's responses shows that talking out of turn and blurting out still constituted over 30 per cent of her deviant responses during Weeks 7 to 9. However Carole was in her seat more, sitting properly, responding more relevantly to teacher, and was on task 50 per cent of the time. We were not satisfied with her improvement and felt that Charley (our other target child) while doing well, could also do better.

On April 25th (Week 9) we instituted a program in which ten-cent notebooks were taped to Carole and Charley's desks. Mrs C told the children that every 30 minutes she would put from one to ten points in their notebooks, depending on how hard they worked and how well they followed the class rules. At the end of the day if they had a certain number of points they could exchange the points for a treat. The initial reinforcer was candy. During this phase the rest of the class could earn a candy treat by helping Carole and Charley earn points. In this way they were not left out. The number of points required was based on a shifting criterion geared to Carole and Charley's progress. As noted below and in figure 15.3, Charley responded well to this added incentive and was gradually shifted to saving points over two, then three, then five days to earn puzzles. Carole still resisted. She worked for points for several days, but on May 3rd (Week 10) she announced she was not going to work for points today and she didn't. She was a hellion all day. Over the following two weeks Carole worked for a ring and then the components of a make-up kit. We were seeking stronger reinforcers and were stretching the delay of reinforcement.

On May 17th Mrs C reported that Carole had earned points for three days in a row and was entitled to a component of the make-up kit. The 20 per cent deviant behavior of that week showed that Carole could behave and work. The last week of May, Carole was back to talking and blurting out again. While some of our reinforcers were effective, Carole still needs a classroom where the structure would require her to depend on the teacher for praise and attention and where peer attention to her deviant behavior could be controlled.

Charley was presumed to be age 8 years and 2 months at the start of the study, but in fact was two years older. His I.Q. was given as 91, but with a proper C.A. was 73. He was doing mid first-grade work in most subjects. Charley picked on the girls, hit other boys and bullied them (he was larger), got loud and angry if reprimanded, and at times he sulked and withdrew. No one was going to force him to do anything. Our ratings showed him highest in categories labeled *motor activities* (out of seat), *ignoring* teacher's requests, *turning in seat* and *talking* to peers.

Initially Charley responded very effectively to rules and praise. He loved to receive praise from Mrs C. However, praise was not enough to keep him on task. Also he was still fighting with Donna at recess. As noted above, a point system was initiated April 25th (Week 9) which worked well for the rest of the semester, while the delay of reinforcement was gradually extended to five days. On April 25th Charley was also informed that further fighting with Donna would lead to a loss of the following recess.

Comments on May 10th: 'Charley is great. He ignores others who bother him as well as keeping busy all the time.' May 26th: 'Charley seems much more interested in school work and has been getting help with reading from his sister at home.'

It is not possible to evaluate whether the point system was necessary for Charley. At best we know that social reinforcement helped considerably and that the point system did help to maintain good classroom behavior.

Teacher D

Mrs D teaches a lower intermediate class of about 25 children. One group of her children had been in a slow class where the teacher allowed them 'to do what they wanted'. A brighter group had been taught by a strict teacher who enforced her rules. Since September the class has been divided and subdivided six times and has had seven different teachers.

Mrs D describes the families of her two target children as follows:

Don has average ability and achieves below the average of the class. The father works late afternoons and evenings. The mother, a possible alcoholic, has been known to do some petty shoplifting. She is frequently away from home in the evening. One older brother drowned at the age of seven. An older sister with above average ability left home at the age of fifteen. She later married. Her husband was killed this spring in an automobile accident. Another older sister lost an arm at a very early age and is an unwed mother at the age of fourteen. Another sister attends Junior High School.

Dan's mother is of mixed parentage and has been in the hospital this year. The mother is divorced. The father remarried and it appears that there is a good relationship between the two families; however, the father has been in prison because of 'dope'.

Mrs D was initially quite bothered about being observed, but quickly learned to look more carefully at the way in which her behavior affected that of her class.

Don was 10 years and 4 months old at the start of the study. In April of 1961 he was recommended for placement in the class for slow-learning children. Since kindergarten his performance on intelligence tests had risen from 75 to 102. He was obviously of at least average ability. His level of school achievement was between grades two and three, except for arithmetic reasoning (4.3). Observations revealed a high frequency of moving around the room and talking when he should have been working. He was called 'hyperactive' and said to have poor 'attention'. His talking to other children was quite annoying to his teacher and interfered with classwork. Don appeared to respond to teacher attention, but obtained such attention most often when he was acting up.

The experimental procedures quickly brought Don's level of deviant behavior down from about 40 per cent to under 20 per cent. He was particularly good at working when the task was specifically assigned. When he was left to his own devices (no stimulus control) he would start to play around. These observations suggest that Don would greatly profit from more individualized programming of activities. He was reported to show improved behavior in his afternoon classes involving several different teachers.

Danny was age 10 years, 6 months at the start of the study. He measured near 85 on several I.Q. tests. His classroom behavior was

H

described as being generally disruptive and aggressive. During baseline he scored high on *motor, talking, orienting, ignoring* and *noise*. By all standards Danny was a serious behavior problem. He seldom completed work assignments and was in the slowest reading group. Because of the severity of his behavior and difficulty staying on task, an educational diagnosis was requested during the early part of baseline. The staffing at Week 2 indicated a two-year reading deficit and a one-year arithmetic deficit. The following comments from the psychological report which followed the staffing are of interest:

Danny's lack of conscience development and other intrinsic controls still present a serious problem in controlling his behavior. His immediate impulsive aggressive reaction to threatening situations may hamper any educational remediation efforts. The evidence presented still suggests that Danny, in light of increasing accumulation of family difficulties, lack of consistent masculine identification, his irascible and changeable nature, and educational pressures will have a difficult time adjusting to the educational situation. It is our opinion that unless further action is implemented, i.e. school officials should attempt to refer this boy to an appropriate agency (Mental Health, Institute for Juvenile Research) for additional help and correction, he is likely to become a potentially serious acting out youngster.

The data on Danny presented in figure 15.4 are most interesting. They show a small improvement in his behavior the first two weeks of the experimental phase. Generally the observers felt the whole class was quieter and better behaved. Danny especially stayed in his seat more of the time. However, a most dramatic change occurs when tutoring sessions in reading were begun (Week 8 to 9). It would appear that unless the child is capable of following the assigned activity, social reinforcement for 'on task' behavior is not enough. In Danny's data this point is supported by an analysis of the kinds of activities where he showed the most improvement. Dan was averaging 80 per cent deviant behavior when the activity was workbook assignments related to reading and language. In the reading group, where the teacher was there to help and direct activity, he averaged only 40 per cent deviant behaviors. By early May (Week 11) the amount of deviant behavior during 'seat work' activities had dropped to an average of 15 per cent, with only an occasional bad day.

Well into April, Danny had not shown much improvement in his afternoon classes (with teachers not in our program). Several observations suggested that he would still show high rates of deviant behaviors

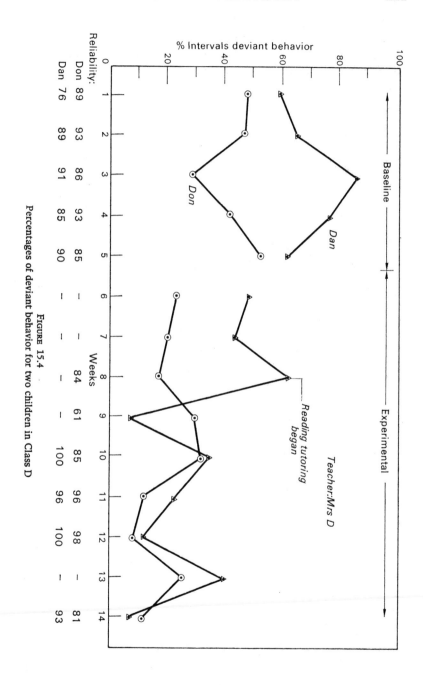

FIGURE 15.4
Percentages of deviant behavior for two children in Class D

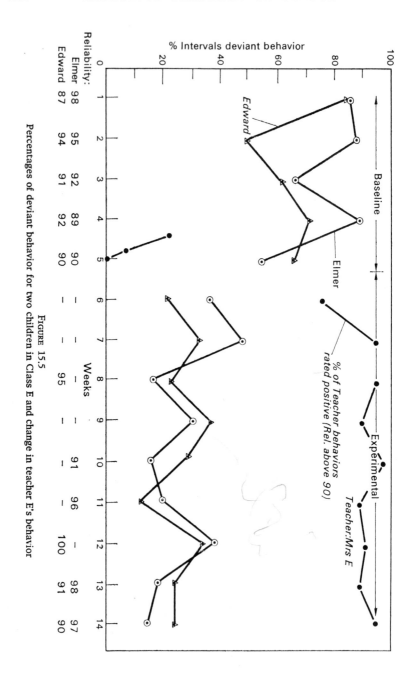

FIGURE 15.5
Percentages of deviant behavior for two children in Class E and change in teacher E's behavior

on days when he was otherwise on task, if the activity shifted to something he could not do. For example, May 5th showed 25 per cent deviant behavior during a period of seat work (*reading*), 30 per cent during *spelling*, and 55 per cent an hour later during *grammar* and *composition*. Danny was just beginning to move in reading, but was not ready for composition. The increase during Week 13 is due to one day where he was rated 40 per cent off task. The rater comments indicate the basis for the 'deviant' rating: 'Danny should have been sitting quietly after doing his work, but, instead of just waiting for the next assignment, he was playing with clay with another child. However, he was very quiet.' Comments from May 9th and 10th give some flavor of the changes which occurred.

May 9th: Mrs D reported that Danny, after he finished reading, immediately started on spelling. This is a highly unusual occurrence. Until now Danny has avoided spelling activities until made to work on them.
May 10th: Danny completely surprised the observer when he was on task the whole observation period, except for one minor talking to neighbor.

In view of the rather dramatic changes Danny has made in classroom behavior through a combination of remediation and social reinforcement, perhaps it is necessary to question the assumptions implicit in the quotation from Danny's psychological report given earlier. It should be noted that no attempt was made to work on family problems, his conscience, his masculine identification, or his 'irascible nature' in changing his adjustment to school.

Teacher E
We have saved until last the most dramatic of all the changes produced in teachers and children. Mrs E had a lower primary class of 23 children.
Observation of February 1, 1966:

Six children were in a reading group and 15 were working on individual projects. The noise level for the entire classroom was extremely high and went higher just before recess. Some behaviors noted included whistling, running around the room (5 occasions), yelling at another child (many times), loud incessant talk, hitting other children (7 times), pushing, shoving, and getting in front of each other in recess line. Mrs E would re-establish quiet by counting to 10, after giving a threat.

Observations suggested that control was obtained mainly by shouting, scolding and the like in an attempt to suppress unwanted behaviors. This approach would work for a while, but there was then a gradual build up in noise until quiet was again demanded. Figure 15.5 shows that Mrs E's responses on three days prior to a shift to positive reinforcement contained very few positive statements. Essentially, there was nothing to maintain appropriate classroom behaviors. The focus was on what not to do rather than what to do. There is a good possibility that the attention given deviant behavior in fact served to reinforce it.

Edward and Elmer were selected as barometers which might reflect changes for the whole class. Mrs E was given the general instructions presented above but no special instructions for Edward and Elmer. They were not to receive more attention than other members of the class. She was to make her rules clear, repeat them as needed, ignore deviant behavior and give praise and attention to behavior which facilitated learning. We wanted to see if a general approach to classroom management would be effective with children showing a high level of deviant behavior. The rating of Mrs E's behavior before and after the change clearly shows an effect of the experimental instructions and training on her behavior.

Edward (age 6:8) tested 95 on the Stanford-Binet. Mrs E considered him to be 'distractible', to have poor work habits, show poor attention and not to comprehend what he read. He never finished assignments. He could sight read and spell first-grade words. The baseline observations showed a high incidence of wandering about the room, turning around in his seat, talking at the wrong time and making odd noises. He also showed little peer play.

A psychological examination in January of 1966 stressed Edward's poor social history (his parents had not talked to each other for three years), his lack of enthusiasm and emotional responsiveness, the apparent restriction on his peer interaction by his mother and his need for better listening and language skills. Edward received speech therapy while in kindergarten. Throughout the baseline and experimental phase of this study, Edward was seen by a social worker and continued in speech therapy. In view of the fact that his (and Elmer's) behavioral changes are found to be directly associated with the change in classroom procedures, rather than time *per se*, these other treatments do not offer convincing alternative explanations for the data.

Edward greatly reduced the time he spent in aimless wandering, twisting in his seat and talking. He responded well to praise in both the reading group and class activities. Mrs E reports that he began to complete assignments. He also showed better give and take with his peers, and would laugh, cry and make jokes. While still 'distractible', he has learned to work independently for longer periods of time.

Elmer (6 years, 10 months) scored 97 on a group I.Q. test. He apparently started out the school year working well, but his work deteriorated. He seemed 'nervous', hyperactive and would not work. He threw several tantrums and would cry if his work was criticized. His twin sister was also in the class and was doing well. By comparison Elmer often lost out. The parents expected as much of Elmer as of his sister. During baseline he was rated as showing inappropriate gross motor behaviors as much as 70 per cent of the time. *Talking* was as high as 50 per cent at times. *Noise* and *turning* in seat were at about 10 per cent each. Initially our observers thought he was brain damaged.

Elmer's rapid response to positive reinforcement and a better structured classroom made it possible for him to stay on task longer. However, he did not improve greatly in his reading group. When the children were silently reading, he would at times clown and make noises. More work on reading will be necessary for academic progress.

Elmer's father came to work as a teacher's aid in one of our other classes just after the shift off baseline. His work with Mrs C and changes in Elmer led slowly to his accepting the value of a positive rather than a punitive approach. Very likely father's attempt to be more rewarding with Elmer contributed to the maintenance of Elmer's improved classroom behavior. More to the point, however, is the fact that Elmer's improved classroom behavior (we showed father the graph during Week 9) served to reinforce father's acceptance of a positive approach.

In her report at the end of the semester Mrs E felt that 12 of 23 children in her class definitely profited from her change in behavior, that six children were unchanged, three somewhat improved and two more deviant. The children who were reported unchanged tended to be the quiet and submissive ones who escaped Mrs E's attention much of the time. From her own comments, it is likely that those reported to be more deviant seem so only because they stand out from the group more now that Elmer and Edward are not such big problems.

Implications

The results of these investigations demonstrate that quite different kinds of teachers can learn to apply behavioral principles effectively to modify the behavior of problem children. These results extend to the elementary classroom, with normal teacher-pupil ratios, the importance of *differential* social reinforcement in developing effective social behaviors in children. Work now in progress suggests that rules alone do nothing and that simply ignoring deviant behavior actually increases such behavior. The combination of ignoring deviant behavior and reinforcing an incompatible behavior seems critical. Nearly all of our teachers found that the technique of praising a child who was showing an incompatible appropriate behavior, when another child was mis-behaving, was especially effective. This action keeps the teacher from attending to the deviant act and at the same time provides vicarious reinforcement for an incompatible behavior. In the future we hope to bring together a group of techniques which various teachers found effective in implementing the general strategy of this project.

These findings add support to the proposition that much can be done by the classroom teacher to eliminate behaviors which interfere with learning without extensive changes in the home, or intensive therapy.

References

Section A The Nature of Behaviour Problems

BARTON HALL, M. (1947) *Psychiatric Examination of the School Child.* London: Edward Arnold.

BEILIN, H. (1959) 'Teachers' and clinicians' attitudes toward the behavior of children—a reappraisal.' *Child Dev., 30,* 9–25.

BRINKMANN, E. H. and BRINKMANN, R. A. (1963) 'Group influence on the individual in the classroom: a case study.' *Merrill-Palmer Quart., 9,* 195–204.

BURT, C. and HOWARD, M. (1952) 'The nature and causes of maladjustment among children of school age.' *Br. J. Psychol. (Statistical Section), 5,* 39–60.

CLARK, E. (1951) 'Teacher reactions toward objectionable pupil behavior.' *Elementary School Journal, 51,* 446–9.

DAVIDSON, S. (1961) 'School phobia as a manifestation of family disturbance: its structure and treatment.' *J. child Psychol. Psychiat., 1,* 270–87.

DEL SOLAR, C. (1949) *Parents and teachers view the child: a comparative study of parents' and teachers' appraisals of children.* New York: Teachers College, Columbia University.

ELLIS, D. and MILLER, L. (1936) 'Teachers' attitudes and child behavior problems.' *J. educ. Psychol., 27,* 501–11.

ENGLISH, O. S. and PEARSON, G. H. (1947) *Emotional Problems of Living.* New York: Norton (3rd edn 1963).

FRICK, W. B. (1964) 'School phobia: a critical review of the literature.' *Merrill-Palmer Quart., 10,* 361–74.

GALLAGHER, J. J. and ASCHNER, M. J. (1963) 'A preliminary report on analyses of classroom interaction.' *Merrill-Palmer Quart., 9,* 183–94.

GARDNER, D. E. M. (1942) *Testing Results in the Infant School.* London: Methuen.

GARDNER, D. E. M. (1950) *Long Term Results of Infant School Methods.* London: Methuen.

GARDNER, D. E. M. (1965) *Experiment and Tradition in Primary Schools.* London: Methuen.

GARRISON, K. C., KINGSTON, A. J. and BERNARD, H. W. (1967) *The Psychology of Childhood.* New York: Scribner's.

H*

228 BEHAVIOUR PROBLEMS IN SCHOOL

GRIMES, J. W. and ALLINSON, W. (1961) 'Compulsivity, anxiety, and school achievement.' *Merrill-Palmer Quart.*, 7, 247–72.

HADFIELD, J. A. (1950) *Psychology and Mental Health.* London: Allen and Unwin.

HALMOS, P. (1958) (ed.) 'Papers on the teaching of personality development.' *Sociol. Rev. Monogr.*, 1.

HEMMING, J. (1948) 'Standards of social health in the school community.' *New Era*, 29, 121–7.

HERBERT, E. L. (1955) 'Human problems in the educational field.' *New Era*, 36, 102–6.

HERSOV, L. A. (1961a) 'Persistent non-attendance at school.' *J. child Psychol. Psychiat.*, 1, 130–6.

HERSOV, L. A. (1961b) 'Refusal to go to school.' *J. child Psychol. Psychiat.*, 1, 137–45.

HILDRETH, G. A. (1928) 'A survey of problem pupils.' *J. educ. Res.* 18, 1–14.

HUNTER, E. C. (1957) 'Changes in teachers' attitudes toward children's behavior over the last thirty years.' *Ment. Hyg. NY*, 41, 3–11.

JOHNSON, R. C. and MEDINNUS, G. R. (1965) *Child Development.* New York: Wiley.

LEVY, D. M. (1943) *Maternal Overprotection.* New York: Columbia University Press.

McCLURE, W. E. (1929) 'Characteristics of problem children based on judgments of teachers.' *Journal of Juvenile Research*, 13, 124–40.

MITCHELL, J. C. (1942) 'A study of teachers' and mental hygienists' ratings of certain behavior problems.' *J. educ. Res.*, 36, 292–307.

MOORE, T. W. (1959) 'Studying the growth of personality: a discussion on the uses of psychological data obtained in a longitudinal study of child development.' *Vita hum.*, 2, 65–87.

MOORE, T. W., HINDLEY, C. B. and FALKNER, F. (1954) 'A longitudinal research in child development and some of its problems.' *Br. med. J.*, II, 1132–7.

PECK, L. (1935) 'Teachers' reports of the problems of unadjusted school children.' *J. educ. Psychol.*, 26, 123–38.

POPPER, E. (1952) 'The difficult child at school.' *New Era*, 33, 197–200.

RAVEN, J. C. (1958) *Guide to using the Mill Hill Vocabulary Scale and the Progressive Matrices Scales.* London: H. K. Lewis.

Registrar General (1950) *Classification of Occupations.* London: HMSO.

SARASON, S. B. et al. (1960) *Anxiety in Elementary School Children.* New York: Wiley.

SNYDER, L. M. (1934) 'The problem child in the Jersey City elementary schools.' *J. educ. Soc.*, 7, 343–59.

SPARKS, J. N. (1952) 'Teachers' attitudes toward the behavior problems of children.' *J. educ. Psychol.*, 43, 284–91.

STOUFFER, G. A. W., Jr. (1952) 'Behavior problems of children as viewed by teachers and mental hygienists.' *Ment. Hyg. NY, 36,* 271–85.

STOUFFER, G. A. W., Jr. (1956) 'The attitudes of secondary school teachers toward certain behavior problems of children.' *School Review, 64,* 358–66.

TAYLOR, P. H. (1962) 'Children's evaluation of the characteristics of the good teacher.' *Br. J. educ. Psychol., 32,* 258–66.

THOMPSON, G. G. (1962) *Child Psychology.* Boston: Houghton-Mifflin.

TIBBLE, J. W. (1959) 'The concept of adjustment.' *New Era, 40,* 198–204.

WALL, W. D. (1955) *Education and Mental Health.* Paris: UNESCO; London: Harrap.

WATSON, G. A. (1933) 'A critical note on two attitude scales.' *Ment. Hyg. NY, 17,* 59–64.

WATSON, R. Y. (1965) *Psychology of Childhood.* New York: Wiley.

WICKMAN, E. K. (1928) *Children's Behavior and Teachers' Attitudes.* New York: Commonwealth Fund.

Section B   Identification of Maladjusted Behaviour

BELLER, E. K. (1962) *Clinical Process: A New Approach to the Organisation and Assessment of Clinical Data.* Illinois: Free Press of Glencoe.

BOWER, E. M. (1958) 'A process for early identification of emotionally disturbed children.' *Bulletin of California State Department of Education, 27,* 1–65.

BOWLBY, J., AINSWORTH, M. B. and ROSENBLUTH, D. (1956) 'The effects of mother-child separation: a follow-up study.' *Br. J. med. Psychol., 29,* 211–47.

BURT, C. (1933) *The Subnormal Mind.* London: Oxford University Press.

BURT, C. (1937) *The Backward Child.* London: University of London Press.

BURT, C. and HOWARD, M. (1952) 'Nature and causes of maladjustment among children of school age.' *Br. J. Psychol. (Statistical Section), 5,* 39–59.

CAMERON, K. (1955) 'Diagnostic categories in child psychiatry.' *Br. J. Psychol., 28,* 67–71.

CATTELL, R. B. and COAN, R. W. (1957) 'Personality factors in middle childhood as revealed in parents' ratings.' *Child Dev., 28,* 439–58.

CHAZAN, M. (1963) 'Maladjustment, attainment and sociometric status.' *University College of Swansea, Faculty of Education Journal,* pp. 4–7.

CUMMINGS, J. D. (1944) 'Emotional symptoms in school children.' *Br. J. educ. Psychol., 14,* 151–61.

DOUGLAS, J. W. B. (1964) *The Home and the School.* London: MacGibbon and Kee.

EISENBERG, L., LANDOWNE, E. J., WILNER, D. N. and IMBER, S. D. (1962)
'The use of teacher ratings in a mental health study: a method for
measuring the effectiveness of a therapeutic nursery programme.' Am. J.
publ. Hlth., 52, 18–28.

GLIDEWELL, J. C., DOMKE, H. R. and KANTOR, M. B. (1963) 'Screening in
schools for behaviour disorder: use of mothers' reports of symptoms.'
J. educ. Res., 56, 508–15.

HAGGERTY, M. E. (1952) 'The incidence of undesirable behaviour in public
school children.' J. educ. Res., 12, 102–22.

LAPOUSE, R. and MONK, M. (1958) 'An epidemiological study of behaviour
characteristics in children.' Am. J. publ. Hlth., 48, 1134–44.

MACFARLANE, JEAN W., ALLEN, L. and HONZIK, M. P. (1954) A Developmental Study of the Behaviour Problems of Normal Children. Berkeley:
University of California Press.

McFIE, B. S. (1934) 'Behaviour and personality difficulties in school children.'
Br. J. educ. Psychol., 4, 30–46.

MEEHL, P. E. and ROSEN, A. (1955) 'Antecedent probability of the efficiency
of psychometric signs, patterns or cutting scores.' Psychol. Bull., 52,
194–216.

Ministry of Education (1955) Report of the Committee on Maladjusted
Children. London: HMSO (Underwood Report).

MITCHELL, SHEILA (1965) 'A Study of the Mental Health of School Children
in an English County.' Unpublished Ph.D. thesis, University of London.

MULLIGAN, D. G. (1963) Personal communication cited in RYLE, A., POND,
D. A. and HAMILTON, M. (1965) 'The prevalence and patterns of psychological disturbance in children of primary age.' J. child Psychol. Psychiat.,
6, 101–13.

MULLIGAN, D. G. (1964) 'Some correlates of maladjustment in a national
sample of school children.' Ph.D. thesis, University of London.

MULLIGAN, D. G., DOUGLAS, J. W. B., HAMMOND, W. A. and TIZARD, J. (1963)
'Delinquency and symptoms of maladjustment: the findings of a longitudinal study.' Proc. R. Soc. Med., 56, 1083–6.

OLSON, W. C. (1930) Problem Tendencies in Children: A Method for Measurement and Description. Minneapolis: University of Minnesota Press.

PEARSON, G. H. J. (1952) 'A survey of learning difficulties in children.'
Psychoanal. Study Child, 7, 322–86.

PILTZER, E. (1952) 'Disturbed children who make good school adjustment.'
Smith Coll. Stud. Soc. Wk., 22, 193–210.

PRITCHARD, M. (1963) 'Observation of children in a psychiatric in-patient
unit.' Br. J. Psychiat., 109, 572–8.

RICHMAN, N. (1964) 'The prevalence of psychiatric disturbance in a hospital
school for epileptics.' D.P.M. dissertation, University of London.

ROGERS, C. R. (1942) 'Mental health findings in three elementary schools.' *Educ. Res. Bull.* (Ohio State University), *21*, 69–79.

ROSS, A. O., LACEY, H. M. and PARTON, D. A. (1965) 'The development of a behaviour checklist for boys.' *Child Dev.*, *36*, 1013–27.

RUTTER, M. (1965) 'Classification and categorization in child psychiatry.' *J. child Psychol. Psychiat.*, *6*, 71–83.

RUTTER, M. (1966) 'A children's behaviour questionnaire for completion by teachers: preliminary findings.' *J. child Psychol. Psychiat.*, *8*, 1–11.

RUTTER, M. and GRAHAM, P. (1966) 'Psychiatric disorder in 10- and 11-year-old children.' *Proc. R. Soc. Med.*, *59*, 382–7.

RUTTER, M. and GRAHAM, P. (1968) 'The reliability and validity of the psychiatric assessment of the child. I. Interview with the child.' *Br. J. Psychiat.*, *114*, 563–79.

SCHONELL, F. J. (1952) 'The development of educational research in Great Britain: Part 7. Maladjusted children.' *Br. J. educ. Psychol.*, *22*, 30–9.

Scottish Education Department (1964) *Ascertainment of Maladjusted Children:* Report of the Working Party appointed by the Secretary of State for Scotland. Edinburgh: HMSO.

STOTT, D. H. (1958) *The Social Adjustment of Children.* Manual to the *Bristol Social Adjustment Guides.* London: University of London Press, (4th edn, 1971).

TIZARD, J. (1966) 'Mental subnormality and child psychiatry.' *J. child Psychol. Psychiat.*, *7*, 1–15.

ULLMAN, C. A. (1952) 'Identification of maladjusted school children.' *Publ. Hlth. Monogr.* (U.S.), No. 7.

VERNON, P. E. (1964) *Personality Assessment: A Critical Survey.* London: Methuen.

WICKMAN, E. K. (1928) *Children's Behaviour and Teachers' Attitudes.* New York: Commonwealth Fund.

YULE, W. and RUTTER, M. (1968) 'Educational aspects of childhood maladjustment.' *Br. J. educ. Psychol.*, *38*, 1, 7–9.

Section C   Causes of Maladjustment

AINSWORTH, M. D. and BOWLBY, J. (1954) 'Research strategy in the study of mother-child separation.' *Courrier du Centre International de l'Enfance*, *4*, 105–31.

ALLEN, F. (1955) 'Mother-child separation—process or event?' In G. CAPLAN (ed.), *Emotional Problems of Early Childhood.* New York: Basic Books.

ALLPORT, G. W. (1938) *Personality: A Psychological Interpretation.* London: Constable.

BETTLEHEIM, B. (1967) *The Empty Fortress.* New York: Free Press.

232   BEHAVIOUR PROBLEMS IN SCHOOL

BODMAN, F., MACKINLAY, M. and SYKES, K. (1950) 'The social adaptation of institution children.' *Lancet*, 258, 173–6.

BOWLBY, J. (1946) *Forty-four juvenile thieves, their characters and home life.* London: Baillière, Tindall & Cox.

BOWLBY, J. (1951) *Maternal care and mental health.* Monograph Series of the World Health Organization, No. 2, Geneva.

BOWLBY, J., AINSWORTH, M. D., BOSTON, M. and ROSENBLUTH, D. (1956) 'The effects of mother-child separation; a follow-up study.' *Br. J. med. Psychol.*, 29, 211–44.

BURT, C. (1925) *The Young Delinquent.* London: University of London Press.

BURT, C. (1933) *The Subnormal Mind.* London: Oxford University Press.

BURT, C. (1946) 'The assessment of personality.' *Egypt. J. Psychol.*, II, 1–21.

CALDWELL, B. M. and RICHMOND, J. B. (1964) 'Programmed day care for the very young child.' *J. Marriage and the Family*, 26, 481–9.

COOLIDGE, J. C., TESSMAN, E., WALDFOGEL, S. and WILLER, M. (1962) 'Patterns of aggression in school phobia.' *Psychoanal. Study Child*, 17, 319–33.

DAVIDSON, S. (1961) 'School phobia as a manifestation of family disturbance.' *J. child Psychol. Psychiat.*, 1, 270–87.

DOLL, E. A. (1953) *The Measurement of Social Competence; a manual for the Vineland Social Maturity Scale.* Minneapolis, U.S.A.: Educational Test Bureau.

EISENBERG, L. (1958) 'School phobia: a study in the communication of anxiety.' *Am. J. Psychiat.*, 114, 712–18.

ESTES, H. R., HAYLETT, C. H. and JOHNSON, E. M. (1956) 'Separation anxiety.' *Am. J. Psychother.*, 10, 682–95.

FITZGERALD, O. W. S. (1948) 'Love deprivation and hysterical personality.' *J. ment. Sci.*, 94, 701–17.

FORD, D. (1955) *The Deprived Child and the Community.* London: Constable.

GARVEY, W. and HEGRENES, S. R. (1966) 'Desensitization techniques in the treatment of school phobia.' *Am. J. Orthopsychiat.*, 36, 147–52.

GOLDBERG, T. (1953) 'Factors in the development of school phobia.' *Smith College Studies in Social Work*, 23, 227–48.

GOLDFARB, W. (1943) 'Infant rearing and problem behaviour.' *Am. J. Orthopsychiat.*, 13, 249–65.

GORDON, R. G. (1939) (ed.) *A Survey of Child Psychiatry.* London: Oxford University Press.

HALL, M. B. (1947) *Psychiatric Examination of the School Child.* London: Arnold.

HARMS, E. (1947) (ed.) *Handbook of Child Guidance.* New York City: Child Publications.

HARROWES, W. (1949) *Human Personality and its Minor Disorders.* Edinburgh: Livingstone.

HENDERSON, D. K. and GILLESPIE, R. D. (1933) *Textbook of Psychiatry.* London: Oxford University Press.

Home Office (1946) *Report of the Care of Children Committee.* Cmd. 6922. London: HMSO (Curtis Report).

JOHNSON, A. M., FALSTEIN, E. I., SZUREK, S. A. and SVENDSEN, M. (1941) 'School phobia.' *Am. J. Orthopsychiat., 11,* 104–27.

KESSLER, J. W. (1966) *Psychopathology of Childhood.* Englewood Cliffs, New Jersey: Prentice-Hall.

LAFORE, G. G. (1945) 'The practices of parents in dealing with pre-school children.' *Child Development Monographs,* No. 31. New York: Teachers College, Columbia University.

LAZARUS, A. A., DAVISON, G. C. and POLEFKA, D. A. (1965) 'Classical and operant factors in the treatment of a school phobia.' *J. abnor. Psychol., 70,* 225–9.

LEVENTHAL, T. and SILLS, M. (1964) 'Self image in school phobia.' *Am. J. Orthopsychiat., 34,* 685–95.

LEVENTHAL, T., WEINBERGER, G., STANDER, T. J. and STEARNS, R. P. (1967) 'Therapeutic strategies with school phobics.' *Am. J. Orthopsychiat., 34,* 67–70.

MABERLEY, A. (1946) 'A symposium on personality. II. Personality of the problem child.' *Br. J. educ. Psychol., 16,* 5–12.

MESSER, A. A. (1964) *Treatment of the Child in Emotional Conflict.* New York: McGraw-Hill.

MEYER, A. (1935) 'The psychobiological point of view.' Ap. National Research Council, *The Problem of Mental Disorder.* New York: McGraw-Hill.

Ministry of Education (1945) *Handicapped Pupils and School Health Service Regulations.* London: HMSO.

PRINGLE, M. L. KELLMER (1957) 'Differences between schools for the maladjusted and ordinary boarding schools.' *Br. J. educ. Psychol., 27,* 29–36.

PRINGLE, M. L. KELLMER (1958) 'Learning and emotion.' *Educ. Rev., 10,* 146–68.

PRINGLE, M. L. KELLMER and BOSSIO, V. (1958) 'A study of deprived children. Part 2. Language development and reading attainment.' *Vita hum., 1,* 142–70.

RAVEN, J. C. (1948) *Mill Hill Vocabulary Scale.* London: H. K. Lewis.

RAVEN, J. C. (1951) *Controlled Projection for Children.* (2nd edn) London: H. K. Lewis.

RHEINGOLD, H. L. (1943) 'Mental and social development of infants in

234   BEHAVIOUR PROBLEMS IN SCHOOL

relation to the number of other infants in the boarding home.' *Am. J. Orthopsychiat., 13*, 41–4.

ROGERS, C. R. (1942) 'A study of mental health problems in three representative elementary schools.' *Bureau of Educational Research Monographs,* No. 25. Ohio: Ohio State University.

SAIY, B. and HARLOW, H. F. (1965) 'Maternal separation in the rhesus monkey.' *J. nerv. ment. Dis., 140,* 434–41.

SANDIFORD, P. (1938) *Foundations of Educational Psychology.* London: Longmans.

SCHONELL, F. J. and SCHONELL, F. E. (1956) *Diagnostic and Attainment Testing. (Silent Reading Test B).* 3rd edn. London: Oliver & Boyd.

SHRYOCK, R. H. (1948) *The Development of Modern Medicine: An Interpretation of the Social and Scientific Factors Involved.* London: Gollancz.

SPITZ, R. A. (1945) 'Hospitalism; an inquiry into the genesis of psychiatric conditions in early childhood.' In *Psychoanalytic Study of the Child, I,* 53–74. London: Imago Publishing Co.

STOTT, D. H. (1956) 'The effects of separation from the mother in early life.' *Lancet,* 624–8.

STOTT, D. H. (1958) *The Social Adjustment of Children;* manual to the *Bristol Social Adjustment Guides.* London: University of London Press (4th edn, 1971).

SULLY, J. (1886) *Teachers' Handbook of Psychology.* London: Longmans.

SUTTERFIELD, V. (1954) 'School phobia: a study of five cases.' *Am. J. Orthopsychiat., 24,* 368–80.

United Nations, Department of Social Affairs (1952) *Children Deprived of a Normal Home Life.* New York.

WALDFOGEL, S., TESSMAN, E. and HAHN, P. B. (1959) 'A program for early intervention in school phobia.' *Am. J. Orthopsychiat., 29,* 324–33.

WARREN, W. (1960) 'Some relationships between psychiatry of children and adults.' *J. ment. Sci., 106,* 815–26.

WECHSLER, D. (1949) *Wechsler Intelligence Scale for Children.* New York: Psychological Corporation.

YARROW, L. J. (1964) 'Separation from parents during early childhood.' In M. I. HOFFMAN and L. W. HOFFMAN (eds.), *Review of Child Development Research.* New York: Russell Sage Foundation.

Section D   Methods of Treatment

ALLEN, K. E., HART, B. M., BUELL, J. S., HARRIS, F. R. and WOLF, M. M. (1964) 'Effects of social reinforcement on isolate behavior of a nursery school child.' *Child Dev. 35,* 511–18.

ALLEN, K. E. and HARRIS, F. R. (1966) 'Elimination of a child's excessive scratching by training the mother in reinforcement procedures.' *Behav. Res. Ther.*, *1*, 305–12.

ALLEN, K. E., HENKE, L. B., HARRIS, F. R., BAER, D. M. and REYNOLDS, N. F. (1967) 'The control of hyperactivity by social reinforcement of attending behavior in a preschool child.' *J. educ. Psychol.*, *58*, 231–7.

ANNESLEY, P. T. (1961) 'Psychiatric illness in adolescence: presentation and prognosis.' *J. ment. Sci.*, *107*, 268–78.

BENDER, L. and GUREVITZ, S. (1955) 'The results of psychotherapy with young schizophrenic children.' *Am. J. Othopsychiat.*, *25*, 162–70.

BIJOU, S. W., PETERSON, R. F., HARRIS, F. R., ALLEN, K. E. and JOHNSTON, M. S. (1969) 'Methodology for experimental studies of young children in natural settings.' *Psychol. Rec.*, *19*, 177–210.

BLOCH, D. D. and ROSENFELD, E. (1962) 'Evaluation (process-outcome) studies of the psychiatric treatment of children. Progress report and research plans for the years 1962–1964.' Unpublished memorandum, Jewish Board of Guardians, New York.

BUCKLE, D. and LEBOVICI, S. (1960) *Child Guidance Centres.* Geneva: World Health Organization.

CATTELL, R. B. and COAN, R. W. (1957) 'Personality factors in middle childhood as revealed in parents' ratings.' *Child Dev.*, *28*, 439–58.

CHARNY, I. W. (1961) 'Regression and reorganization in the "isolation treatment" of children: a clinical contribution to sensory deprivation research.' Paper presented at the meeting of the American Psychological Association, New York.

CHESS, S. (1957) 'Evaluation of the effectiveness of an interracial child guidance clinic: diagnosis and treatment.' Unpublished paper, New York.

CUNNINGHAM, J. J., WESTERMAN, H. H. and FISCHHOFF, J. (1956) 'A follow-up study of patients seen in a psychiatric clinic for children.' *Am. J. Orthopsychiat.*, *26*, 602–11.

CYTRYN, L., GILBERT, A. and EISENBERG, L. (1960) 'The effectiveness of tranquilizing drugs plus supportive psychotherapy in treating behaviour disorders of children: a double blind study of 80 outpatients.' *Am. J. Orthopsychiat.*, *30*, 113–28.

DORFMAN, E. (1958) 'Personality outcomes of client-centred child therapy.' *Psychol. Monogr.*, *72*, No. 456.

EISENBERG, L., MARLOWE, B. and HASTINGS, M. (1958a) 'Diagnostic services of maladjusted foster children: an orientation toward an acute need.' *Am. J. Orthopsychiat.*, *28*, 750–63.

EISENBERG, L. (1958b) 'School phobia: a study in the communication of anxiety.' *Am. J. Pschiat.*, *114*, 712–18.

EISENBERG, L. and GRUENBERG, E. M. (1961) 'The current status of secondary prevention in child psychiatry.' *Am. J. Orthopsychiat.*, *31*, 355–67.

FERSTER, C. B. and DeMYER, M. K. (1961) 'The development of performances in autistic children in an automatically controlled environment.' *J. chron. Dis.*, *13*, 312–45.

FILMER-BENNETT, G. and HILLSON, J. S. (1959) 'Some child therapy practices.' *J. clin. Psychol.*, *15*, 105–6.

GLIDEWELL, J. C., DOMKE, R. H. and KANTOR, M. B. (1963) 'Screening in schools for behaviour disorders: use of mothers' reports of symptoms.' *J. educ. Res.*, *56*, 508–15.

HALL, J. and JONES, D. C. (1950) 'Social grading of occupations.' *Br. J. Sociol.*, *1*, 31–55.

HAMILTON, D. M., McKINLEY, R. A., MOORHEAD, H. H. and WALL, J. H. (1961) 'Results of mental hospital treatment of troubled youth.' *Am. J. Psychiat.*, *117*, 811–16.

HARING, N. G., HAYDEN, A. H. and ALLEN, K. E. (1968) *Building Social Skills in the Preschool Child.* 16 mm colour film. Experimental Education Unit, Child Development and Mental Retardation Center, University of Washington.

HARING, N. G., HAYDEN, A. H. and NOLEN, P. A. (1969) 'Accelerating appropriate behaviors of children in a Head Start program.' *Exceptional Children*, *35*, 773–84.

HARRIS, F. R., JOHNSTON, M. K., KELLEY, C. S. and WOLF, M. M. (1964) 'Effects of positive social reinforcement on regressed crawling in a pre-school child.' *J. educ. Psychol.*, *55*, 35–41.

HARRIS, F. R., WOLF, M. M. and BAER, D. M. (1964) 'Effects of adult social reinforcement on child behavior.' *Young Children*, *1*, 8–17.´

HART, B. M., ALLEN, K. E., BUELL, J. S., HARRIS, F. R. and WOLF, M. M. (1964) 'Effects of social reinforcement on operant crying.' *J. exp. Child. Psychol.*, *1*, 145–53.

HAWKINS, R. P., PETERSON, R. F., SCHWEID, E. and BIJOU, S. W. (1966) 'Behavior therapy in the home: amelioration of problem parent-child relations with the parent in a therapeutic role.' *J. exp. Child Psychol.*, *4*, 99–107.

HEINICKE, C. M. (1960) 'Research on psychotherapy with children: a review and suggestions for further study.' *Am. J. Orthopsychiat.*, *30*, 483–93.

HERSOV, L. A. (1960) 'Refusal to go to school.' *J. child Psychol. Psychiat.*, *1*, 137–45.

HOOD-WILLIAMS, J. (1960) 'The results of psychotherapy with children: a revaluation.' *J. consult. Psychol.*, *24*, 84–8.

KANE, R. P. and CHAMBERS, G. S. (1961) 'Improvement: real or apparent? A seven year follow-up of children hospitalized and discharged from a residential setting.' *Am. J. Psychiat.*, *117*, 1023–6.

KANNER, L. (1957) *Child Psychiatry.* (3rd edn) Springfield, Ill.: C. C. Thomas.

KANNER, L. (1960) 'Do behavioural symptoms always indicate psycho-pathology?' *J. child Psychol. Psychiat.*, *1*, 17–25.

KAUFMAN, I., FRANK, T., FRIEND, J., HEIMS, L. W. and WEISS, R. (1962) 'Success and failure in the treatment of childhood schizophrenia.' *Am. J. Psychiat.*, *118*, 909–13.

KLEIN, J. W. (1969) 'Innovative approaches in project Head Start.' Paper presented at the Council for Exceptional Children, Special Conference on Early Childhood Education, New Orleans.

LAKE, M. and LEVINGER, G. (1960) 'Continuance beyond application inter-views in a child guidance clinic.' *J. soc. Casework*, *91*, 303–9.

LAPOUSE, R., MONK, M. A. and STREET, E. (1964) 'A method for use in epidemiological studies of behaviour disorders in children.' *Am. J. publ. Hlth.*, *54*, 207–22.

LAVIETES, R. L., HULSE, W. and BLAU, A. (1960) 'A psychiatric day-treat-ment center and school for young children and their parents.' *Am. J. Orthopsychiat.*, *30*, 468–82.

LAZARUS, A. A. and ABRAMOVITZ, A. (1962) 'The use of "emotive imagery" in the treatment of children's phobias.' *J. ment. Sci.*, *108*, 191–5.

LEVITT, E. E. (1957a) 'Results of psychotherapy with children: an evalua-tion.' *J. consult. Psychol.*, *21*, 189–96.

LEVITT, E. E. (1957b) 'A comparison of "remainers" and "defectors" among child clinic patients.' *J. consult. Psychol.*, *21*, 316.

LEVITT, E. E. (1958a) 'A comparative judgmental study of "defection" from treatment at a child guidance clinic.' *J. clin. Psychol.*, *14*, 429–32.

LEVITT, E. E. (1958b) 'Parents' reasons for defection from treatment at a child guidance clinic.' *Ment. Hyg. N.Y.*, *42*, 521–4.

LEVITT, E. E., BEISER, H. R. and ROBERTSON, R. E. (1959) 'A follow-up evaluation of cases treated at a community child guidance clinic.' *Am. J. Orthopsychiat.*, *29*, 337–47.

LEVITT, E. E. (1960) 'Reply to Hood-Williams.' *J. consult. Psychol.*, *24*, 89–91.

MACFARLANE, J. W., ALLEN, L. and HONZIK, M. P. (1954) *A Developmental Study of the Behaviour Problems of Normal Children Between 21 months and 14 years.* Berkeley: University of California Press.

MICHAEL, C. M., MORRIS, H. H. and SORAKER, E. (1957) 'Follow-up studies of shy, withdrawn children—II. Relative incidence of schizophrenia.' *Am. J. Orthopsychiat.*, *27*, 331–7.

MILLER, D. H. (1957) 'The treatment of adolescents in an adult hospital: a preliminary report.' *Bull. Menninger Clin.*, *21*, 189–98.

Ministry of Education (1955) *Report of the Committee on Maladjusted Children.* London: HMSO (Underwood Report).

MITCHELL, SHEILA (1965) 'A Study of the Mental Health of School Children in an English County.' Unpublished Ph.D. thesis, University of London.

MORRIS, H. H., ESCOLI, P. J. and WEXLER, R. (1956) 'Aggressive behavior disorders of childhood: A follow-up study.' *Am. J. Psychiat.*, 112, 991–7.

NOLEN, P. A., HULTEN, W. J. and KUNZELMANN, H. P. (1968) 'Data diagnosis and programing.' In JOHN I. ARENA (ed.), *Successful Programing: Many Points of View*. Boston: Fifth Annual International Conference of the Association for Children with Learning Disabilities, 409–18.

O'LEARY, K. D. and BECKER, W. C. (1967) 'Behavior modification in an adjustment class: a token reinforcement program.' *Exceptional Children*, 33, (9), 637–42.

O'NEAL, P. and ROBINS, L. N. (1958a) 'The relation of childhood behavior problems to adult psychiatric status.' *Am. J. Psychiat.*, 114, 961–9.

O'NEAL, P. and ROBINS, L. N. (1958b) 'Childhood patterns predictive of adult schizophrenia.' *Am. J. Psychiat.*, 115, 385–91.

PHILLIPS, E. L. (1957) 'Some features of child guidance clinic practice in the U.S.A.' *J. clin. Psychol.*, 13, 42–4.

PHILLIPS, E. L. (1960) 'Parent-child psychotherapy: a follow-up study comparing two techniques.' *J. Psychol.*, 49, 195–202.

PHILLIPS, E. L. (1961) 'Logical analysis of childhood behavior problems and their treatment.' *Psychol. Rep.*, 9, 705–12.

REXFORD, E. N., SCHLEIFER, M. and VAN AMERONGEN, S. T. (1956) 'A follow-up of a psychiatric study of 57 antisocial young children.' *Ment. Hyg. N.Y.*, 40, 196–214.

RODRIGUEZ, A., RODRIGUEZ, M. and EISENBERG, L. (1959) 'The outcome of school phobia: a follow-up study based on 41 cases.' *Am. J. Psychiat.*, 116, 540–44.

ROSS, A. O. and LACEY, H. M. (1961) 'Characteristics of terminators and remainers in child guidance treatment.' *J. consult. Psychol.*, 25, 420–4.

RYLE, A. (1963) 'Psychotherapy by general practitioners.' *Proc. R. Soc. Med.*, 56, 834–7.

SEIDMAN, F. (1957) 'A study of some evaluation variables in a child guidance center.' Paper presented at the meeting of the American Association of Psychiatric Clinics for Children.

STRUPP, H. (1962) 'Psychotherapy.' *Ann. Rev. Psychol.*, 13, 445–78.

WAHLER, R. G., WINKEL, G. H., PETERSON, R. F. and MORRISON, D. C. (1965) 'Mothers as behavior therapists for their own children.' *Behav. Res. Ther.*, 3, 113–24.

WINNICOTT, D. W. (1965) *The Family and Individual Development*. London: Tavistock.

ZAUSMER, D. M. (1954) 'The treatment of tics in childhood.' *Arch. Dis. Childh.*, 29, 537–42.

Some Suggestions for Further Reading

Books

The suggestions which follow are not intended to constitute a bibliography. They are offered as a short list of selected books which will enable the interested student to carry forward his interest in the different sections of this reader. For this purpose the sections of the reader on which these selections have most bearing are indicated.

BOWER, E. (1969) *Early Identification of Emotionally Handicapped Children in School* (2nd edn). Springfield, Ill.: C. C. Thomas.
This is a practical book which describes the author's methods for identifying children with emotional problems. His suggestions are comprehensive and the American context is not too limiting.

B

CASHDAN, A. and WILLIAMS, P. (1972) *Maladjustment and Learning*, Vol. 5 of 'Personality, Growth and Learning, a second-level course in Educational Studies.' Bletchley, England: Open University Press.
This is a teaching text, which sets out to meet a list of defined objectives, and should be considered as enrichment rather than extension of the material in this reader.

A B C

CHAZAN, M. (1968) 'Children's Emotional Development': in BUTCHER, H. J. (ed.) *Educational Research in Britain* 1. London: University of London Press.
This is a valuable survey of British work in the field of emotional development, a somewhat wider area than is covered by this reader. But Section I which relates to causation and Section 3 which contains material on treatment are particularly relevant.

C D

CHAZAN, M. (1970) 'Maladjusted Children': in MITTLER, P. (ed.) *The Psychological Assessment of Mental and Physical Handicap*. London: Methuen.
The various techniques which can be used to assess maladjustment are

surveyed in this chapter. It is useful as a source of reference, although it is not written for teachers.

B

GROPPER, C. L. and KRESS, G. C. (1970) *Managing Problem Behavior in the Classroom.* New York: New Century.
This set of materials consists of a programmed learning text, a workbook and a handbook. The materials deal with a range of examples of children's problem behaviour, provided from the experiences of Pittsburgh teachers. The authors follow a learning theory approach.

D

ROE, M. C. (1965) *Survey into Progress of Maladjusted Pupils.* Inner London Education Authority.
This reports a study of the development of children attending special schools and special classes for the maladjusted in the ILEA. It is one of the very few enquiries into the efficiency of special educational treatment for the maladjusted.

D

RUTTER, M., TIZARD, J. and WHITMORE, K. (1970) *Education, Health and Behaviour.* London: Longmans.
Much of this book, which describes a survey of children aged 9 to 12 years on the Isle of Wight, is relevant reading. Section 10, 'Selection of Children with Psychiatric Disorder', is particularly interesting for its bearing on the nature of behaviour problems.

A

SHEPHERD, M., OPPENHEIM, B. and MITCHELL, S. (1971) *Childhood Behaviour and Mental Health.* London: University of London Press.
The authors report a research study related to articles 7 and 13 in this reader. This study is one of the few well-designed British investigations concerned with children's behaviour.

A B D

STOTT, D. H. (1969) 'Personality and Adjustment': in MORRIS, J. F. and LUNZER, E. A. (eds.) *Contexts of Education.* London: Staples.
This is an original and unusual analysis of behaviour and of the mechanisms which operate when it is disturbed. Sections III, IV and V are perhaps the most relevant to this reader.

A B

WOODY, R. H. (1969) *Behavioral Problem Children in the Schools.* New York: Meredith Corporation.

The contents of this book cover fairly closely the whole field of interest of this reader. The approach to identification and diagnosis is eclectic, but the book is committed to treatment via behaviour modification.

A B C D

Journals

Articles concerned with children's behaviour problems are scattered in a wide range of journals, as the sources for the articles in this reader testify. Interested students will find that the journals below publish relevant articles, although they also cover many other areas of interest.

The list is far from exhaustive. For example, those British journals concerned with medical aspects of children's behaviour have been omitted, as have many, less available, American journals which carry material in our field of interest. But the eight journals listed probably contain a good proportion of the important and relatively easily available articles concerned with children's behaviour.

British Journal of Educational Psychology
Behavioural Research and Therapy
Child Development
Educational Research
Exceptional Children
Journal of Child Psychology and Psychiatry
Journal of Special Education
Special Education

For the research worker who is making a more thorough survey of current published work, one effective method is to consult *Current Contents* (Behavioural, Social and Educational Sciences). This weekly periodical lists the titles of articles appearing in a very large number of journals. Thus relevant articles can easily be located. But titles are sometimes misleading and some disappointments have to be faced as the penalty for speedy retrieval.

The *Education Index* appears monthly, but lists titles by subject and includes books as well as journal articles. Other publications also take longer to appear than *Current Contents* but often contain a brief summary of the books and articles listed. *Psychological Abstracts* is an example of a publication which is always worth consulting for details of recent work in this field, although its coverage is very wide.

Questions and Activities

The questions and activities below are prompted by the papers in this reader. They are intended to stimulate discussion in seminars and tutorials, rather than as titles for long essays and term papers, though a few could serve this latter purpose too. The order of questions follows in general the order of the readings.

One of the purposes here is to suggest that research findings on behaviour problems are too often accepted uncritically. The answers which any study provides to its own questions will depend to some extent upon individual interpretation. The relationship between these answers and those of other studies is not only a matter of interpretation, it is also often a point of departure for learning.

There are many other questions which can be asked on the basis of the material in the reader, and the inventive teacher will be able to pick up those points in which he particularly wishes to interest his class. The list is not exhaustive.

1. Consider the questions raised at the very end of the first paper, page 15. How do Wickman's findings as stated in the second paper illuminate these questions?

2. Ziv (page 42) notes a high relationship ($\rho = +0\cdot84$) between the rankings of severity by children and the rankings of severity by teachers. How would you account for this?

3. Would you agree with Ziv's interpretation (page 44) of the similarity between the rankings of severity given by teachers and psychologists respectively?

4. Moore (page 49) notes that girls exhibit a consistently lower average number of areas of difficulty than boys. Why might this be?

5. Do you agree with Moore's classification (page 49) of the eight areas of difficulty? Specifically, what other areas of difficulty would you expect to be mentioned if you were extending Moore's approach to secondary school children?

6. What practical steps can be taken to ease the areas of difficulty elicited by Moore's enquiry?

7. Use the method of Birch's article to carry out a small-scale survey (on

about 30 children in one age group) of nail-biting. Does your incidence
of (a) all categories of nail-biters

    (b) severe biters

agree approximately with Birch's?

If not, what hypotheses can you suggest to explain the difference?

8. Should 'nail-biting' be used as an item in methods of assessing
behavioural or emotional problems? (Note item 13 in the Scale in
paper 6, page 94, and item *h* in Appendix to paper 7, page 103.
Remember the reasons given in paper 6 for selecting items.)

9. Use the Scale in paper 6 (p. 94) to rate a child known to you. Obtain a
total score and, where appropriate, 'antisocial' and 'neurotic' sub-scores.
Do you think that (a) the exercise is useful?

                (b) the total score is informative (remember the
                    cut-off at 9, which Rutter suggests)?

                (c) the relationship between the 'antisocial' and
                    'neurotic' scores is interesting (if applicable)?

10. How far does Tizard's article (paper 8) support Rutter's view (page 93)
that the teachers' questionnaire may usefully be used as a 'screening
instrument to detect children likely to show some emotional or
behavioural disorder?' (Note Rutter's own reservations in the following
paragraph on pages 93–5.)

11. Rutter (page 95) suggests that the overlap between disorders perceived
by teachers and disorders perceived by parents is surprisingly small.
Comment on this suggestion in the light of the Mitchell and Shepherd
paper.

12. Make a comparison of the content of the two questionnaires which
are given in excerpts 6 and 7 respectively. Have the different approaches
of the constructors led to differences in content?

13. Look at table 7.1, page 99. Total the *rows* to find, separately, the
number of boys and girls who have none, 1, 2, 3 or more problems
underlined by teachers. Enter your findings in the table below. Two of
the cells have been completed as a check.

Number of problems underlined by teacher	Boys	Girls
None	1,729	
1		
2		271
3 or more		
Total	3,076	3,001

In the table below, enter the *column* totals of table 7.1 to show, again separately, the numbers of boys and girls who have none, 1–3, 4–6, 7 or more problems underlined by parents. Again, two cells have been completed for you.

Number of problems underlined by parents	Boys	Girls
None	1,199	
1–3		
4–6		
7 or more		105
Total	3,076	3,001

Examine the two tables you have constructed.

Contrast the relative behaviour of the boys and the girls as assessed by teachers with their behaviour as assessed by parents. Discuss any differences you find. (Remember Moore's article, paper 4, especially page 49, 'Results'.)

14. Burt and Howard list (page 136) the conditions which they find show the most important relationships with maladjustment. Go through table 9.2, pp. 126–7, listing the size of the correlations associated with each of the conditions. Set out your findings as shown in the table below.

Conditions	Correlation
In the school	
Uncongenial teacher	$+0.23$
Class work too difficult	$+0.17$
In the home	
Lack of affection	$+0.34$
Adolescent instability	$+0.21$

(a) Suppose that *all* conditions which gave rise to correlation coefficients as low as $+0.17$ had been included in your table. Would you want to modify Burt and Howard's interpretation of their findings?

(b) Suppose that only conditions which gave rise to correlation coefficients of $+0.30$ or more had been listed. How would this affect your interpretation of the findings?

15. Discuss Burt and Howard's views on the importance of 'school conditions' associated with maladjustment.

16. Pringle and Bossio contrast the experiences of (a) rejection (lack of affection?) with those of (b) physical separation in small groups of

stable deprived children and maladjusted deprived children. Can their findings be reconciled with those of Burt and Howard?

17. Levitt (page 169) argues that there is no support for the contention that psychotherapy facilitates recovery from emotional illness in children. Comment on this finding in the light of Burt and Howard's views on the likely causes of maladjustment in children.

18. How well do the figures for improvement ratios of treated and non-treated children quoted by Shepherd, Oppenheim and Mitchell in table 13.3 agree with those quoted in Levitt's article? Do you accept their suggestion that 'many so-called disturbances of behaviour are no more than transient exaggerations of widely distributed reaction patterns' (page 183)?

19. Instead of comparing the effectiveness of clinical treatment of behaviour problems with non-treatment of those problems, we should really be trying to specify those types of problems which are most responsive to particular kinds of clinic treatment.
Do readings 12 and 13 vitiate this point of view?

20. Papers 14 and 15 describe ways in which a behaviour modification approach can be used to deal with classroom behaviour. Discuss the ways in which these two papers differ in their method from the two previous papers (12 and 13) in their concern to evaluate the effectiveness of the clinical approach to treatment. (Consider, for example, questions such as the size of the samples, the presence of control groups, etc.)

21. Is it fair to say that behaviour modification deals with symptoms, not causes?

22. Consider the last sentence of paper 15, page 226: 'These findings add support to the proposition that much can be done by the classroom teacher to eliminate behaviours which interfere with learning without extensive changes in the home, or intensive therapy.'
Is this statement consistent with the findings of Burt and Howard (paper 9)?

Index